FULLY GROWN

DIETRICH VOLLRATH

Fully Grown

WHY A STAGNANT

ECONOMY IS A SIGN

OF SUCCESS

THE UNIVERSITY OF CHICAGO PRESS Chicago and London

The University of Chicago Press, Chicago 60637

The University of Chicago Press, Ltd., London

© 2020 by The University of Chicago

Published 2020

Printed in the United States of America

29 28 27 26 25 24 23 22 21 20   1 2 3 4 5

ISBN-13: 978-0-226-66600-6 (cloth)

ISBN-13: 978-0-226-66614-3 (e-book)

DOI: https://doi.org/10.7208/chicago/9780226666143.001.0001

Library of Congress Cataloging-in-Publication Data

Names: Vollrath, Dietrich, author.

Title: Fully grown : why a stagnant economy is a sign of success / Dietrich Vollrath.

Description: Chicago : The University of Chicago Press, 2020. | Includes bibliographical references and index.

Identifiers: LCCN 2019024282 | ISBN 9780226666006 (cloth) | ISBN 9780226666143 (ebook)

Subjects: LCSH: Economic development—United States. | Economic development—Technological innovations. | Economic development—Econometric models.

Classification: LCC HC110.E44 V65 2019 | DDC 330.973—dc23

LC record available at https://lccn.loc.gov/2019024282

♾ This paper meets the requirements of ANSI/NISO Z39.48-1992 (Permanence of Paper).

CONTENTS

Preface *vii*

1 Victims of Our Own Success *1*

2 What Is the Growth Slowdown? *12*

3 The Inputs to Economic Growth *26*

4 What Accounts for the Growth Slowdown? *40*

5 The Effect of an Aging Population *55*

6 The Difference between Productivity and Technology *70*

7 The Reallocation from Goods to Services *81*

8 Baumol's Cost Disease *93*

9 Market Power and Productivity *105*

10 Market Power and the Decline in Investment *116*

11 The Necessity of Market Power *126*

12 Reallocations across Firms and Jobs *139*

13 The Drop in Geographic Mobility *155*

14 Did the Government Cause the Slowdown? *170*

15 Did Inequality Cause the Slowdown? *185*

16 Did China Cause the Slowdown? *195*

17 The Future of Growth *206*

Appendix: Data and Methods *217*

References *249*

Index *257*

At the turn of the millennium in 2000, you could be forgiven for thinking that stable economic growth was something like a law of nature. The average growth in the late 1800s, when the US economy was dominated by agriculture, was about 2% per year. Between 1900 and 1950, as the United States turned into an industrial powerhouse, the average growth was also 2%. For the rest of the twentieth century, the average growth rate was 2%. This is true despite all the fluctuations and changes that occurred in the economy over this time, including the Great Depression, two world wars, globalization, high tax rates, low tax rates, and the arrival of electricity, air travel, and computers. A lot of economic theory, and practical policy, was built around the fact that growth always averaged out to about 2% per year.

Always, that is, until now. For nearly two decades, the average growth rate of per capita gross domestic product (GDP) has been around only 1%, half of what several generations of Americans experienced in the past. It has been going on too long to be just a temporary blip, and it has forced economists and policy makers to recalibrate their expectations of how fast the economy will grow in the future.

At the same time, if you didn't know growth had slowed down but instead focused on the *level* of material living standards, you wouldn't guess there was a problem. Real GDP per capita, our way of assessing the value of the goods and services produced in the economy, was roughly 20% higher in 2018 than in 2000. It was more than three times higher than in 1950, more than eight times higher than in 1900, and more than fifteen times higher than in 1870, which is as far back as we can track. So what gives? Does this mean that the growth rate doesn't matter?

No—it matters. But the drop in growth isn't what you think. In this book, I'm going to share the surprising story of why growth slowed down—and why that's a good sign.

I wish there were a nifty anecdote about how I hit upon this idea, an "aha!" moment in the shower or a pointed conversation with a cab driver. The truth is that there isn't. I sort of stumbled into this project over the course of the past few years. In 2011, Charles (Chad) Jones asked me to collaborate on a new edition of his undergraduate textbook on economic growth. At that point, I was mainly focused on my research related to long-run growth and population change, which was something Chad was hoping to incorporate. But he also was hoping to update the book's material on theories of innovation, and to bring the data on growth rates and living standards up to date. As I worked on the book and then started teaching from an early draft of it, I found that I had accumulated a set of stories, data, and math that was useful in explaining topics in economic growth, and not all of it could find its way into the textbook.

As others started using the book, I realized that I could share some of that additional material I had and perhaps make adopting the book more attractive to others. So in the spring of 2014 I started publishing the very unimaginatively named *Growth Economics Blog*. I posted ideas about how to explain or understand simple concepts in economic growth and started commenting on current research. Although the blog did not become an overnight sensation, there turned out to be a decent audience of people interested in topics related to growth.

One topic in particular that drew a lot of readers was the growth slowdown, which in 2014 was becoming noticeable in the aftermath of the financial crisis. The interest in that was mirrored in the courses I was teaching, and I started to dig more into the underlying reasons why growth had not accelerated as expected after the recession that crisis caused. It was around that same time that I read some research by John Fernald, who established that the growth slowdown was not just a result of the recession; rather, it was a long-run phenomenon that started around the turn of the twenty-first century.

At the same time, more and more stories were coming out regarding the growth slowdown, and a trope in those stories was a failure of innovation. Most of this was just angry-old-man ranting about how the kids with their FaceTweets were ruining the economy, as far as I could tell. It also confused the notion of productivity, which I'll define clearly in this book, with technology. I ended up writing a number of posts about how productivity growth had slowed down, but that this might reflect not a failure of technology but rather changes in the market power of firms and the shift of economic activity between sectors.

Because of some of my own research on historical shifts of workers out of agriculture, I was also playing around with data and theories related to the industrial composition (e.g., manufacturing, health care, retail) of what we produce. That got me reading more deeply the work of William Baumol, his "cost disease" of services, and its plausible role in slowing down economic growth.

Reading Baumol may have been the point at which I first conceived of writing a book about the subject of the growth slowdown. I had acquired a lot of disparate material on the subject, and I thought I saw some common threads running through all of it. First there was the notion that productivity growth had more to do with how we allocate our workers and capital across different activities—firms or industries—than with technology per se. Second was the idea that an increase in market power may be a reasonable explanation for why those allocations changed so much over time.

As I started to work on the outlines of that book, though, I realized that my original concept of the growth slowdown was not going to hold up. Some simple accounting showed me that I had entirely underestimated the role that demographic changes played, and that a story based just on productivity growth would be something of a waste of time. I also was absorbing research on the influence of market power on growth and realized it was far more subtle than I had originally thought. Both things left me wavering about whether it was worth it to continue to work on a book. I had all these bits and pieces of explanations for the growth slowdown, but they didn't seem to fit together.

Here is where it would be really nice if I had that neat anecdote about how, with despair in my heart, I had a key flash of inspiration. But like I said, I don't have a good story. I put aside the whole project for a few weeks. Then, probably trying to procrastinate from doing work on a different project, I pulled the material on the growth slowdown back up one day. Looking at it fresh, it seemed more obvious that the demographics and the shift into services described by Baumol were the main culprits. The break had allowed me to clear my head, and the underlying success that drove both of those phenomena looked obvious. Everything else slotted into place at that point, and here we are.

I didn't set out to write a book with an optimistic or positive outlook, but that is where I ended up. That might seem incongruous with day-to-day commentary on the state of the economy, which focuses a lot on failures of innovation, failures of competition, and failures of policy. I still spend a good part of the book exploring these failures, in part to establish that they did not drive the growth slowdown but also to make clear that they are still failures despite the lack of a direct effect on the growth rate. The overall message of the book is thus not complacent or naively optimistic. To use a term coined by the recent Nobel Prize winner Paul Romer, I would say that this book is conditionally optimistic. If we pursue fixes to perceived economic failures, we should be optimistic that we can, in fact, fix them. The successes behind the growth slowdown mean we have even more reason to debate and address the failures we see in the economy. We have the means to take action, if we want.

While Chad Jones was the one indirectly implicated in bringing this book about, it has relied on a series of intellectual connections and friendships. This goes back to graduate school, where my advisers Oded Galor, Peter Howitt, and David Weil impressed on me the value of taking a long-run view. That was reinforced over time by interactions—electronic or in person—with Areendam Chanda, German Cubas, David Cuberes, Carl-Johan Dalgaard, Ryan Decker,

Markus Eberhardt, Lennart Erickson, Jim Feyrer, Doug Gollin, Robert Gordon, Mike Hsu, Greg Ip, Remi Jedwab, Mike Jerzmanowski, Sebnem Kalemli-Ozcan, Jenny Minier, Chris Papageorgiou, David Papell, Noah Smith, Bent Sorensen, Liliana Varela, and Kei-mu Yi.

Alex Tabarrok, Garett Jones, and Brad DeLong all deserve a special mention, as they were willing to read an original draft of this book and offered a series of thoughtful comments and criticisms. They'll all find changes they suggested scattered throughout. I also appreciate the positive feedback I got from all of them, as my own conviction wavered—often on a day-to-day basis—as to whether I could turn this into something worth reading.

Last, I want to thank my wife, Kirstin, who never let all that wavering get out of control. She never doubted that I could write this book but let me decide if I should. I appreciate every sacrifice she made, big or little, to let me pursue this.

VICTIMS OF OUR OWN SUCCESS

1 In the aftermath of the financial crisis and Great Recession, one of the noticeable outcomes was a lack of any acceleration in economic growth. From our past experience, we would have expected to see several quarters, if not several years, of above-average growth rates as the economy clawed back what it lost during the crisis. This had been true of every earlier recession, including the Great Depression. It was the economic equivalent of doing seventy-five miles per hour to make up lost time after a slowdown in a construction zone. But while economic growth was positive in every year since 2010, it struggled to crack 2% on an annual basis, meaning that the economy remained well below the trend established before the financial crisis. It's like we decided to stick to fifty-five miles per hour after getting free of the roadwork.

This growth slowdown has not escaped the attention of, well, anyone with even a passing interest in economics. Robert Gordon's recent history of economic growth in the United States is entitled *The Rise and Fall of American Growth*, not *The Rise and Continued Pretty Good Rate of American Growth*. You can find multiple stories on slow economic growth in past issues of the *Wall Street Journal*, the *Economist*, the *Atlantic*, the *New York Times*, and the *Financial Times*, just to name a few. During the 2016 Republican presidential primary, Jeb Bush made a campaign promise of achieving 4% growth in gross domestic product (GDP), something we haven't seen in twenty years. There is an ongoing argument over whether the US economy is experiencing "secular stagnation," but no one disputes that stagnation exists. Recurring debates about government spending and debt hinge on claims that certain policies can, or cannot, increase the growth rate of GDP.

The slowdown is easy to see in the data. The growth rate of GDP per capita, which is what I focus on in this book, averaged 2.25% per year from 1950 to 2000. But the average growth rate of GDP per capita from 2000 to 2016 was only 1%. That difference of 1.25 percentage points of growth per year means that GDP per capita today is about 25% *lower* than if we had matched the twentieth-century growth rate throughout the twenty-first century. It represents a significant deceleration of economic growth, but it started well before the recession in 2009. Federal Reserve economist John Fernald argues that the growth slowdown is close to twenty years old already, and what the financial crisis did was bring it to our attention.

The immediate reaction to the slowdown is that there must be something *wrong*. We have somehow fallen behind, with respect to either other nations or our own past. And given that sense, it is natural to look for the causes of the growth slowdown. Who or what should we blame for it, and is there something we can do to reverse it?

SOME SIMPLE ACCOUNTING

To answer these questions, we need to account for what drives economic growth in the first place. Because economic growth is an increase in the output of goods and services, it depends on the growth in inputs. One of those inputs is physical capital, which is poorly named, as it consists not only of the stock of physical assets like buildings and machines but also of intellectual property like software. The data shows that the growth rate of physical capital declined by a small amount in the twenty-first century compared to the twentieth. And as I explain in more detail later, this effect is probably overstated, meaning that slower growth in physical capital did not account for much of the growth slowdown.

This is in contrast to the second input, human capital, which depends on the number of workers, the hours they put in, their experience, and the skills they bring with them. Human capital growth was slower in the twenty-first century than in the twentieth, and by itself this can explain at least 0.8 percentage points of the 1.25 point decline in the growth rate that constituted the growth slowdown. The sources of this drop in human capital growth will be key to explaining the growth slowdown.

Human capital is not the only explanation, though. The combination of slower growth in these inputs is not enough to explain the overall decline in economic growth. There is some residual explanation that these two stocks cannot account for, such as the effect of innovations, changes in which industries produce the majority of GDP, the reallocation of workers between firms or locations, the influence of regulation and taxation on business decisions, and an almost infinite number of other possibilities. In short, residual growth captures everything else involved in economic growth that is *not* due to growth in human and physical capital. It is common to use the term *productivity* for this residual, but it is important to remember that this means productivity growth depends on more than just technological change. Regardless, much like human capital, the productivity growth rate was lower in the twenty-first century than in the twentieth. It can account for the remainder of the growth slowdown.

This accounting exercise, which takes up chapters 3 and 4, will tell us how the slowdown happened, but it won't tell us why. The remainder of the book is an exploration of the underlying reasons for the drop in both human capital growth and productivity growth during the twenty-first century.

THE CONSEQUENCES OF OUR CHOICES

When we dig into the reasons for drops in growth, it will become apparent that the growth slowdown has less to do with things that went wrong, and more to do with things that went right. Step back from the focus on the growth slowdown itself, or on recent events like the financial crisis, and the evidence shows that GDP per capita has been growing, with very few interruptions, for as far back as the data goes. The value of goods and services we produce every year, per person, is about three times larger than it was in 1950 and about seven times larger than it was in 1900. And that doesn't quite capture the expansion in living standards that occurred over those same periods. Goods and services that didn't exist or were available to only a select few seventy years ago, like air-conditioning, refrigerators, televisions, computers, smartphones, air travel, antibiotics, and the internet, are now ubiquitous. Even running water and flush toilets were available in only about two-thirds of households in 1940. Whatever is happening with the growth rate today, the economy has had incredible success in meeting the material needs of almost every single person in the United States.

That success, though, is one of the primary drivers of the growth slowdown. It changed how we build our families, for starters. All the available evidence shows that as material living standards improve, fertility rates fall. The explanations for this are legion, but the relationship is almost universal across time and across countries. Alongside this, the successful introduction of reliable contraceptives, like the pill, that were under the control of women themselves, gave them more control over their own fertility. This in turn allowed women more control over their participation in the labor force, marriage, and schooling. The result was more education for both women and men, later marriage, and delayed childbearing. Taken together, rising GDP per capita and reproductive rights led to a steady fall in the birth rate from the baby boom until today.

The drop in human capital growth in the twenty-first century, and hence much of the growth slowdown, is the result of that fall in birth rates. When the baby boomers were finishing their schooling and entering the labor force in the 1960s and 1970s, there was a rapid increase in the amount of human capital. Their entry into the workforce raised the proportion of workers to population, and along with the acceleration of college graduation rates, this led to rapid growth in the stock of human capital we used to produce GDP during the late twentieth century.

But because those baby boomers, on average, did not have large families of their own, when they began to exit the labor force in the twenty-first century there was no way to keep up the momentum. The ratio of workers to population fell, and hence the growth rate of human capital fell during the twenty-first century. The growth slowdown is, in large part, a consequence of the family decisions made by people thirty or forty years ago. And those decisions were informed by the success of rising living standards and innovation in contraception.

Beyond demographics, increased living standards had another significant consequence for economic growth, which worked through our choices about the kinds of products we purchase. In 1940 you might have spent your money installing plumbing for running water or a toilet, if you didn't already have those things. The same went for air-conditioning, a TV, or a computer at other points in time during the twentieth century. But once we had those goods, then what did we spend our money on? Did people install an extra toilet in their bathroom? Probably not. Instead, as goods became cheaper and we filled up our houses with them, our spending turned toward services. We took advantage of the falling prices and availability of basic goods to take longer and better vacations, to take classes, to see medical specialists, to get some physical therapy, to put more data on our phone plans, or to subscribe to Netflix and Hulu. We took advantage of our success in providing goods to buy more and more services. And in an unsurprising response, the economy shifted more and more workers into firms that provide them. The flow of workers out of producing goods didn't signal some kind of failure; it is a consequence of our own choices about what to spend our money on.

There is nothing new about the shift from goods to services. It has been going on for the entire history of the United States as labor shifted away from agriculture and then manufacturing. What changed in the twenty-first century was that these shifts became a drag on economic growth. It turns out that most service industries have relatively low productivity growth, and most goods-producing industries have relatively high productivity growth. As we shifted our spending from goods to services, then, this pulled down overall productivity growth, which is just a weighted average of productivity growth across different industries.

The reasons for the difference in productivity growth across industries were first explored by William Baumol in several papers published in the 1960s. The key idea is the role of labor in production.

Labor is necessary to produce goods, but it is not part of the product itself. The person who assembled your fuel injector does not have to be there for you to drive your car. In contrast, for services labor is part of the product itself. You need to interact with a doctor, lawyer, waiter, personal trainer, financial adviser, or teacher to receive the service. This means that in services it is harder—though not impossible—to reduce the amount of labor used and increase productivity. It isn't some kind of failure that service productivity growth is low; it is rather an inherent feature of those kinds of activities.

The combination of the shift into services and the decline in fertility rates can account for the vast majority of the growth slowdown, and both of these are clear consequences of success. We made choices beginning in the middle of the twentieth century about family size and the composition of our spending that reflected high average living standards. These choices born of success had the unintended consequence of putting a drag on the growth rate in the twenty-first century.

TURNOVER, MARKET POWER, AND GROWTH

It's important not to confuse the claim that success brought us to where we are today with the claim that there are no problems in the economy or that higher growth is impossible. There were several changes to the economy over the past few decades that contributed to the growth slowdown—even if they were not the dominant reason for it—that could well be qualified as failures of one kind or another.

In particular, over the past few decades there has been a distinct decline in the volume of turnover in the number of firms and jobs in the economy, with fewer new firms entering the economy, fewer old firms exiting, and fewer movements of people from one job to another. There was also a distinct decline in the geographic mobility of workers, which might be either a cause or a consequence of the fall in worker turnover.

On average, workers tend to get moved into more-productive jobs, and more-productive establishments tend to replace less-productive establishments. More turnover is therefore associated with faster productivity growth. The decline in mobility and turnover played some role in the growth slowdown, although the data will show that it was a smaller role than the combination of demographic change and the shift into services.

The reasons for this decline in turnover are not clear. One possible source is the rise in the market power of firms over the past few decades. I'll review the evidence that economic profits—the extra income that is earned from selling goods and services over and above the cost of producing them—have risen steadily since at least the early 1990s. Those economic profits are the outward sign of increased market power.

It's possible that market power could explain the slowdown in turnover. With market power, firms react less to shocks that occur to the costs of, or the demand for, their products. They won't hire and fire workers, or shutter and open new locations, as quickly as firms in more competitive markets. And there is some evidence to back this up.

But that isn't the whole story with market power. Some of the rise in market power comes from a shift in our spending away from firms and industries with little market power, and toward firms and industries with a lot of market power. The shift in market power may have been driven by forces similar to the ones that caused the shift from goods to services. This leads to the somewhat counterintuitive finding that the rise in market power was good for productivity growth during the twenty-first century, as it meant we were putting our resources to work producing goods and services that we implicitly put a high value on.

In the end, the effect of the increase in market power was ambiguous. This doesn't change the fact that the rise in market power could represent a very serious distributional issue for the economy and society, or that we might still want to reverse it. A reversal, however, would have to be undertaken with care, as some market power is necessary to generate economic growth at all, a key finding that I'll explain in more detail as we go.

THE USUAL SUSPECTS

Many popular explanations for the growth slowdown turn out to have little real content. Like the increase in market power, they tend to be important for how the economic pie is divided up but have no effect on how big the pie is.

One common worry is that the growth slowdown reflects a failure of ingenuity or innovation. We hear this in complaints that the things we do invent are frivolous or trivial, as in PayPal founder and venture capitalist Peter Thiel's famous quotation "We wanted flying cars, and all we got was 140 characters," or in some of Robert Gordon's analysis in his recent book. At the same time, techno-optimists say we are in the middle of an unprecedented explosion in technological creativity, often associated with the massive increase in computing power available to firms and researchers, and the possibilities of artificial intelligence and robotics.

Neither side in this argument has much support from the evidence on economic growth. That is because our technological growth, whatever you think of it, is not synonymous with our productivity growth. The latter depends as much on the allocation of workers and capital across industries and firms as it does on the specific technologies we employ. The simple observation that productivity growth fell does not imply much of anything about whether we were better or worse at technological innovation.

That said, there is evidence that the effort necessary to produce new technologies—such as faster semiconductors, higher plant yields, or new drugs—rose over time. Have we perhaps reached a point at which it is too hard to innovate? That could make sense, except that the rise in research effort has been going on since at least the middle of the twentieth century. It has *always* been the case that it takes more research and development resources to achieve each new rung on the innovation ladder, and there was nothing that changed right around the turn of the century to make this worse.

Another obvious place to look for a source of the growth slowdown is the government, which includes everything related to taxes and regulation at any level, from federal on down to local. Perhaps onerous regulation forced productive firms to shut down or entrepreneurs to give up on opening new firms in the first place. Corporate taxes may have played a similar role in limiting new firm entry, and individual tax rates might explain why the number of workers declined relative to population—it wasn't demography alone.

While these theories are plausible, there is little to no evidence that either regulation or taxation had a significant effect on the growth slowdown. At the federal level, dividend tax rates and the tax rates on individual income both fell at the beginning of the twenty-first century. That should have increased the number of workers and investment by firms, but the exact opposite happened. Across states, there is no evidence that those with tighter regulatory conditions or higher tax rates grew at a slower rate than those with what are considered better business environments. California and Massachusetts are still two of the most productive states and continue to have some of the most rapid economic growth in the country, despite scoring low on "business-friendly" metrics. Research on the effect of regulation shows that industries with more restrictions on them in the federal code did not have lower productivity growth. If anything, they grew faster.

Trade, in particular with China, is another place to lay blame. There is good evidence that trade with China resulted in significant losses of jobs in specific manufacturing subindustries, such as furniture and clothing. The effect of this trade is clear in those towns or cities that lost significant employers and struggled to find replacements. Even if those workers who lost jobs did find new employment, it might well have been in service industries with lower productivity levels of their own, and that would have been part of the drag on growth. Much like the government explanation, however, the effect of trade with China is plausible in theory but not very big in the data. Results from studies of the effect of China indicate that it did cause workers to exit the labor force or move to other industries, but the totals are just too small to show up as much more than rounding error in the growth slowdown of the twenty-first century.

A last potential explanation is the clear rise in inequality in the past few decades. Again, it appears plausible that inequality could provide an explanation for the growth slowdown, for example, by changing the composition of spending across different industries. It is a regularity in the data that as people get richer, they spend a smaller share of their income on goods and a larger share on services. As inequality concentrated income in the hands of relatively rich people, it would also have concentrated spending into services. But again, the rise in inequality wasn't large enough, and the difference in spending patterns wasn't strong enough, to provide much of an explanation for the shift toward services. A different possibility is that inequality slowed the growth of human capital, in particular through the ability of people to obtain an education or provide it for their children. However, the plausible effects of inequality on educational attainment are not large enough to explain the slowdown in human capital growth that accounts for the growth slowdown.

Much like market power, perceived failures in the areas of technology, government taxation or regulation, trade, and inequality may have had significant distributional effects, but they did not drive the growth slowdown. The most plausible explanation remains the successes embedded in the aging population and the shift into services.

SO IS THIS A GOOD THING?

It may be hard to wrap your head around the idea that the growth slowdown is a sign of success and not the consequence of some failure in either policy or ingenuity. But don't confuse the word *success* with *good* or *fair*. The steady increase in GDP per capita that drove the demographic changes and shift in spending toward services represented a substantial improvement in material living standards, but that doesn't mean that everyone enjoyed the same improvement, or that there were no consequences for the environment, politics, or society in general. Think of GDP per capita like a pedometer for economic activity. Just as achieving ten thousand steps in a day does not tell you everything about your health, the successes behind the growth slowdown do not tell you everything about society or the economy.

But because it is ultimately rising living standards that lie behind the growth slowdown, we may not be able to—or even want to—reverse it. Would it be worth it to destroy everyone's car just to boost both employment in the automotive industry and the growth rate of GDP per capita for a little while? Would you want to roll back living standards and women's rights to reverse population aging in the hopes of increasing growth decades in the future? On the presumption that the answer to both questions is no, this leaves us without a clear villain for the growth slowdown. In its place we've got a somewhat boring accumulation of changes in markets, spending patterns, and family decisions that took place over decades. The fact that we'd be unwilling to roll back all those changes just to achieve slightly higher growth is why I refer to the slowdown as a success. We have the growth rate we wanted.

To make this case, I'm going to provide a lot of data and reference quite a lot of recent economic research. That said, this is not a technical book. There are no equations and no dense footnotes. The appendix at the end of the book does contain explanations of points I make in the text, if you care to dig into the subject further and don't mind a little math. As for the data itself, all the data and the code I used to produce the figures and tables are publicly available. I think the conclusions in the book follow clearly from the data, and an advanced degree isn't required to understand the logic of how success led to the growth slowdown.

WHAT IS THE GROWTH SLOWDOWN?

2 Before we even get into the how and why, I want to lay out the basic facts behind the growth slowdown so that the timing and implications of it are clear. I cited some numbers in chapter 1 about the growth rate falling from around 2.25% in the twentieth century to around 1.0% in the twenty-first, but let's put those numbers in context. In figure 2.1, I've plotted two separate series. The dashed line is the annual growth rate of real GDP per capita in the United States from 1950 (meaning the growth rate from 1949 to 1950) through 2016 (meaning the growth rate from 2015 to 2016). As you can see, this jumped all over the place, with some very high growth rates of over 5% per year in the 1950s, 1960s, and even the 1980s. There were also some very low growth rates, including negative growth in recessions during the 1950s, 1970s, 1980s, and most noticeably, in 2009.

Because of the way the growth rate fluctuates, it is hard to see any trends in the growth rate itself. So the solid line I've plotted is the ten-year average growth rate. In 1960 (meaning the annualized growth rate from 1950 to 1960), the growth rate was about 2.6% per year. That ten-year growth rate reached close to 4% per year in the late 1960s, and then settled down to around 2.4% per year until the early 2000s.

At that point, around 2006, the average growth rate dropped. Remember, these are backward-looking averages, so when the average growth rate started to dip in 2006, that meant that the average growth rate fell for the period 1996–2006. The decline was not just due to the financial crisis and re-

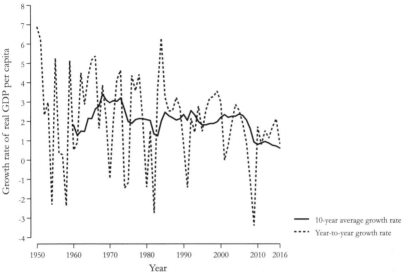

Figure 2.1. Growth rate of real GDP per capita
Note: Real GDP per capita is from the Bureau of Economic Analysis. The year-to-year growth rate is the percentage change in real GDP per capita from year *t* – 1 to year *t* (e.g., for 2016 this is the percentage growth in real GDP per capita from 2015 to 2016). The ten-year average growth rate is the annualized percentage change in real GDP per capita from year *t* – 10 to year *t* (e.g., for 2016 this is the annualized growth rate of real GDP per capita from 2006 to 2016).

cession in 2008–2009. That event did help accelerate the drop in average growth rates to 2010, at which point the growth rate settled down around 1%. But even excluding the years of the recession, the growth rate of real GDP per capita in the twenty-first century has been at least 1 percentage point lower than during the twentieth.

The "growth slowdown," then, refers to this drop in the ten-year average growth rate around 2006, and that drop implies that growth rates dropped starting in the late 1990s and early 2000s. Different economists or authors may provide slightly different definitions and dates, but the rough idea is always the same. Starting around the early 2000s, the growth rate of real GDP in the United States dropped compared to the historical norm of around 2.25% per year, and now is somewhere around 1.0% per year. And while the financial crisis and recession have not helped the average growth rate, the general consensus is that the drop in the growth rate was not simply a manifestation of that event.

THE LEVEL AND GROWTH OF REAL GDP PER CAPITA

The drop in the growth rate is clear from figure 2.1, but the relationship of that drop to the level of living standards is not so obvious. A common misinterpretation of the fall in the growth rate, which I've even heard from professional economists, is that the actual size of GDP per capita dropped as well. That's wrong. It did not fall, it just didn't go up quite as fast as before.

To see this, let's take a look at some numbers. In figure 2.2 I've plotted what I call growth of real GDP per capita. This is the absolute change in real GDP per capita from one year to the next, as opposed to the growth rate, which is the percentage change in real GDP per capita. In the figure, each bar shows the absolute change in real GDP per capita in a year relative to the absolute change in the year 2000. In 1950, as an example, the growth of real GDP was about 0.75, meaning that the change in GDP per capita that year was equivalent to three-quarters of the change in GDP per capita in the year 2000. What's important here is not the actual number, but comparing the height of the bars across the years.

Notice that the absolute growth in real GDP per capita got a little larger over time. Up until about 1980, every year real GDP per capita went up an amount equal to about half the growth in 2000. But after 1980, the growth of real GDP per capita was around three-quarters or more of 2000 growth. This was true even in the twenty-first century during the growth slowdown. Despite a lower growth rate, growth in real GDP per capita was about as large as it ever was. I plotted the average growth over this whole period with the dashed line, and even in 2014, 2015, and 2017 real GDP per capita grew by more than that average.

Now, the flip side of growth being larger over time is that when things go bad, as in 2009, the loss of GDP per capita was also larger. You can see that in 2009 real GDP shrank by about 1.3 times as much as real GDP per capita grew during 2000. It was enough to wipe out almost all the growth that had occurred in 2005, 2006, and 2007.

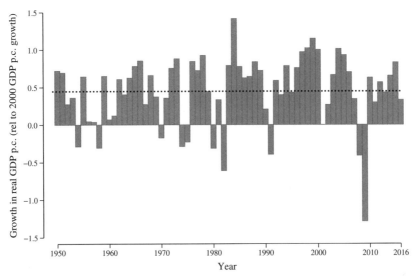

Figure 2.2. Growth in real GDP per capita

Note: Real GDP per capita is from the Bureau of Economic Analysis. Growth in real GDP per capita is the absolute change in real GDP per capita from year $t - 1$ to year t, divided by the absolute change in real GDP per capita from 1999 to 2000, so that the figure shows absolute growth in real GDP per capita relative to the growth from 1999 to 2000. The dashed line shows the average of this percentage across all years.

Compared to the other years in which real GDP shrank (like 1954 or 1974 or 1982), the loss in 2009 was massive. In absolute terms, the recession in 2009 eliminated more than twice as much real GDP per capita as the recession in 1981.

The growth slowdown from figure 2.1 did not mean that the absolute growth in real GDP per capita fell, only that this growth was a smaller percentage of the existing level of real GDP per capita. The level of living standards kept going up despite the growth slowdown. You can see this in figure 2.3, which plots the level of real GDP per capita over time. In the figure, I've set the level of real GDP per capita in 2009 to equal 100, and then plotted each year relative to that value. Compared to the other figures, this one isn't nearly as exciting, as it shows the steady climb in real GDP over time. Back in 1950, real GDP was only about 30% of the level in 2009. But despite the occasional recession here or there that lowered real GDP per capita from one

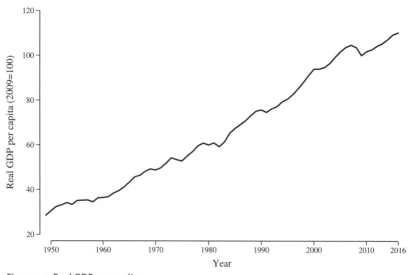

Figure 2.3. Real GDP per capita
Note: Real GDP per capita is from the Bureau of Economic Analysis. For each year, real GDP per capita is indexed to equal 100 in the year 2009.

year to the next, from 1950 forward, real GDP increased. By the mid-1980s real GDP per capita was 70% of the 2009 level, and in the year 2000 it was 94% of the 2009 level. In 2007 real GDP per capita was 105, meaning that it was 5% higher than in 2009. Then the financial crisis hit, and real GDP shrank. Once the recession was over, real GDP per capita started growing again. Real GDP per capita in 2016 was 110, or about 10% higher than in 2009. Despite the growth slowdown, real GDP per capita was still 17% higher in 2016 (110) than it was in 2000 (94).

The level of real GDP per capita certainly could have been much higher in 2016 if the growth slowdown hadn't occurred. The growth slowdown represented a significant loss of potential economic activity. But that isn't the same as saying the growth slowdown represented a significant loss of *actual* economic activity.

THE MEANING OF REAL GDP PER CAPITA

You may have noticed that I've been repetitive in saying *real GDP per capita* throughout this chapter. That is because I want to keep clear that what I'm discussing here is not growth in the *dollar* value of all the goods and services produced in the economy, but their real value. As you are no doubt aware, an increase in the dollars you spent doesn't necessarily mean that you got more goods and services. It might just reflect inflation in prices over time. We can calculate real GDP by stripping out inflation, which leaves us with a measure of growth in the actual number of goods and services produced. If we made sixteen hamburgers and seven hours of yoga classes last year, and twenty hamburgers and nine hours of yoga classes this year, there was *real* growth in the goods and services we produced. Real GDP is meant to measure that increase, whether the dollar cost of those hamburgers and yoga classes went up or down from one year to the next.

As you might imagine, this calculation can get sort of hairy when you start thinking about the millions of different goods and services produced in the economy in any given year. There are issues with how to deal with products that change characteristics over time (e.g., a forty-two-inch TV today is not the same thing as a forty-two-inch TV from 1995), products that didn't exist in the past but do now (e.g., a Fitbit), and products that existed in the past but don't any more (e.g., a DeLorean). I'm going to return to some of those issues later in the book, as one explanation for the growth slowdown is that it reflects a failure of our measure of real GDP to keep up with changes in the quality of products. For the moment, it's important just to be aware that what the concept of real GDP does is strip out the effects of pure price inflation and capture real changes in the quantities of goods and services we produce each year.

Real GDP is a narrow concept. It measures the real quantities of goods and services, and only those. It isn't an index of unemployment, or how well the stock market is doing, or the profit margins of firms, or whether firms are making profits or losses at all. It doesn't measure the size of your bank balance or retirement account. There may be some tendency for things like profits or stock prices to rise rapidly when real GDP growth is large, but there is no necessary connection. Real GDP is related to things like the stock market or the unemployment rate in the same way that the final score of a football game is related to time of possession. Yes, there is a tendency for the team with more time of possession to outscore its opponent, but that doesn't mean that points are awarded for each minute a team holds the ball. I'm harping on this because when I get to talking about how higher real GDP per capita represented a success in terms of raised living standards, I don't mean to imply that everyone also experienced financial success as well.

The last thing to note is that I'm showing you everything in terms of real GDP *per capita*, because this gives us a rough measure of material living standards per person. It doesn't mean that every single person in the economy has enjoyed the same increase in living standards over time, of course. It does serve as a rough index of how average living standards have changed for most people.

ARE WE FALLING BEHIND?

Leaving aside the minutiae of measuring real GDP per capita, we can pick back up with implications of the growth slowdown. One common reaction is that the slowdown means the United States is falling behind other nations in some capacity. But compared to other developed economies, the growth slowdown in the United States is not extraordinary. Figure 2.4 plots the ten-year average growth rate of real GDP per capita for five major economies. In looking at the years since 2000, you can see that the growth slowdown occurred in all of them, although the exact timing differed by a few years. The slowdown became apparent in Japan in the early 2000s, whereas the other countries experienced it at around the same time as the United States. In the last few years shown in the figure, Germany and France appear to have growth rates that were higher than that of the United States but lower than their values in the decades leading up to 2000.

In those prior decades, though, the US experience looked very different from that of other countries. France had a higher growth rate than the United States in the 1960s and 1970s, as did Germany. The German experience started out similar to that of Japan, which maintained a very high growth rate well into the 1970s of close to 8% per year. That kind of very rapid growth rate of real GDP per capita rela-

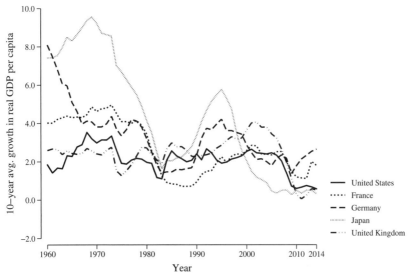

Figure 2.4. Growth in real GDP across countries
Note: Real GDP per capita for all countries is from the Penn World Tables, Version 9. The ten-year average growth was calculated by the author as the annualized growth rate from year t – 10 to year t (e.g., the reported growth rate in 2016 is the annualized growth rate from 2006 to 2016).

tive to the United States in the 1960s and 1970s calls to mind a similar comparison to the growth rate of China in more recent decades.

To highlight this, in figure 2.5 I've plotted the ten-year average growth rate of real GDP per capita for the United States, China, and Japan. You can see the growth slowdown for the United States, in the solid line, just as before. Compared to that, the growth rate for China in the past few decades was immense, at around 8% per year in the 2000s. Even in the 1990s, China's growth rate was around 4% per year for real GDP per capita. It was only back in the 1960s and 1970s, before most of the economic reforms of Deng Xiaoping in the late 1970s, that the growth rate was similar to that in the United States, or even below it. China's growth rate of real GDP per capita accelerated for more than two decades and only recently looks to have slowed a little.

It's informative to compare China's growth rate to Japan's, which

Figure 2.5. Growth in real GDP in the United States, China, and Japan
Note: Real GDP per capita for all countries is from the Penn World Tables, Version 9. The ten-year average growth was calculated by the author as the annualized growth rate from year $t - 10$ to year t (e.g., the reported growth rate in 2016 is the annualized growth rate from 2006 to 2016).

was the growth superstar during the 1960s and 1970s. Japan also had growth rates around 8% at one point, and then growth slumped around the early 1980s, before another spike in the 1990s to growth rates of around 5% or 6%. But since the early 2000s, the growth rate in Japan declined, and Japan's growth slowdown preceded that in the United States by about five to ten years. The growth rate of Japanese real GDP per capita fell to well below 1% in the twenty-first century and has remained below that of the United States. Whether China will experience a similar growth slowdown remains to be seen. The point of figure 2.5 is that this is not the first time that US growth rates lagged those of an apparent economic powerhouse.

But lagging behind Japan or China in growth rates does not mean that the United States was lagging behind in growth or in level of real GDP per capita. Figure 2.6 plots the absolute growth of real GDP per capita in both China and the United States. Everything is relative to US growth in 2000, and so each bar compares growth in a given year or country to growth in the United States in that year. I also dropped Japan from the figure—including Japan got very messy—and the message comes through just using China as the comparison. The growth of real GDP per capita in the United States (dark bars) was much higher than growth in China (light bars) until the past few years. Even recently, the growth in real GDP per capita in the United States and China is similar. In a few years, 2011 and 2013, growth in China was higher. In other years, 2012 and 2014, absolute growth in real GDP per capita in the United States was higher. Our average standard of living improved in an increment similar to China's. Those increments represent a much larger percentage increase in China, which is why China's growth rate looks so much higher than that of the United States.

Stepping back to look at the level of real GDP per capita reinforces the idea that the United States did not fall behind in an appreciable

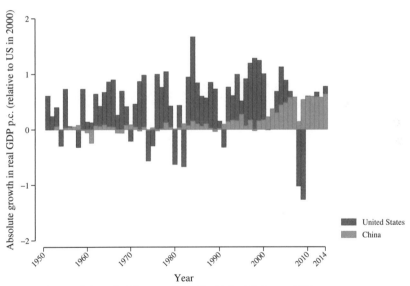

Figure 2.6. Growth in real GDP per capita in the United States and China
Note: Real GDP per capita for both countries is from the Penn World Tables, Version 9. Growth is the difference in real GDP per capita from year *t* – 1 to year *t* (e.g., growth for 2010 is the change in real GDP per capita from 2009 to 2010), divided by the growth in real GDP per capita in the US from the year 2000. The values thus show absolute growth relative to the United States in that year.

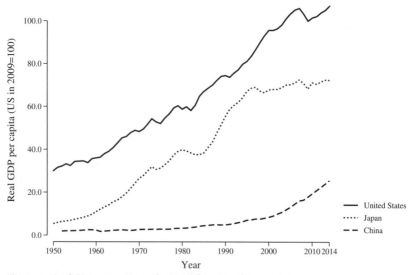

Figure 2.7. Real GDP per capita in the United States, China, and Japan
Note: Real GDP per capita for all countries is from the Penn World Tables, Version 9. For each year, real GDP per capita is indexed to the US real GDP per capita in 2009, with real GDP per capita in 2009 set to 100.

way. Figure 2.7 shows the level of real GDP per capita in the United States, China, and Japan. Starting in 1950, real GDP per capita in the United States was about 30% of what it was in 2009, and it rose over time, with a number of dips along the way, as we have seen. In comparison, both Japan and China were extremely poor in 1950. Japan's real GDP per capita in 1950 was only 5% of the US level in 2009, meaning that it was only about 25% of the US level of real GDP per capita in 1950. China was even poorer. In 1952, the first year for which Chinese data is available, real GDP per capita in China was only 1.8% of that in the United States in 2009, or only about 6% of the US level in 1952.

From the starting point of 1950, real GDP per capita grew in each of the three countries. For Japan, this growth surged first in the 1960s and 1970s, and the gap in real GDP per capita closed with the United States, reaching the closest value in about 1995. But from that point forward, as growth rates in Japan slowed down, the level of real GDP per capita reached something of a plateau, so that it was only about 70% of the US value in 2009.

The experience of China, even with its dramatic surge in growth rates, is more striking. China was, and remains, very poor in relative terms when compared to the United States. Despite having growth rates notably higher than the United States for thirty years, the level of real GDP per capita was still only about 25% of that in the US in 2009. In fact, the absolute gap in the level of real GDP per capita between China and the US was bigger in 2014 than it was in 1990, 1980, 1970, 1960, or 1950. If Chinese real GDP per capita tripled tomorrow, it would still be smaller than real GDP per capita in the United States.

Yes, China's real GDP per capita grew very, very quickly compared to that of the United States in the past twenty years. But that is not an indication that the US fell behind in the level of living standards. Even if China manages to retain its high growth rate, it will still be another twenty-five years before real GDP per capita catches up to the US level. And the likelihood that China's growth rate will remain so high is small. Note that it has already started to decline, and remember the growth rate for Japan in figure 2.5. No country has ever been able to sustain growth rates of 8% for very long, or growth rates of 5%–6% for more than a decade. More realistically, it will at best be fifty years before real GDP per capita catches up to the level in the United States. And that assumes it does not reach a plateau similar to Japan's before then.

SO WHAT IS WRONG?

It may seem like I'm sabotaging my own book by pointing out that the growth slowdown didn't translate into significant declines in average living standards and doesn't mean that China is somehow surpassing us. If we are going to understand the growth slowdown, though, it doesn't do any good to mischaracterize the effects of it. The problem with the growth slowdown is not so much with what is as with what could have been.

By growing more slowly, real GDP per capita in the US is lower than what we might have predicted in, say, 2000. And the effect of slow growth compounds over time, so that in the past two decades, we've left some significant gains in real GDP per capita on the table.

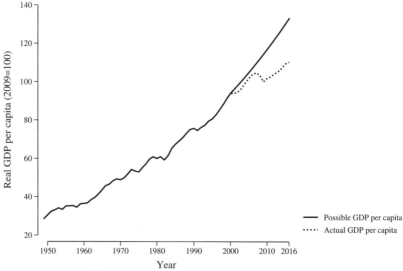

Figure 2.8. Actual and possible levels of real GDP per capita
Note: Real GDP per capita is from the Bureau of Economic Analysis. The figure shows the reported values of real GDP per capita from 1950 to 2000, all indexed to the year 2009. From 2000 to 2016 the dashed line plots the reported values of real GDP per capita, again indexed to the year 2009; the solid line shows what real GDP per capita would have been in each year, if the growth rate of real GDP per capita had remained at 2.2% per year, the average growth rate from 1960 to 2000.

We can play a little game of "what if" by asking what real GDP per capita would have been if, from 2000 on, it had continued to grow at its earlier rate.

Let's assume that, starting in 2000, the growth rate of real GDP per capita was equal to the average growth rate in the 1990s, 2.2%. Figure 2.8 shows what real GDP per capita could have looked like along with its actual level. The actual level of real GDP per capita was roughly 110 in 2016. With 2.2% growth, though, it would have been more like 136. In relative terms, that is about 23% higher. There is a significant amount of real GDP per capita that we are not producing because of the slowdown in growth rates.

These figures illustrate a missed opportunity to have higher material living standards. The gap between the two lines represents something like the "cost" of the growth slowdown. But as I'll discuss as we go through the book, this cost looks like something we chose to pay willingly as we adapted our spending patterns and family structure to the high level of living standards we acquired. Living standards in 2016 were not as high as they could have been given past growth rates. But that doesn't mean that living standards were low in 2016. The increase from 1950 to 2000 was substantial and had a significant effect on our economy in the twenty-first century.

THE INPUTS TO ECONOMIC GROWTH

3 Before I make the case that the growth slowdown is a sign of success, I need to establish what drives growth in the first place. And to understand what drives growth, we need to understand what drives the production of real goods and services, because growth is just the increase in those real goods and services. Production depends on the amounts of inputs we use — *stocks* in the parlance of economics — and the two most important are physical and human capital. We could also consider the stocks of natural resources that we used, but in practice those turn out to be a bit player in this story, so I'm going to set them aside for this analysis. The stocks of human and physical capital are not the only things that matter for production, and so they are not the only things that matter in explaining the growth slowdown. But as I'll explain in the next chapter, to explain the other driver of growth, we first need to know how big the stocks of human and physical capital were and how fast they were growing. This chapter is all about those capital stocks, what goes into them, and how to measure them.

THE COMPONENTS OF HUMAN CAPITAL

The easiest part of human capital to get your head around is time. To produce goods and services, we need people to commit some of their time. That time could be spent busing tables, writing legal briefs, teaching a class, running a drill press, or driving a truck. But the goods and services people want — clean tables, legal briefs, an education, a piece of

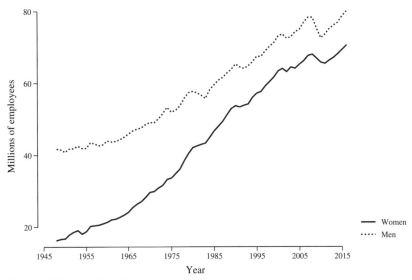

Figure 3.1. Number of employees
Note: Data is from the Bureau of Labor Statistics.

metal with a hole in it, or some boxes moved from El Paso to Denver—don't happen without people putting in their time.

The total amount of time provided depends on the number of people working and the hours they each put in. Figure 3.1 plots the raw number of employees over time, by sex. In the late 1940s, there were about 40 million men working for wages in the US and about 17 million women. Over the following seven decades, the number of men working just about doubled, to 80 million, which roughly tracked the doubling of the US population in this period of time. For women, the number working was close to 70 million in 2015, four times more than in the 1940s. This reflected both population growth and a significant shift in women's rate of participation in the labor force over time. Together, the stock of employees in the US grew from about 57 million in the late 1940s to almost 150 million in 2015.

Even though the number of employees went up by a factor of about 2.5 in this period, the average hours worked per week by those employees fell over time. Comprehensive data for hours worked doesn't extend back as far, but figure 3.2 plots the data from 1965 until today. In 1965 a worker's average weekly hours were around 38.5. By 2015,

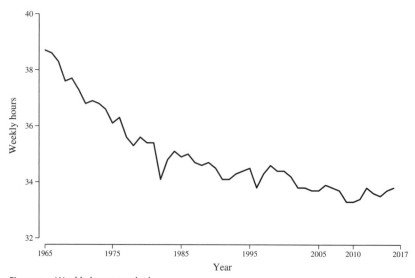

Figure 3.2. Weekly hours worked
Note: Data is from the Bureau of Labor Statistics.

this was 33.7 hours per week. If we assume that hours worked in the 1940s were about 40 per week, which seems a reasonable extrapolation given figure 3.2, then the drop in hours was not enough to offset the rise in the number of employees, which means that the total input of time provided by workers doubled between the 1940s and 2015.

There is more to human capital than just the time people put in; they also contribute their skills. The effective amount of human capital provided may have risen much faster than indicated by time alone if skills were growing. But there isn't a clear and objective way to measure skills like there is to measure time. How do I compare or add the skills of an oral surgeon to the skills of a bartender? In the absence of an obvious metric, the most common way is to look at years of schooling, with the presumption that workers with higher levels of education possess more skills. This isn't true in every individual case, of course. There are highly skilled high school graduates, and there are PhDs who can't find their way out of a paper bag. But in general we think that skills are correlated with education, if only because we see higher educated workers receive higher wages, an indication that they bring something extra to employers.

Figure 3.3 plots the share of prime working-age workers, age 25 and older, with different levels of education over time. Around 1940, less than 20% of those people had completed high school, and 60% had finished elementary school. Less than 10% had completed college or even attended some college. Over time the educational achievement of the adult population changed. By 2010, around 33% had completed only high school, and 5% had completed only elementary school. In contrast, about 33% had completed college, and another 30% had completed some postsecondary schooling. As a whole, the workforce in the United States had a much higher level of general skills in 2010 than in 1940.

Another component of human capital to consider is the role of experience in the workforce, which we can measure by the number of years a worker has been in the labor force. Just like education, there is no clear way to measure how experience translates into human capital. One could imagine that as individuals work, they gain additional human capital, either from explicit on-the-job training or from im-

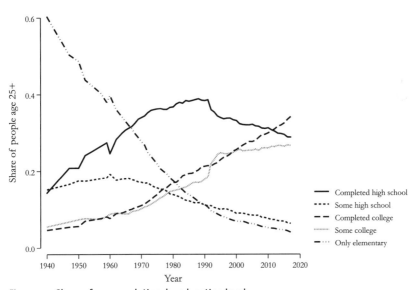

Figure 3.3. Share of 25+ population, by education level
Note: Data is from the US Census Bureau, Current Population Survey. The shares were calculated by the author.

plicit acquisition of skills and habits that make them more productive. Of course, at some point more experience might become a detriment to workers' human capital, perhaps if they tend to rely on their usual way of doing things rather than being willing to adapt. We'll see some evidence shortly on how experience translates to human capital, but let's start by examining how the level of experience has changed over time.

In 1960, the average age of a worker was about 42, but that had fallen to 40.5 by 1980. After that, it rose again, reaching just over 43 in 2010, and it will probably increase a little further by 2020. These do not look like monumental changes, but we can see something a little more dramatic if we consider the distribution of workers by age in more detail. In 1960, about 36% of the working-age population was between 20 and 34 years of age. By 1980, that share rose to 46%, but by 2010 it was back down to 34%. For several decades in the late twentieth century, the US economy had a relatively young and inexperienced workforce, compared to both the twenty-first century and the period not long after World War II. Depending on just how experience affects human capital, this will help determine how the entire stock of human capital moved over time.

MEASURING THE STOCK OF HUMAN CAPITAL

We'd like to have a way of combining all this information about the number of workers, their hours, their education, and their experience into a single measure of the human capital stock. Multiplying the number of workers times the average hours of a worker in a given year gives us the total hours of work, which is straightforward. But those hours of work were being performed by more educated workers over time, as well as by workers who at first had a little less experience (on average) and then a little more. How do we adjust the raw measure of hours worked to reflect the change in the human capital of workers?

Labor economists have found, over and over again, that each year of schooling tends to raise someone's wage by a certain percentage. You could spend a whole semester in graduate school arguing about what the right percentage was, but a common number to use is 10%. This works like compound interest, so that someone with a high school education, or twelve years of education, would be presumed to have about 213% more human capital than someone who had not attended school at all. A person with a college education is presumed to have about 46% more human capital than someone who only graduated high school. From 1920 to 2010 the average worker went from seven years of schooling to thirteen years. The additional six years of schooling imply that human capital per worker was about 77% higher in 2010 than in 1920.

The calculation of the effect of experience is similar, in that the estimated gain in wages from additional experience changes as workers age. There are again a host of different estimates, and from my review of the literature I've drawn out the following numbers. When workers are new, each additional year of experience adds about 5% to their wage. But by the time workers have about ten years of experience, that number is down to about 3.6% per year, and it drops to 2.2% after twenty years. By the time a worker has more than thirty years of experience, the return on an additional year is down to zero. This is consistent with the fact that most workers reach their peak earnings in their late forties or early fifties.

Again, assuming that wages are proportional to human capital, these estimates of the effect of experience enable us to infer the human capital of workers at different ages as well. So we can assume that a worker with ten years of experience has 53% more human capital than one with no experience, and a worker with twenty years of experience has about 105% more human capital than a new worker. What this all means for us is that the amount of human capital being used in the economy fluctuates with the age structure.

The estimates of human capital from education and experience can be combined with the data on number of workers and hours worked to come up with a total stock of human capital in each year. Now, because what we care about in the end is production of real GDP *per capita*, what really matters to us is the stock of human capital per capita. Notice that we measure the human capital stock based on the number and characteristics of workers, but we divide that stock by the total number of people, regardless of whether they are work-

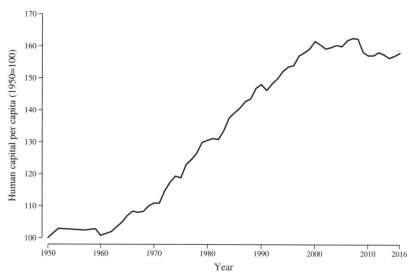

Figure 3.4. Stock of human capital per capita over time
Note: The level of human capital per capita was calculated by the author from data on the number of employees (from the Bureau of Labor Statistics), hours worked per week (from the Bureau of Labor Statistics), educational attainment (from the Current Population Survey), worker experience (from the Current Population Survey), and total population (from the census). The details of the calculation can be found in the appendix.

ing. So part of what determines human capital per capita is the ratio of workers to population, and as we'll see later, that is driven in large part by the age structure. For the moment, let's just focus on the resulting index of human capital per capita.

The index doesn't have any natural units, so in figure 3.4 I've scaled it to be equal to 100 in 1950, and you can see how the human capital stock compared to that value over time. By 2016, human capital per person was about 60% higher than in 1950. The major pattern visible here is the leveling out of the stock of human capital per capita starting around 2000. It stayed flat for a few years and then took a distinct dip in 2009 as a result of the drop in work hours during and after the financial crisis. This dip did not wipe out the major gain in human capital that occurred during the twentieth century, but the value of human capital per capita in 2016 was about the same as in 1998, indicating that the human capital stock per capita did not grow during those eighteen years.

Figure 3.4 doesn't quite give a clear indication of the role of human capital in the growth slowdown. In figure 3.5, I've plotted the ten-year average growth rate of human capital. In the early 1960s this growth rate was negative, which reflects the rapid growth of population as a result of the baby boom, which added babies but not workers. From the mid-1960s to about 2000, the growth rate of human capital per capita was about 1%–1.5% per year, in part because those baby boomers grew up and started to enter the workforce. But around the early 2000s—before the financial crisis of 2008–2009—that growth rate started to fall. The big dip in the growth rate in 2010 reflects the severe drop in total hours worked during the recession, and since then, the growth rate has stayed negative. This reflects, in part, the fact that the baby boomers are starting to retire.

Because human capital is one of the inputs to GDP production, the growth slowdown in human capital is part of the reason for the growth slowdown in GDP. And as you can tell, and as I'll lay out in much more detail later, a lot of that is because of the baby boomers'

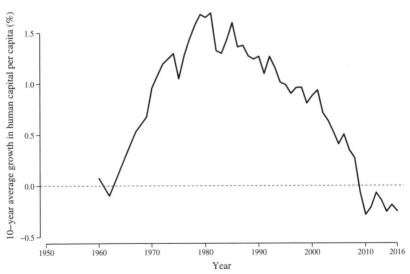

Figure 3.5. Ten-year average growth rate of human capital

Note: The figure shows the annualized growth rate from year *t* – 10 to year *t* (e.g., the growth rate in 2016 is the annualized growth rate from 2006 to 2016) of human capital per capita, and that data is drawn from figure 3.4.

move into retirement. Is this slowdown in human capital growth the only reason for the growth slowdown? No. To find out how important it is, though, we'll have to do a little more work describing how human capital is related to producing GDP. We'll get to that in the next chapter, but for now let's look at how the other big input to production, physical capital, grew over time.

THE COMPONENTS OF PHYSICAL CAPITAL

In imagining physical capital, most people think of things like bull-dozers and steel mills, and those are both part of the stock of physical capital. But also included are things like the computer you use for work, as well as the desks and lectern in the lecture room where I hold class. The kitchen equipment at your favorite restaurant is physical capital, as is the massage table at a day spa. The buildings all these pieces of equipment sit in are part of the physical capital stock, so every factory, warehouse, strip mall, school and office building, and Starbucks counts. Also included is residential housing, both apartment buildings that are rented out and single-family homes.

As a rough guide, physical capital consists of all the things that can be used to produce more GDP and are not used up in the process — they will still be around after they are used. This separates physical capital from stuff like raw materials. But this also leads to some fuzziness in definitions. Your house counts as physical capital because it produces real services to you, in the form of a place to live, and because even though there is wear and tear, your house will continue to provide services in the future. Durable goods, things like washing machines, refrigerators, and cars, also provide services to you on an ongoing basis. So they can be counted in the capital stock, and we can try to include an estimate of the value of those services in GDP. Officially, the Bureau of Economic Analysis (BEA) doesn't do this, but that is because it seems almost impossible to keep track of the value of those appliances, not because there is a bright line dividing durable goods from physical capital. Honestly, almost anything you own could be counted as part of the physical capital stock if it provided an ongoing service. My pants, for example, are not currently included in the official physical capital stock. But they provide an ongoing service to me, keeping my legs warm when it is cold outside and catching all the stuff I spill on myself during lunch.

Despite the caveats, we'll stick with the accepted definition of the physical capital stock, which includes residential housing but excludes durable goods. Having made this decision, we have a problem of how to add up all the different kinds of physical capital used in the economy. How do you add my house to the desks in my classroom, and then add both of those to the robot assembly units at the Toyota plant in Tennessee? This is a lot like the problem of measuring GDP and trying to add up the value of different goods and services. The solution for physical capital is to add up the total amount of real GDP spent on acquiring the capital in the first place, adjusted for some depreciation. The stock of physical capital we measure is thus the sum of the real GDP spent on capital goods each year, with an adjustment for the fact that some of that capital purchased in the past is now obsolete or broken. Allowing for that physical depreciation—which may not be identical to depreciation in the financial value of the asset—the measured stock of physical capital in any given year is mainly determined by spending on capital goods over the past decade or so.

This definition of the stock of physical capital misses the actual usefulness of each unit of capital for production, similar to how our stock of human capital misses the subtleties of each person's skill. What we are doing here with physical capital is assuming that a $1,000 laptop provides the same capital input to production as four $250 office chairs. That probably isn't right, but in the absence of keeping track of every activity done by every employee in every business to know precisely how capital goods are used, we need a rough way of summing up different capital purchases.

Figure 3.6 plots the level of physical capital over time, separating it into four categories to give some idea of what kinds of capital goods we have purchased. Because there are no natural units for the size of the capital stock, I set the total stock of capital in 2009 equal to 100, and the series shows how large each type of capital is relative to total capital in 2009. The most noticeable part of this figure is that structures, both residential and nonresidential, were by far the big-

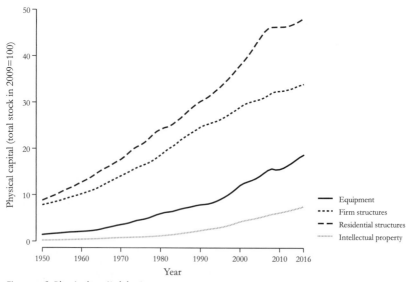

Figure 3.6. Physical capital, by type
Note: Data is from the Bureau of Economic Analysis. Each series is indexed to the total capital stock in 2009. "Residential structures" are homes. "Firm structures" are commercial real estate, including manufacturing plants, warehouses, and office buildings. "Intellectual property" includes intangible assets such as software. "Equipment" includes goods used in production such as computers, industrial machinery, and business vehicles.

gest components of the overall capital stock. Private residences have always been the largest stock of capital, equivalent to 45% of the entire capital stock in 2009. Nonresidential structures—things like factories, strip malls, and office buildings—were about one-third of the total capital stock in 2009.

Equipment is the kind of thing you would normally think of as capital: bulldozers and drill presses and computers. But this stock is small compared to the structures such items are housed in. The last category, intellectual property, is something not typically associated with the capital stock. Most recently, the stock of intellectual property includes the value of software, which has no tangible presence but does constitute an asset that provides ongoing services for firms. You can see that this stock was insignificant until the late 1980s, and although it has grown since then, it is still much smaller than the stock of structures.

Where figure 3.6 showed the level of the capital stocks at work in the economy, figure 3.7 shows the growth rates of the capital stock components year by year. Here, the ranking of the growth rates is almost a perfect inverse of the size of each capital stock. Intellectual property had growth rates of about 5%–6% per year throughout the twentieth century, but growth dipped below 4% in the twenty-first. Regardless, it still grew faster than almost any other type of capital over time. Equipment experienced large fluctuations in its growth rate but overall moved from around 5% in the 1960s to under 3% in the twenty-first century. Both residential and nonresidential structures grew at about 3% in the twentieth century but dipped below 2% in the past few years. The drop in the growth rate of residential housing after the 2009 recession is apparent in figure 3.7.

What you can see from all four series in figure 3.7 is that the growth rate of physical capital declined over time. The only exception is that the early 1950s had growth in structures that was about as slow as it

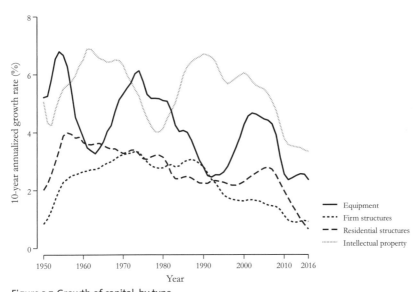

Figure 3.7. Growth of capital, by type
Note: The figure shows the annualized growth rate from year *t* – 10 to year *t* (e.g., the growth rate in 2016 is the annualized growth rate from 2006 to 2016) of each type of physical capital. Data is drawn from figure 3.6, and the definitions of the capital types can be found in that figure as well.

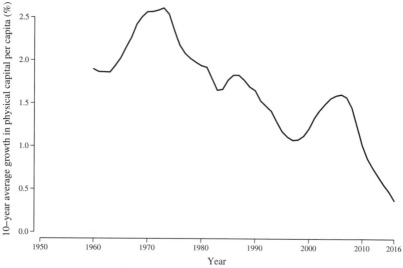

Figure 3.8. Growth rate of physical capital per capita
Note: Data on the total stock of physical capital is from the Bureau of Economic Analysis, and population data is from the census. The figure shows the annualized growth rate from year *t* – 10 to year *t* (e.g., the growth rate in 2016 is the annualized growth rate from 2006 to 2016) of physical capital per capita.

was in the twenty-first century, but otherwise the growth rates have all tended to trend downward starting in 1960.

THE GROWTH RATE OF AGGREGATE CAPITAL

We'd like to see how important physical capital is to the growth of GDP over time, and to do that, we want a single measure of the physical capital stock that combines the different categories shown in the prior figures. We'll come up with that by adding together the value of each kind of capital stock. As I mentioned, this method is imperfect, but it gives us a good idea of the gross stock of capital goods available for use in production. Given the aggregate capital stock, I'll again divide it by population so that we can track the stock of physical capital per capita.

Figure 3.8 plots the growth rate of physical capital per capita, again using ten-year averages. Here, the combined drop in growth rates for the different types of capital is clear. In the 1960s, the physical capital stock grew at around 2%–2.5% per year, falling to around 1.5%–2.0% per year from the 1980s to the early 2000s. The average growth rate started to fall in the early 2000s and took a big dive during the financial crisis. Unlike the growth rates of real GDP or human capital, though, the growth rate of physical capital has not rebounded since the financial crisis. This is largely because of the lack of a rebound in investment in structures, residential and nonresidential.

This long-run decline in the growth rate of physical capital per capita cannot, by itself, explain the growth slowdown in real GDP because it started well *before* the growth slowdown. But the failure of the growth rate of physical capital to rise back up after the financial crisis is one source of continued slow growth in real GDP. As with human capital, it is not the only source of slow growth. To know how important the slower growth in both physical and human capital was for the growth slowdown, we need to take into account how relevant both are for production. And that's what we turn to in the next chapter.

WHAT ACCOUNTS FOR
THE GROWTH SLOWDOWN?

The prior chapter showed that the growth rate of both major inputs to production—physical and human capital—fell in the past few decades. What it didn't tell us, though, was whether the lower growth rate of those inputs was the only explanation for the slowdown in the growth rate of GDP per capita. In this chapter I'll show you a simple accounting exercise that looks at how important these inputs were for growth. This will demonstrate that slower growth in physical and human capital can explain much, but not all, of the growth slowdown. This means that the growth rate of GDP per capita fell by even more than we might expect, meaning there must be some residual explanation for the growth slowdown that the two capital stocks cannot explain. Defining this residual growth, and understanding what drives it, will take up a few chapters later in the book.

EVERYBODY LOVES CAKE

This accounting can get very dry, so let me give you an analogy that may help illustrate what I'm trying to do. Imagine that you are making a cake, and you are interested in the total value of the cake you are baking, which is some combination of the size of the cake and how good it tastes. We could measure that value using a price, if you sold the cake, or we could measure that value by letting my kids rate the cake on both taste and size (they care deeply about both the quantity and quality of the cake they get to eat). But let's say that however we measure it, we see that the total value of your cake today was 4% larger than the cake you made yesterday. Now we want to know why.

When you look back over what you did, you see that the amount of flour you used today was 2% more than yesterday. The amount of baking powder you used today was 1% more than yesterday. As an experienced baker, you know that the size of your cake depends on both the amount of flour and the amount of baking powder, and that they matter equally. You calculate that the additional flour and baking powder should have increased the size of the cake by the average of those two growth rates, 1.5%, because the two changes matter equally. Holding quality constant, the additional quantity of cake due to baking powder and flour should have raised the total value of the cake by 1.5% as well.

But the actual cake value went up by 4%, which means that you still have to explain 2.5% of the growth in value. That 2.5% is the residual growth in cake value, over and above what you could attribute to the extra flour and baking powder. What explains residual growth? Everything you did differently except for the flour and baking powder. Maybe you used larger eggs, or more vanilla, or extra sugar. Maybe you stirred the batter less, or more, or with a whisk rather than a spoon. Maybe you switched from vegetable oil to melted butter or yogurt. Maybe you mixed everything together at once instead of combining the wet ingredients before adding the flour. Maybe you changed the flavor entirely from vanilla to chocolate or added sprinkles, nuts, or fruit. Maybe you baked it at 400 degrees rather than 375, or for twenty-two minutes rather than twenty-eight. Maybe you used a different kind of flour than yesterday, which doesn't show up in your simple calculation of using 2% more.

The point is that once we account for the role of flour and baking powder, everything else that matters to the value of a cake comes out in this residual growth of 2.5%. The story of accounting for growth in real GDP is similar. Physical and human capital are the flour and baking powder of real GDP per capita. We're going to use a rule of thumb about how to average physical and human capital growth to figure out how much they contributed to the growth rate of real GDP per capita. But that won't tell us the whole story, and there is going to be a significant amount of residual growth in real GDP per capita that physical and human capital cannot account for. That residual growth in real GDP per capita is just like the residual growth in the value of cake. It incorporates everything else about real GDP that isn't due to physical or human capital.

WEIGHTS FOR PHYSICAL AND HUMAN CAPITAL

To do all these calculations, we need several pieces of information. We already looked at the growth rate of real GDP per capita a few chapters ago. That is the equivalent of the growth in the value of the cake. And in the previous chapter, we looked at the growth rate of both physical and human capital per capita, and saw that both of those have grown more slowly in recent decades. Now, to calculate how much growth in real GDP per capita these two stocks of inputs were responsible for, I need something similar to that rule of thumb we used in evaluating the change in cake value. There we said that flour and baking powder were equally responsible for cake size, meaning that we put a weight of one-half on each and just averaged the growth rates.

Unlike flour and baking powder, though, we don't necessarily think that physical and human capital are equally important to producing real GDP per capita. So what are the weights we should use to average their growth rates? The weight we want is the *elasticity* of real GDP per capita with respect to each input. And to figure out what I mean by that term, let's try a little mental experiment. If I could magically double the amount of physical capital per capita in the economy, by how much would real GDP per capita go up? Would it double as well? Probably not. Yes, we'd have twice as many computers, semitrucks, and office buildings. But what would you do with twice as much office space for each person? Most of it would just sit empty. Same with the trucks and computers. Some of them would be useful, but a lot of them would end up sitting idle because there just aren't enough people around to work with them. GDP would go up, but it would not double. We'd get a similar answer if I told you that I doubled the amount of human capital per capita in the economy. Real GDP per capita would go up, as we'd have more workers, or workers who were each more skilled, or some combination of the two. But GDP per capita wouldn't double. We'd have a lot of extra workers floating around without anything to do because there wasn't enough physical capital to work with.

The elasticity of real GDP with respect to a capital stock measures the percentage by which real GDP would rise if we raised an input by 1%. If the elasticity of real GDP per capita with respect to physical capital per capita is 0.4, for example, then this means a 1% increase in the stock of physical capital increases real GDP per capita by only $0.4 \times 1\% = 0.4\%$. That this elasticity is less than 1 captures the idea that doubling the input doesn't double output. More generally, if we know the elasticities, we can figure out how much GDP went up over time as a result of the increase in the stocks of human and physical capital.

To figure out these elasticities, we need to make a few mild assumptions about how the economy works, and these tell us how to find these elasticities using some observable data. The first assumption is that the elasticities for physical and human capital have to add up to 1. This means that if we doubled both physical and human capital per capita, we'd get exactly twice as much real GDP per capita. All those extra workers would use all those extra office buildings and trucks and computers, and we wouldn't have to worry about empty buildings or idle workers.

To give you an example of how this works, let's say the elasticity for physical capital is 0.4 and the elasticity for human capital is 0.6, so they add up to 1. Now, raise the amount of both physical and human capital by 1%. Real GDP per capita will go up by 0.4% because of the increase in physical capital. Real GDP per capita will go up by 0.6% because of the increase in human capital. Together, real GDP per capita has gone up by 0.4% + 0.6% = 1.0%. A 1% increase in all inputs to production raises GDP by 1%. This assumption that the elasticities add up to 1—which is called constant returns to scale—is handy because if I can find just one of the elasticities, I can immediately solve for the other.

The second assumption we need is that the firms operating in the economy are not totally stupid. Formally, an economist might say that

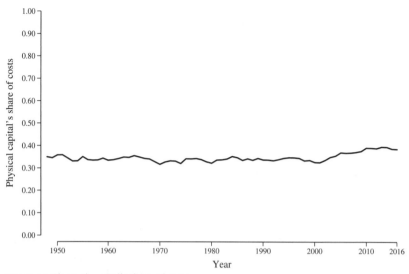

Figure 4.1. Physical capital's share of costs
Note: Data is from the Bureau of Labor Statistics multifactor productivity data set. Physical capital's share was calculated by the author using data on nominal costs for both physical capital and wages.

we can assume that firms are cost minimizers. That means that they are using the cheapest possible combination of human and physical capital to produce an output, even if management is using hundred-dollar bills to light their cigars in the boardroom. This assumption about firms has an interesting implication; namely, that the amount spent on human capital (e.g., wages) as a share of spending on all inputs (e.g., wages plus physical capital costs) is equal to the elasticity of output with respect to human capital. For example, if the elasticity for human capital is 0.6, then a cost-minimizing firm will spend 0.6 (i.e., 60%) of its costs on human capital in the form of wages and the other 0.4 (i.e., 40%) on physical capital.

We can use this assumption to go backward from data on costs to figure out the elasticities. Combined with the first assumption about the two elasticities adding up to 1, I just need data on the share of costs going to physical capital, and I can infer both elasticities.

Figure 4.1 shows physical capital's share of costs. This data is for private businesses only, which leaves out government and residential housing, both of which are major sectors of the economy. But allowing this share to vary with their inclusion would not change the basic pattern. As it is, the data series is pretty boring. The share of costs that are paid to physical capital stayed at about 0.35 the whole time, with a slight tick up toward 0.40 by 2015. The implied share of costs being paid to human capital is therefore about 0.65 over the same period, with a slight tick down toward 0.60 by 2015. Given this data, I'm going to stick with using a cost share for physical capital of 0.35 and 0.65 for human capital to do all the calculations. Nothing important will happen to the conclusions if you use the actual shares from each year, as we're going to be looking mainly at long periods of time. And the basic conclusions won't change much if I use 0.33 or 0.37 for physical capital, either.

As an aside, you may be familiar with the idea that human capital's share of GDP fell over the past few decades. That fact is consistent with the idea that human capital's share of costs was stable over time. The difference arises from growth in the share of profits in GDP over time, which I cover in more detail later in the book.

RUNNING THE NUMBERS

With the elasticities for physical and human capital, we can finally calculate how important their growth rates were for the growth rate of real GDP per capita. Let's start with average growth over the twentieth century, from 1950 to 2000. The average growth rate of physical capital per person was about 1.83% per year. Multiplied by the elasticity of 0.35, this means that real GDP per capita should have grown at the rate of 0.64% per year because of the accumulation of physical capital alone. Human capital per person grew at 0.96% per year. With an elasticity of 0.65, this means that real GDP per capita should have grown at 0.62% per year solely because of growth in human capital. Together, real GDP per capita should have grown at 0.64% + 0.62% = 1.26% per year just because we accumulated more of both stocks of capital.

But real GDP per capita grew at about 2.25% per year in the twentieth century. That means that there was residual growth of 2.25% − 1.26% = 0.98% per year (the difference isn't exact because of rounding). The growth rate was higher than we'd have expected given the

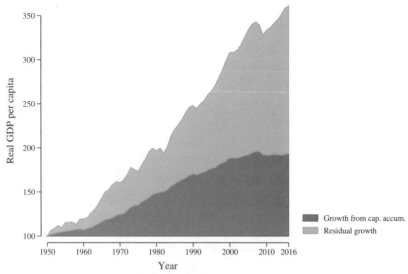

Figure 4.2. Accounting for real GDP per capita

Note: The top line of the figure plots actual real GDP per capita, normalized to equal 100 in 1950, using data from the Bureau of Economic Analysis. The middle line that defines the dark gray area below it is the hypothetical path of real GDP per capita, calculated by the author, assuming that only physical capital and human capital accumulation occurred. The dark gray area shows how much of the increase in real GDP per capita was due to capital accumulation; the light gray area shows how much of the increase was due to residual growth.

increase in capital stocks. That residual growth of 0.98% per year is like the residual growth in the value of the cake from the beginning of this chapter. It captures all the *other* things that were generating growth in the amount of economic activity per person. That might be better technologies, or changes in how capital was allocated between firms and industries, or changes in our demand for different goods and services. For the moment, let's just concentrate on the fact that this residual growth exists and see how important it was as a contributor to economic growth.

Figure 4.2 shows how real GDP per capita grew over time. It rose by a factor of just over 3.5 between 1950 and 2016, from 100 to 350. Of that increase, the lower, dark portion is what can be accounted for by the increase in the use of physical and human capital. If we had frozen the technology, allocations, and our preferences at 1950 levels, and then just loaded more and more physical and human capital into the economy, by 2016 real GDP per capita would have been about 180, or only 1.8 times larger than in 1950. The additional growth in real GDP per capita that occurred is captured by the light gray area, which shows residual growth in real GDP. As you can see, much of the growth in living standards over time was due to the increase in this residual, and not due to physical and human capital accumulation. The residual is not just an accounting error; it is fundamentally important to an explanation of how real GDP per capita grew.

DOES THIS EXPLAIN THE GROWTH SLOWDOWN?

Figure 4.2 showed the importance of the residual for growth in real GDP per capita in the long run. But does residual growth help explain the growth slowdown? To see the importance of the residual, consider table 4.1, which shows all of this accounting for real GDP per capita growth for different time periods. The top row replicates the growth calculation we just did for 1950 to 2000. The first column shows average growth in real GDP per capita (2.25%). The second and third columns show the *weighted* growth in physical capital (0.64%) and human capital (0.62%), using our elasticities to figure out how important each of them was to producing GDP growth. The last column is average growth in the residual (0.98%), which is the first column minus the second and third ones.

In the middle of the table, you'll see the accounting for each individual decade of the twentieth century. Growth was a little slower in the 1950s (1.78%) and a little faster in the 1960s (2.92%), but for the most part the growth rate of real GDP per capita stayed close to the average of 2.25%. The growth in all decades was driven by a combination of the accumulation of physical capital, accumulation of human capital, and some residual growth. Residual growth varied across the decades, from a low of 0.33% in the 1970s to a high of 1.41% in the 1960s, but it was always a significant contributor to growth.

In the second-to-last row of the table you can find the accounting for the "long decade" of 2000 to 2016. I excluded the decade from 2000 to 2010 because the end point of that period is dominated by effects of the financial crisis, which skews the information on long-

Table 4.1 Accounting for growth in the United States, by time period

Time period	GDP per capita	Physical capital per capita	Human capital per capita	Residual
		Growth rate (%)		
1950–2000	2.25	0.64	0.62	0.98
1950–1960	1.78	0.66	0.05	1.07
1960–1970	2.92	0.89	0.62	1.41
1970–1980	2.07	0.67	1.06	0.33
1980–1990	2.32	0.57	0.82	0.93
1990–2000	2.17	0.42	0.57	1.18
21st century, 2000–2016	1.00	0.27	−0.10	0.82
Last 10 years, 2006–2016	0.61	0.13	−0.16	0.64

Note: The table shows the breakdown of actual growth in real GDP per capita (column 1) into the contribution from physical capital (column 2), human capital (column 3), and residual growth (column 4). The contributions of physical and human capital are calculated from their actual annualized growth rate over the given period of time, multiplied by their associated elasticity (0.35 for physical capital and 0.65 for human capital). The residual is simply the growth rate of real GDP per capita minus the listed contributions of physical and human capital. Because of rounding, columns 2–4 may not add up precisely to column 1. Each row of the table shows the same kind of accounting but limited to a given time period.

run trends. Regardless, we can see that the average growth rate of real GDP per capita was lower (1.00%) in the twenty-first century than in any other decade in the postwar era.

If you look across the columns for the twenty-first century, you can see where that growth slowdown came from. For 2000 to 2016, the contribution of growth in physical capital per person was only 0.27% per year, well below the average in the twentieth century of 0.64%. In raw terms, the drop in the growth rate of physical capital shaved 0.37 percentage points (0.64 minus 0.27) off the growth rate in the twenty-first century compared to the twentieth century. There is a similar story for human capital per capita. In the twentieth century human capital contributed about 0.62% per year, but from 2000 to 2016 it subtracted 0.10 percentage points each year. The drop in the human capital growth rate cut 0.72 percentage points (0.62 minus −0.10) from the growth rate in 2000–2016 compared to the twentieth century. Together, physical and human capital reduced growth in real GDP per capita by 1.09% per year in the twenty-first century compared to the twentieth.

But overall growth fell from 2.25% per year in the twentieth century to 1.00% in the twenty-first, a difference of 1.25%. The remaining drop in the growth rate is accounted for by a decline in how fast that residual grew. In the twentieth century it averaged 0.98% per year, but in 2006–2016 only 0.82%, a difference of 0.16%. It's not sufficient for us just to focus on why physical and human capital growth declined; we'll also have to consider what drove down the residual growth rate.

The final row of table 4.1 shows the accounting from 2006 to 2016. The last ten years of data show an even more severe slowdown in economic growth, to 0.61% per year. In comparison to the twentieth century, and even to the accounting for 2000 to 2016, the slow growth in this last period can be attributed more to the residual than to the accumulation of capital stocks. From 2006 to 2016, the contribution of residual growth was only 0.64% per year, down from the twentieth-century average of 0.98%. That drop of 0.34 percentage points was a significant part of the reason that growth in real GDP per capita fell from 2.25% to 0.61%. Regardless of the exact time frame we use as a comparison, residual growth contributed to the slowdown.

PHYSICAL CAPITAL MATTERS LESS THAN IT SEEMS

The accounting in table 4.1 indicates that all three contributors to economic production led to the growth slowdown. But the table also overstates the importance of physical capital to some extent. The reason is that producing new capital goods—like buildings, bulldozers, and laptops—is part of producing real GDP. If growth in real GDP slowed for some other reason—say, because human capital growth stalled or residual growth fell—then this would in turn slow the growth rate of physical capital.

To get your head around this, think of the economy as being like a garden where you grow tomato plants. The number of tomatoes your plants yield depends on some "physical capital" like tomato seeds and the amount of nutrients in the soil, as well as on the human capital you provide in terms of planting and weeding, and some residual growth, which depends on the amount of rain and sunshine the plants get. Each year, from your tomato harvest, you set some of your output aside to add to your capital stock. You can save some of the tomatoes to provide seeds for new tomato plants the next year, and then compost the vines and mix them in with the soil to replenish the stock of nutrients. The better your crop of tomatoes in a given year, the more you can "invest" in building up your capital stock.

If one year there is a severe drought (e.g., low or negative residual growth), then you'll get fewer tomatoes, and the number of seeds and the amount of composted vines will fall as well. This will make your capital stock fall, and so the following year, even with normal amounts of rain, your output of tomatoes will be lower. If we did a simple accounting, then we'd attribute some of the drop in tomato production this year to the decline in the capital stock of seeds and compost. But that isn't quite right, is it? The real source of that decline in your tomato yield was the drought the year before, which in turn affected your ability to invest.

The tomato analogy is oversimplified, but the same principle applies to talking about physical capital accumulation in the economy. Because physical capital depends on our ability to produce real GDP, the drop in the growth rate of physical capital in the twenty-first century may be as much a consequence of the growth slowdown as it is a cause. While arguments could be made that both human capital and the residual suffer from the same issue, they suffer far less than physical capital does. Lower growth in real GDP could, for example, limit the resources available to staff schools or universities, but most of the changes in human capital growth are driven by the demographics of people aging into or out of the labor force. And although lower

Table 4.2 Accounting for growth in the United States, adjusting for capital

	Growth rate (%)			
Time period	GDP per capita	Physical capital	Human capital per capita	Residual
1950–2000	2.25	−0.22	0.96	1.51
1950–1960	1.78	0.05	0.08	1.65
1960–1970	2.92	−0.21	0.95	2.17
1970–1980	2.07	−0.08	1.64	0.51
1980–1990	2.32	−0.37	1.26	1.43
1990–2000	2.17	−0.52	0.88	1.81
21st century, 2000–2016	1.00	−0.12	−0.15	1.26
Last 10 years, 2006–2016	0.61	−0.13	−0.25	0.99

Note: The table shows the breakdown of actual growth in real GDP per capita (column 1) into the contribution from physical capital (column 2), human capital (column 3), and residual growth (column 4). The contribution of physical capital is adjusted here for the fact that physical capital is produced using real GDP, which adjusts the implied elasticities used to do the calculation. Full details are in the appendix. The residual is simply the growth rate of real GDP per capita minus the listed contributions of physical and human capital. Because of rounding, columns 2–4 may not add up precisely to column 1. Each row of the table shows the same kind of accounting but limited to a given time period.

growth in real GDP could limit the resources available for things like research and development that might influence residual growth, residual growth depends on many things beyond just R&D.

If table 4.1 overstates the importance of the growth rate of physical capital, can we correct it? The answer is yes, and doing so involves some tedious but simple adjustments to the results in that table. Briefly, we need to know how fast physical capital per capita grew relative to the growth of GDP per capita, and not just how fast it grew overall. I've shown the result of doing this in table 4.2, which has the same overall structure as table 4.1. The growth rates of real GDP per capita in the first column are all identical, because I don't change that observable outcome, only how I account for that outcome in the other columns.

The "physical capital" column shows the adjusted effect of capital on growth in real GDP per capita. For the twentieth century, this effect was negative, at –0.22% per year. That doesn't mean the capital stock was falling, only that the growth in the capital stock was not keeping up with growth in real GDP. To go back to the tomatoes, what this indicates is that even though the tomato crop was growing over time, you were plowing a smaller and smaller share of it back into the garden every year. Jumping all the way down to the period 2000–2016, the effect was only –0.12% per year. This implies that the effect of capital was less negative than in the twentieth century, and by itself this should have made growth *higher*. The implication of table 4.2 is that changes in our accumulation of physical capital had little to no effect on generating the growth slowdown. Physical capital accumulation was a small net drag on growth from 1950 onward.

In contrast, once we've done this adjustment on physical capital, it pushes up the implied effects of human capital and the residual. We're blaming, so to speak, the drought and not the effect it had on our stocks of seeds and compost. For human capital, the contribution to economic growth in the twentieth century was 0.96%. But by 2000–2016, this contribution was negative, at –0.15%. By itself, the decline in human capital growth can account for a 1.11% (0.96 minus –0.15) drop in the growth rate of real GDP per capita. This accounts for almost all of the growth slowdown. The remainder was due to the decline in residual growth. Properly accounted for, the residual grew at about 1.51% per year in the twentieth century, but at only 1.26% per year from 2000 to 2016, meaning the growth rate fell by about 0.25% per year because residual growth declined. This residual growth accounts for the remainder of the growth slowdown.

The final row of table 4.2 tells a similar story for the period 2006–2016. Again, the drop in the growth rate of human capital per capita, from 0.96% to –0.25%, can account for a huge part of the growth slowdown, whereas residual growth, which fell from 1.51% to 0.99%, can account for the rest. Using 2006–2016 as the comparison period, residual growth accounted for almost one-third of the slowdown, and human capital accounted for the rest. It is clear that the slowdown in human capital growth and the slowdown in residual growth are responsible for the growth slowdown.

If you were to compare the twenty-first century—either 2000-2016 or just 2006-2016—to the decade of the 1990s alone, you'd come up with a similar answer for what drove the growth slowdown. It was predominantly a function of slower growth in human capital per capita combined with an additional drop in residual growth. With all this evidence, I'll spend most of the rest of the book explaining why human capital growth and residual growth fell during the twenty-first century, with less focus on what drove changes in physical capital growth.

BEWARE OF FALSE ACCURACY

A last note is that we do not need to get hung up on the exact numbers in tables 4.1 and 4.2. The tables show answers with two decimal places, but none of these numbers is that precise. The accountings I've done depend on the assumptions I put into them, including how the stock of human capital is defined and how big the elasticities are. I've laid out all the assumptions behind these calculations in the appendix, and the code and data I used are available online, so you can investigate this yourself. Any adjustments you make would alter the exact numbers in the tables. One particular adjustment that may be relevant is the measurement of human capital, which had a lot of assumptions built in. In the appendix, you can see how things come out in the accounting if I use an alternative series on human capital that some researchers favor. The conclusion about the relative importance of human capital for the growth slowdown remains intact, though.

Perhaps more relevant, I've done all my accounting for the growth rate in real GDP per capita, but very often economists focus on accounting for the growth rate in real GDP per worker. In my accounting, the growth rate of real GDP per capita is affected by how many workers there are per capita, and that in turn will be driven in large part by demographic shifts, like the aging population. In contrast, if you do the accounting only for real GDP per worker, you set aside the demographic effects but gain the ability to see what is driving the growth slowdown among actual workers. I happen to favor the broader approach, as I believe real GDP per capita is a more relevant measure of our living standards.

John Fernald has done some of the most respected work on accounting for the growth slowdown, often building on his work with Susanto Basu and Miles Kimball. He focuses on real GDP per worker while also incorporating nuances like factor utilization (e.g., a shuttered factory doesn't count as part of the capital stock), and he makes some different choices about some parameters, like elasticities. His work, including a recent working paper with Robert Hall, James Stock, and Mark Watson, also tends to focus only on the business sector, as opposed to the whole economy. Fernald's results, across his work, do not question the presence of the growth slowdown. But they do give a slightly different accounting for it. Nevertheless, they show that physical capital played a muted role in accounting for the slowdown, but in terms of real GDP per worker, the role of human capital was smaller, and the role of the residual larger. Either way, the successes behind the drop in human capital and residual growth that I'll explain remain important to understanding the growth slowdown.

THE EFFECT OF AN AGING POPULATION

The accounting in the last chapter showed that the single most important explanation for the growth slowdown was the decline in the growth rate of human capital per person. Human capital per capita went from a growth rate of 0.96% during the twentieth century to a growth rate of –0.15% during the twenty-first. As I'll explain in this chapter, it is best to see this decline in the growth rate of human capital as a success along several dimensions, and thus much of the growth slowdown is a consequence of success as well.

These successes accrued over many decades, but they manifested in the twenty-first century as an aging population. The most obvious outcome of aging was a decrease in the number of workers relative to population, which in turn reduced the amount of human capital per person. But beyond that, there were more subtle effects of the age structure on growth in education and worker experience.

FALLING FERTILITY

The origin of the aging population of the twenty-first century is the decline in fertility that started decades ago. Figure 5.1 plots two different measures of fertility. The first, the crude birth rate (measured on the left axis), is simply the number of babies born in a given year per thousand women. There were almost thirty babies per thousand in 1910, but this declined into the 1930s, when it reached about seventeen babies per thousand. The baby boom is visible in the middle of the 1940s, with the crude birth rate

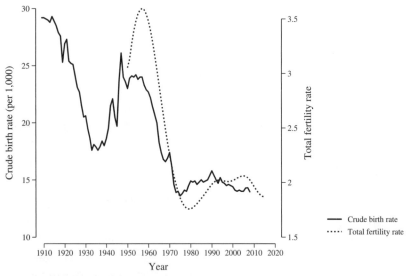

Figure 5.1. Different fertility measures over time
Note: Data on both crude birth rate (left axis) and total fertility rate (right axis) is from Mitchell (2013).

shooting up to above twenty-five babies per thousand in 1947 and staying high into the 1950s, before dropping again in the 1960s. By the 1970s, the crude birth rate had hit about fifteen babies per thousand, and it has stayed around that number ever since. If you look over the whole time period, you can see that the baby boom interrupted a steady decline in the crude birth rate.

The crude birth rate is a good measure of the raw number of kids added to the population, but the fall over time could have been due to changes in the age structure of the population and not to a change in fertility behavior. For example, if in 1960 there happened to be a lot of women age 20–35, this would tend to indicate a high crude birth rate, as these women would be of prime childbearing age. Today, these women would be age 80–95 and incapable of having more kids. Even if women age 20–35 *today* were having as many kids as their mothers or grandmothers did, there would be few of them relative to the number of women age 80–95, so the crude birth rate—babies born per thousand women—would be low.

To confirm that the drop in crude birth rate reflected a change in behavior, and not just an echo of a large cohort of mothers in the 1950s and 1960s, we can look at total fertility rate. This is plotted in figure 5.1 against the axis on the right. The total fertility rate is a synthetic measure that captures how many children each woman would be expected to have if she had children at the age-specific rates prevailing in a given year. So in 1960, when the total fertility rate was above 3.5, a woman entering childbearing age (say, age 15–45) would be expected to have 3.5 kids, on average, if the age-specific rates of fertility in 1960 *stayed constant over time.* That is, if a woman made all the same fertility choices that women of different ages in 1960 were making, then she'd have about 3.5 kids in her lifetime.

Although the data does not go back as far for total fertility rate, you can see that it tracks the crude birth rate. In 1950, the total fertility rate was 3, but it jumped to over 3.5 by the late 1950s, and then it plunged, just like the crude birth rate. After bottoming out around 1980, the total fertility rate recovered to around 2 children per woman by 2010. What this tells us is that fertility behavior, and not just the number of women capable of having children, changed over time. By 1980, the women in each age group were having fewer kids than women were from 1950 or 1960. This meant that a woman entering childbearing age in 1980 was expected to have only 1.75 kids, not 3.5.

The decline in the crude birth rate was driven largely by a shift in the preferences of families regarding the number of children to have. This behavioral change is a prime mover of population aging and the growth slowdown. After looking over those phenomena, I'll return to the question of why this behavioral change in fertility occurred, why it can be seen as a sign of success, and why we shouldn't expect it to change any time soon.

THE AGE DISTRIBUTION

Figure 5.2 shows the raw effects of the fertility decline on the size of age cohorts over time. The figure plots, in millions, the number of people in the United States in a series of five-year age cohorts, denoted by the minimum age in the cohort along the horizontal axis.

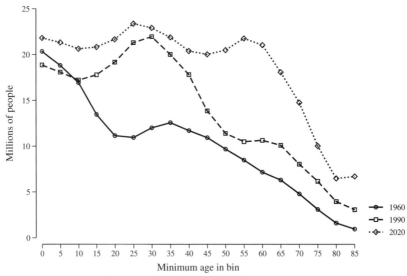

Figure 5.2. Age structure over time

Note: Data is from the Organisation for Economic Co-operation and Development population statistics database. Horizontal axis labels refer to the lowest age in a given bin, so that "5" indicates the number of people age 5–9. The "85" bin includes all people 85 years old and older.

For example, the cohort labeled "5" refers to the number of people age 5–9. The last cohort, 85, is a little different and includes all people at least 85 years old.

From this figure, you can see from the shift up in the curves that the absolute size of the population became larger from 1960 to 1990, and it is projected to be larger in 2020 than in 1990. Despite the aging population, we will have, in absolute terms, more kids age 0–4 and 5–9 in 2020 than we've ever had. However, we also will have a lot more elderly people than ever before.

There were few elderly people in 1960 both in absolute terms and in relation to younger ages. By 1990, the absolute number of elderly people was much larger. For example, in 1960 there were about 5 million people in the 70–74 age range, but by 1990 there were 7.5 million. By 2020, there will be about 15 million people age 70–74, double the number from 1990. And if we examine the age groups from 50 to 75, it's clear that they all are poised to grow by substantial numbers by 2020, which will make the US age distribution much more "flat" than it was in the past.

This aging population changed the proportion of working-age adults to people in "dependent" categories, such as children (age 0–20) and the elderly (age 65 and older). Take a look at the curve for 1990 in figure 5.2, for example. There was a big bulge of people in the range of 20–24 to 40–44, which are prime working ages. In comparison, in 1990 the number of children was small compared to that bulge, and there were very few elderly people. The ratio of potential workers to nonworkers was high.

Take a look at 2020, though, and you can see how this will change. Yes, there will be a large number of potential workers in the economy, but notice the proportion of older workers and elderly, everyone age 50 and older, will be much higher compared to the prime working-age labor force ranging from 20 to 44. We are in the middle of a significant shift in the relationship of the number of workers to the total number of people.

Figure 5.3 shows this in what are termed *dependency ratios*. The solid line near the top of the graph shows the number of kids, age 0–20, as a percentage of the total number of working-age people, age 20–64. The effect of the baby boom is visible around 1960, as the number of kids exploded to equal almost 80% of the working-age population. At the same time, the old-age dependency ratio, which is the number of people 65 and older as a percentage of the working-age population, was less than 20%.

From 1960 to almost 2010, as fertility declined so did the youth dependency ratio. It is now around 45%, almost half its peak in 1960. And for much of that same period, the old-age dependency ratio also stayed constant at around 20%. This means that the ratio of workers to total population rose throughout the twentieth century and into the twenty-first. But as the figure shows, we then entered a period of profound change as the baby boom generation entered retirement. By 2030 the old-age dependency ratio will approach 40%, whereas the youth dependency ratio is not projected to fall much at all. This

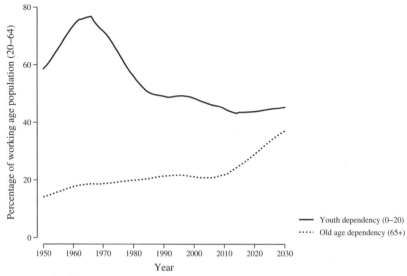

Figure 5.3. Dependency ratios over time
Note: Data is from the Organisation for Economic Co-operation and Development population statistics database. Youth dependency is the ratio of people age 0–20 to the working-age population, 20–64. Old-age dependency is the ratio of those age 65 and older to the working-age population, 20–64.

means that the proportion of workers to total population, which had already begun to drop because of the rise in the old-age dependency ratio in the early 2000s, will continue to fall.

I attributed this all to a decline in fertility, but of course changes to mortality rates have played a role as well. In 1960, life expectancy in the United States was roughly age 70, but by 2015 it had reached age 79. Life expectancy works a lot like total fertility rate, in that it captures a snapshot of the mortality rates acting on people of different ages in a given year. A life expectancy of age 70 means that someone born in 1960 would expect to live seventy years, if age-specific mortality rates never changed. The increase in life expectancy indicates that those age-specific mortality rates fell from 1960 to 2015. Much of the decline in mortality took place among the elderly, meaning that people age 70–80 could expect to live another ten or fifteen years rather than just another zero to five years. That increased the number of very old people in the United States, but it didn't increase the stock of workers, thus contributing to the decline in the ratio of workers to population.

EXPERIENCE AND EDUCATION

A few chapters back we covered how the stock of human capital depended not just on how many workers there were but on their schooling and experience as well. And if you look at figure 5.2, you can guess that population aging had some impact on both schooling and experience.

Think about experience first, for which the role of aging is most apparent. From 1960 to 1990, there was a huge surge in the number of workers age 20–45. These are the people who get the most out of initial job experience, and so the human capital stock of the economy grew as these workers entered the workforce and started to learn on the job. But from 1990 to today, the greatest increase in the workforce came from older cohorts age 45–65. These workers are still obtaining experience, but the gain for human capital from their experience is much lower, if not negative. Younger workers did keep adding themselves into the mix during the twenty-first century, but the average worker in the economy was becoming much older, and thus the growth of human capital from people acquiring experience fell during the twenty-first century.

Now, we might imagine that the drag coming from experience could be overcome if education levels increased at the same time. This is possible in theory, but it does not appear to be the case in practice. Over the past few decades educational outcomes have stalled. In particular, the rate of high school graduation stagnated starting around 1980. Richard Murnane collected data on completion rates by the cohort age 20–24. In 1970, 80.8% of this group (those born in 1946–1950) graduated from high school or received a GED. In 1990 (those born in 1966–1970), 78.5% had graduated or received a GED. By 2010 (those born in 1986–1990), the rate was 83.7%. There was some increase in the 2000s, after a few decades of stalling, but the increase was not a massive shift in educational achievement. Ever since 1970 about four-fifths of each generation has completed basic secondary schooling.

Before that, of course, the achievement rates were far worse, as high school education was not universal in the United States. But the years between 1900 and 1970 did see enormous growth in secondary schooling. The United States was, for much of the twentieth century, far and away the leading country in terms of expanding high school graduation rates. Work by Claudia Goldin and Lawrence Katz shows that the high school graduation rate for 18-year-olds was only about 9% in 1910. But by 1940, just thirty years later, that rate was 50%. From there it climbed up to the roughly 80% mark that Murnane found for the 1970s. This continual rise in high school graduation rates meant significant growth in human capital during much of the twentieth century, which contributed to rapid economic growth in that century.

While high school completion stalled starting around 1980, there has been growth over the past few decades in college attendance and completion. When I first discussed the human capital stock, I showed you figure 3.3, which plotted the percentage of people older than age 25 who had completed different levels of education. In the early 1990s, only about 20% of those age 25 and older had completed four years of college or more. By 2015, that completion rate was 32.5%. That is the result, in part, of the death of older cohorts, who were kids in the early twentieth century, when college attendance was rare. They were being replaced by new cohorts of 25-year-olds each year who had much higher rates of college attendance.

However, because of the fertility decline, the speed at which more-educated kids replaced less-educated older folks in the workforce stalled. Goldin and Katz calculated that between 1960 and 1980, the supply of workers with college degrees relative to those with just high school degrees grew at 3.77% per year. This contributed to human capital growth by raising the average skill level of workers. From 1980 to 2005, though, the relative supply of college-educated workers grew by only 2.0% per year. Thus the stock of human capital grew but at a slower rate than before.

ACCOUNTING FOR THE SLOWDOWN
IN HUMAN CAPITAL GROWTH

Let's put some firmer numbers on all the sources of slow human capital growth. In table 5.1, I've done a breakdown of the growth in human capital per person, by decade, similar to what we did in the prior chapter accounting for the growth slowdown. In the first column, you can see the same exact numbers that we found earlier. The growth rate of the human capital stock, by itself, produced growth of 0.96% per year in real GDP per capita from 1950 to 2000. Looking down that column, you can see that from 2000 to 2016, the contribution of human capital was −0.15% per year, and this drop is the reason human capital is such a major explanation for the growth slowdown.

Looking over the remaining columns, I've broken down the growth

Table 5.1 Accounting for growth in human capital per person, over time

| | Contribution to growth (%) | | | | |
| | Human capital per capita | Components of human capital | | | |
Time period		Education	Experience	Workers	Hours
1950–2000	0.96	0.70	0.05	0.45	−0.24
1950–1960	0.08	0.62	0.23	−0.63	−0.13
1960–1970	0.95	0.87	−0.18	0.54	−0.28
1970–1980	1.64	0.92	−0.27	1.62	−0.64
1980–1990	1.26	0.57	0.11	0.70	−0.12
1990–2000	0.88	0.55	0.35	0.01	−0.03
2000–2016	−0.15	0.31	0.08	−0.35	−0.19

Note: The table shows the breakdown of growth in human capital per capita (column 1) into the contribution from education (column 2), experience (column 3), workers per population (column 4), and hours worked per worker (column 5). The data is from the Current Population Survey, Bureau of Economic Analysis, and Bureau of Labor Statistics; see the appendix for details. Because of rounding, the sum of the values in columns 2–5 may not be exactly equal to column 1. Each row of the table shows the same kind of accounting but limited to a given time period.

contribution of human capital into four constituent parts: education, experience, ratio of employment to population, and average hours worked. For the twentieth century, an increase in educational attainment added 0.70% per year to growth in real GDP, but that varied from around 0.55% in the 1980s and 1990s to around 0.90% during the 1960s and 1970s as the baby boom generation entered school and went well beyond their parents and grandparents in the level of education they acquired. But during the twenty-first century, the contribution of education fell to 0.31%. This reflects the forces I discussed in the prior section regarding stagnation in the high school graduation rate and how population aging slowed down the replacement of non-college-educated older workers with younger college-educated workers.

For experience, the average contribution for the twentieth century was only 0.05% per year, and that is in fact lower than the contribution of additional experience during the twenty-first century, 0.08%. But note how much variation there is in the contribution of experience to growth during the twentieth century. During the 1960s and 1970s as baby boomers entered the labor force, this lowered the average level of experience of workers so much that the effect on growth was negative. In the 1980s this popped back up to 0.11% per year, but in the 1990s the baby boomers hit their most productive years, and experience contributed 0.35% to growth. While changes in experience from the twentieth to the twenty-first century do not appear to be a big cause of the growth slowdown, the comparison of the 1990s to the twenty-first century shows that population aging played a big role in the decline in growth rate over that shorter span of time.

The last column of table 5.1 shows that declining hours worked per week subtracted from the stock of human capital over almost the entire period from 1950 to 2016. Note, however, that the decline in hours worked for 2000–2016, while negative, is not much worse than it was earlier in the twentieth century. We are working less per week as we get richer, but it does not appear to be something unique to the period of the growth slowdown.

Compared to education, experience, and hours, the growth rate in workers was much more important in the growth slowdown. During the twentieth century, growth of workers per capita, largely due to the baby boom, added 0.45% to growth in real GDP per capita. You can see the initial negative effect of this generation in the 1950s, as they were not of working age and so lowered the ratio of workers to population. But by the 1970s, the raw effect of baby boomers added 1.62% to the growth rate. After that, though, the effect dissipated. By the 1990s, there was basically zero growth in the ratio of workers to population, and then in the twenty-first century this turned negative, to −0.35%. That twenty-first-century effect is not just a remnant of the financial crisis. Harris Eppsteiner, Jason Furman, and Wilson Powell calculated that population aging alone accounts for four-fifths of the decline in the labor force participation rate from 2007 to 2017, just since the crisis. A different study by Nicole Maestas, Kathleen Mullen, and David Powell identified the effect of population aging by comparing US states with relatively old populations to those with relatively young populations. Their results imply an effect of aging on growth of about 1 percentage point, in line with my numbers here. For the twenty-first century as a whole, the growth slowdown reflects the long-run effect of demographic changes, and not the lingering effects of the recent recession.

THE PREFERENCE FOR SMALLER FAMILIES

Slower human capital growth can explain much of the growth slowdown, and the fall in fertility rates during the twentieth century can explain much of that slower human capital growth. The fertility decline we saw in figure 5.1 is part of a very long-run decline among developed countries that began in the nineteenth century for most, and even earlier for some. The literature attempting to explain the fundamental shift from families that had five to eight children each to families with one to three children each is vast and encompasses economics, sociology, psychology, anthropology, history, demography, political science, and medicine. I will not pretend that I can do justice to all the nuances of this research. Let me give you what I believe are the crucial elements explaining fertility decline in the United States. The short answer is that the fertility decline is a reaction to rising living standards in a very broad sense. It is a symptom of success.

Economists are often accused of turning everything into a cold, lifeless comparison of costs and benefits. And the economics of family size, which Gary Becker is credited with originating, is often cited as the primary example. Becker suggested that the choice of family size was no different from choices about, say, what cereal to buy: it involves preferences and budget constraints. Families have some preference for kids, but the utility that parents get from each additional child declines as they have more. This doesn't mean that parents don't love each child equally, but it does mean that starting a family (i.e., having the first kid) is different from having more kids. There is a fundamental change in the parents' lifestyle—for the better!—when having a first child that doesn't occur again upon having a second.

On the budget side, Becker assumed that the crucial input to raising kids was time. Having a kid decreases the time parents have available to do other activities, which includes working so that they can purchase other non-kid-related goods and spending time on their other kids. That time cost may take the form of having one parent stay home full-time with the kids while the other works, or it could take the form of working part-time, or of working at a lower-paying job that doesn't have demanding hours. Regardless, the cost of each child is thus the earnings forgone by the family because of the time spent raising the child. For Becker, parents choose the number of kids such that the marginal utility of having the last kid is just equal to the marginal cost, those forgone earnings.

From this perspective, the fertility decline is in part a function of economic growth. As wages rose, so did the marginal cost of having an additional child, because parental time became more valuable. And just like any other economic decision, as the marginal cost of a child rose, families chose to have fewer of them. This explanation for fertility decline does not depend on robotic parents running some kind of spreadsheet to decide whether to have a baby. A significant part of the decision on family size comes well before a family even exists. Higher wages are associated with later ages of marriage for both men and women, and smaller family sizes are in part a result of families having fewer years available to have children, not just a conscious decision to limit fertility because of a high wage.

There is a host of evidence to back up these predictions. For almost two centuries, fertility rates have fallen in lockstep with increases in GDP per capita (and wages) across all developed countries. Further, within the United States and other developed nations, at any given time it is the case that fertility rates are lower for those with higher income. Larry Jones and Michele Tertilt have documented the relationship of income and fertility across families over much of US history. Using historical US Census data, they can go back to the cohort of women born in 1828, and in that year and every year they examine afterward, there is a distinctly negative relationship between family income and the number of children a woman has. There is some drift downward in fertility by all women at all income levels over time, but by far the dominant story is that rising income lowers fertility. Associated with this is the consistently negative relationship of the education of women (and men) with the number of children they have. This is all consistent with Becker's theory and indicates that the drop in fertility was indicative of the United States' success in raising living standards (and education) throughout the twentieth century.

On top of the mechanisms outlined by Becker, the nature of the technological change that took place during the twentieth century also contributed to the drop in fertility rates. Jeremy Greenwood, Nezih Guner, and Guillaume Vandenbroucke have reviewed a large literature on how the spread of labor-saving household appliances changed the opportunities available to women. Leaving aside the question of why it was that women were expected to handle the vast majority of household chores in the first place, by reducing the time they spent on chores, these technologies enabled women to more easily enter the workforce. Once in the workforce, this raised the opportunity cost of having kids, similar to Becker's original argument, and fertility fell. Furthermore, these technologies made remaining single a more attractive situation—for both men and women—and contributed to the delay in the age of marriage and a reduction in the marriage rate overall.

Beyond the economic rationales, a major factor behind the fertility decline was the increase in women's control over their own fertility decisions. The most notable example of this was the availability of birth-control pills beginning in the 1960s and 1970s. Yes, contraceptive techniques existed before the pill, but they were less effective, and almost all required a man's cooperation. The pill and other associated contraceptives (e.g., intrauterine devices) allowed women, to a degree unprecedented in history, to make decisions regarding their own fertility. Research by Martha Bailey, along with other work by the same Goldin and Katz I previously cited, has shown the significant effects of the introduction of the pill on a variety of labor market outcomes. For women, access to the pill led to a later age of marriage, increased women's representation in professional occupations (e.g., medicine, law), increased the number of women in the workforce, raised the annual number of hours they worked when in the labor force, and reduced the likelihood of having a first birth before age 22.

For the purposes of thinking about the growth slowdown, what is material here is that the availability of the pill, combined with the continued rise in wages over time, led to a significant and sustained drop in fertility during the twentieth century. That drop in fertility led to a change in the age structure, which had repercussions for the growth of both experience and average education. The fall in the growth in human capital during the past two decades was inevitable, in that the fertility decisions behind it took place starting in the 1950s and 1960s. Once set in motion, the changes in the age structure were unavoidable.

THE CONTRIBUTION TO THE GROWTH SLOWDOWN

The current growth slowdown is, to a great extent, the manifestation of successful economic growth and improved women's rights during the twentieth century. Table 5.1 showed the raw breakdown of the slowdown in human capital growth per person. From a broad perspective, almost all the changes you see in that table are attributable to the shift in family size documented here. That would imply that growth dropped by 1.11 percentage points because of demographic changes alone.

But in the interest of being conservative in my explanation, let me cut that down a bit. The drop in the ratio of workers to population was mainly an effect of population aging, as was the change in experience. However, we could argue that the drop in the growth of education was only partly due to changing demographics and that the effect of the drop in hours worked may well be outside the scope of population aging. To leave with a round number, let's say that population aging due to smaller families accounted for 0.80 percentage points of the growth slowdown. Even with this lower estimate, the twin successes of rising living standards and women's reproductive rights explain about two-thirds of the 1.25 percentage point drop in the growth rate of GDP per capita from the twentieth to the twenty-first century.

THE DIFFERENCE BETWEEN PRODUCTIVITY AND TECHNOLOGY

6

Having accounted for the role of human capital, we can now turn back to the other main source of the growth slowdown, residual growth. All we know for sure about residual growth is what it is *not*. It captures economic growth that was not due to accumulating more physical or human capital. Beyond that, there is no formal definition of residual growth. It is a bit of a dumping ground for all the other forces at work in the economy that may or may not have influenced the growth rate of real GDP per capita. What the accounting in chapter 4 showed was that something happened around the turn of the century that led the residual growth rate to fall. But because there is no single economic activity or concept that the residual measures, it isn't obvious why it fell.

Residual growth does have another name that you may be familiar with: *productivity growth*. Depending on what you read, you might also see it as *total factor productivity growth* or *multifactor productivity growth*. Productivity growth—which I'll stick with from now on given its general usage—is not part of residual growth or an estimate of residual growth. It *is* residual growth. Residual growth and productivity growth are just synonyms. What I will try to do over the next few chapters is provide some of the main explanations for the fall in productivity growth and share why one of them in particular is a sign of success.

DON'T USE THE WORD *TECHNOLOGY*

Before we get into explanations, I want to do a little bit of intellectual weeding. There is a tendency to associate productivity growth with *technology*, and that is at once too broad and too narrow a term. You can see this if you try to decide what constitutes technology. Does a 3-D printer used to produce prototype parts for a car manufacturer count as technology? Sure sounds like it should, doesn't it? It's all sciencey, and it was probably expensive, so it must be a technology. It fits the dictionary definition of *technology*, something along the lines of "the application of scientific knowledge for practical purposes, especially in industry."

But how about cross-docking, in which materials are unloaded from an incoming semitruck right into an outgoing semitruck for delivery? Is that technology? Is there some scientific knowledge that was applied? Or is it just a good idea about how to efficiently shift goods between trucks? What about those upside-down condiment bottles that make it easier to squeeze out ketchup or mayo? Are those technology? Do they not count because the idea was obvious in retrospect? Or do they count as technology because there is some serious fluid mechanics behind their design? Neither cross-docking nor condiment bottles use electricity, so does that make them less technological or more? Is a Cronut technology? Is just-in-time inventory a technology? Is reassigning a top manager to a struggling store a technology?

Before we spend too much time trying to puzzle out what exactly technology is, let me spare you the trouble. From the perspective of economic growth, the word *technology* doesn't mean anything. There is productivity growth, and that's it. Productivity growth tells us how much extra real GDP growth we got beyond the growth in the stocks of human and physical capital we used. It doesn't depend on whether we used electricity, or whether we used techniques designed yesterday or one hundred years ago, or whether there are people in white lab coats involved in any way.

I don't know if Cronuts count as technology, but I do know they raised productivity because they led people to put a higher value on a given set of raw inputs. Cross-docking raised productivity because it allowed firms to produce the same amount while using fewer inputs, like warehouse space (physical capital) and truckers' time (human capital). Just-in-time inventory raised productivity in a similar way, because it allowed firms to avoid costly warehousing and shutdowns due to a lack of parts. Transferring a top manager raised productivity if it turned around a struggling store by getting more production from a given set of inputs.

Whether or not a product or process is high-tech is irrelevant for productivity growth, and hence for economic growth. All we care about is the value of the goods and services produced. Remember the cake example from chapter 4? There is nothing high-tech about making a cake, but the cake still has value. And when the value of your cake has gone up, there is nothing to say that it must be because you used a new high-tech oven with an app to alert you that the cake was finished. Maybe all you did was add nuts. In fact, maybe the value went up precisely because you used a low-tech method, like hand-whipping the egg whites to just the right level of fluffiness. But because the value of your cake went up, so did productivity.

This doesn't mean that technology, per se, is unimportant for economic growth. High-tech 3-D printers that let car manufacturers reduce lead times on new models raise productivity growth too. Advances in solar-cell and battery technologies contribute to productivity growth by lowering costs and allowing firms and individuals to substitute for other sources of energy. The examples go on and on.

But be careful to keep technological change and productivity growth as separate concepts in your head. The slowdown in productivity growth does not mean that we have become less inventive or capable. From the other side, advances in exciting new technologies—self-driving cars, genetic editing, biofuel—don't necessarily mean anything for the productivity growth rate. I have no clue what future technologies will look like or what their fundamental impact on human welfare will be. Maybe we are about to enter some kind of techno-utopia. Or perhaps Skynet will kill us all. What I do know is that the recent slowdown in *productivity growth* tells us very little about the probability of either of those things happening.

IS PRODUCTIVITY GROWTH EVEN SLOWING DOWN?

If technology isn't the only thing behind the slowdown in productivity growth, then what else is there? One possibility is that there is some kind of error in the calculations, and there is no slowdown in productivity growth at all. In particular, somewhere around the year 2000, the measured growth in real GDP stopped keeping up with actual growth in the value of goods and services. If the measured GDP growth rate was understated, but the growth rates of physical and human capital were accurate, this would result in an understated growth rate for productivity, as it is just residual growth. If this is true, the slowdown in productivity growth did not cause the growth slowdown because there was no growth slowdown. Both are just symptoms of a problem in how real GDP was measured.

Martin Feldstein recently published a paper explaining several possible measurement issues. Growth in real GDP is calculated by comparing how much total spending (in dollars) grew to how much prices grew over the same period. If spending grows faster than prices, then real GDP must have gone up. What Feldstein points out is that if we are overstating growth in prices, then we are understating growth in real GDP. And the BEA may be overstating price growth because it too crudely lumps together particular goods or services.

Think about a TV. When my wife and I moved into our house in 2005, I got a great deal on a thirty-two-inch HDTV—a newish technology at the time—for about $800. It had a resolution of 480p, but it was still a tube TV and weighed as much as a Volkswagen. Sometime in 2010, we bought a new forty-two-inch TV, also for about $800. It was an LCD flat screen with 1080p resolution that could be mounted on the wall—I could lift it by myself. Just a few years ago we moved that TV into our bedroom and upgraded once more. Again, we spent about $800. This time we got a forty-six-inch LED, again with 1080p resolution, but it weighed even less and included a bunch of smart-TV apps so that we can get Netflix and HBO without having to use an external device—and we're still behind the curve on TVs. If you headed to Best Buy right now, you could find, for about $800, a sixty-inch LED with 4K resolution and the full range of smart-TV apps.

If we think of each of these as just "a TV," then it looks like the price of TVs has been $800 for more than a decade, or 0% price growth. But that seems too crude, because each of these TVs is an obvious upgrade over the previous one. Let's say that the forty-six-inch TV we bought in 2015 was four times better than the TV from 2005, thanks to the higher resolution and apps. In other words, our 2015 TV was the equivalent of four 2005 TVs. This implies that the price of a 2005 TV, in 2015, was only $200. Which means the growth in the price of 2005 TVs was −75%, as it fell from $800 to $200. But if the BEA used the 0% growth of the price of a TV, it is overstating price growth and understating real GDP growth.

Feldstein's argument is that there are a large number of goods and services that have this problem, and so we are overstating price growth in general and understating real GDP growth. This problem gets even worse when you consider the introduction of entirely new goods or services into the economy. For those new items, we have no way to get a price for them before they were introduced. So the BEA has to group them into a larger category to get prices for years when they didn't exist, and we end up with the same problem. This could be a particular issue in the past few decades, given the introduction of a host of new products (e.g., smartphones) that combine features found in many different categories (e.g., computers, mobile phones, radios, GPS devices).

There are several challenges, though, for this explanation of the growth slowdown. In the same journal issue in which Feldstein published his paper, Chad Syverson published a piece that questioned not the premise of Feldstein's argument but whether the effect is big enough to matter. If mismeasurement of real GDP is what explains the growth slowdown, then it must be that the mismeasurement has become much worse since 2000. But as Syverson explains, these kinds of problems predate the growth slowdown by decades. As far back as 1961, the US created the Stigler Commission (named for economist George Stigler) to study whether measures of GDP were effective at capturing changes in quality over time. In 1996, before the growth slowdown, the Boskin Commission (named for economist Michael Boskin) was asked to study the construction of the Consumer Price Index (CPI) for similar reasons. Measuring real GDP has never been an exact science, and it is not clear why smartphones or 4K TVs or other products of the previous decade would create more problems than refrigerators or cars or air conditioners.

If current products like smartphones *were* more prone to these measurement issues, then we could expect the slowdown of productivity growth to be pronounced in the industries that make those products. For any given industry, we can do a similar kind of accounting as we did for real GDP as a whole, which would allow us to back out a residual that measures productivity growth. Syverson does this for industries producing computers and other electronic goods, and he finds that the slowdown in their productivity growth is no different from that in industries producing all sorts of other goods and services. If all the industries are slowing down at the same time, it is hard to blame mismeasurement in just a few. His conclusion is that, yes, we may be mismeasuring the growth of real GDP, but we've always been mismeasuring it, and there is nothing special about mismeasurement in the past few decades that can explain the growth slowdown.

DID WE RUN OUT OF INNOVATION?

Although technological innovation is not the only thing involved in productivity growth, it definitely plays an important role. A possible explanation of the growth slowdown is therefore that innovations are getting harder to find. Recent work by Nicholas Bloom, Charles Jones, John Van Reenen, and Michael Webb offers a way of looking at that argument. They examined the effort that is put toward research and development, in terms of workers and resources invested in R&D, and how that relates to the speed with which new innovations are produced.

The intriguing thing about their work is that they look beyond residual productivity, and instead bring in data on tangible improvements in technology in a few select fields. One example is an investigation of Moore's law, which is the observation that the density of transistors on integrated circuits that serve as the processing units for computers and a whole range of electronics doubles every two years.

This doubling has been going on from the early 1970s, when there were about two thousand transistors on a chip, to today, when there are somewhere north of 2 billion. What Moore's law implies is that the growth rate of transistor density has been constant (at about 35% per year) for almost fifty years.

What Bloom and his coauthors point out is that while this growth rate has been constant, the research effort necessary to achieve that growth has gone up by a factor of almost 80 in the same time period. As they note, because the growth rate of transistor density has not changed, it is about eighty times harder to double transistor density today than it was in 1970. In that sense, innovation got harder over time.

They find a similar story in other fields. Agricultural yields, which depend on innovation in seed quality, fertilizers, and other areas, have grown at steady rates for the past fifty years. But the research effort put toward raising yields grew by a factor of between 6 and 24, depending on the exact crop studied. In medicine, they track the number of new molecular entities (NMEs) that were registered with the FDA. NMEs are new drugs, and the count includes all the significant drug releases, including a lot of familiar ones, like Prilosec, Claritin, and Prozac. Like integrated circuits and agricultural yields, Bloom and the others find that research effort rose by a factor of 16 between 1970 and 2015, whereas the growth rate of NMEs introduced stayed about the same over time.

From these examples, and several others in their paper, the origin of slower productivity growth may appear to be this increasing difficulty in innovating. But note that in each case the authors document that the growth rate of innovations is in fact constant over time, not falling. Yes, it may take more effort to produce innovations over time, but we have continued to put in that extra effort and maintained the growth rate of innovations in these fields.

One of the coauthors of this paper, Charles Jones, published two papers in the mid-1990s that made a similar point, but he looked at aggregate data. He found that despite a clear increase during the twentieth century in the number of researchers employed not just in the US but across all developed nations, the growth rate of produc-

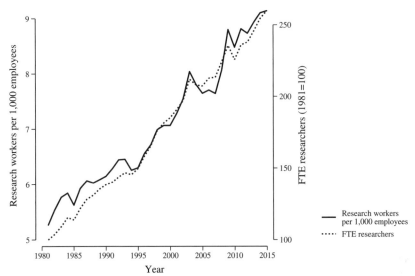

Figure 6.1. Researchers over time

Note: Data on researchers per thousand employees is reported directly by the Organisation for Economic Co-operation and Development. The index for full-time equivalent (FTE) researchers was calculated by the author.

tivity and real GDP per capita was persistent. He used this fact to provide some deeper insights into what determined the long-run growth rate itself—they are fascinating insights, but a bit beyond the scope of this book. An important conclusion for our purposes is that even if innovation requires more and more effort, it is possible to prevent the growth rate of innovation from falling toward zero over the long run.

Both the Bloom paper and Jones's other work suggest that if a drop in the rate of innovation is behind the growth slowdown, then that would have to be driven by a drop in the effort put toward innovation. We can look at some data similar to theirs, but at the aggregate level, to see if there was such a drop.

Figure 6.1 shows two measures of aggregate research effort based on the number of people engaged in research work, as defined by the Organisation for Economic Co-operation and Development. The solid line plots the number of researchers per thousand employees, which grew from about five (i.e., about 0.5% of employees were researchers) in 1981 to about nine by 2015. There is a period around

2003–2007 where this ratio was flat, but it then jumped back up by 2010 to the prior trend. Moreover, across the whole time frame, there is no indication that the growth of the number of researchers changed in a fundamental way around 2000.

The dashed line tracks the absolute number of researchers (in full-time equivalents, indexed to equal 100 in 1981) over time. By 2015, the number of researchers was a little more than 2.5 times higher than in 1981. Again, there is little evidence that the climb in research workers changed or was interrupted around the turn of the century. We continued to put more and more effort into research, at least in terms of employment, during the growth slowdown. Combined, the data in figure 6.1 gives no reason to suspect that there was a fundamental drop in research effort around the turn of the century. Despite innovation becoming harder over time, that does not appear to be a plausible explanation for the growth slowdown.

IS THERE AN ANSWER IN HERE ANYWHERE?

All I've done so far is tell you about a few things that do *not* explain the slowdown in productivity growth. And the frustrating part is that I'm not able to tell you for sure why productivity growth slowed down. Because productivity is a residual, we have a nearly infinite number of candidate explanations, and I cannot provide a definitive accounting of the slowdown in productivity growth. But I will show you that a few explanations for it have significant empirical support.

The first explanation involves the long-run shift in the composition of our spending away from goods and toward services. As I'll explain, this is something we should consider a success. The shift occurred because we became so good at producing goods that they are now very, very cheap, so we don't *need* to spend much on goods any more. That shift in spending had direct consequences for productivity growth, however.

Productivity growth for the whole economy, which is the residual I calculated in chapter 4, is a weighted average of the productivity growth of all the individual industries that make up the economy, like manufacturing, health care, and retail. For each of those industries, we can compute the residual productivity growth by comparing actual output growth to the predicted growth from their use of physical and human capital, just like we did for the economy as a whole. What that shows is that productivity growth in service-producing industries tends to be lower than in goods-producing industries. As our spending shifted toward services, we were shifting toward lower productivity growth as well. This shift can account for about half the drop in economy-wide productivity growth. But that drop is a consequence of the success we had in making material goods inexpensive.

The second big idea for explaining slower productivity growth was the rise in market power of firms over the past few decades. The available evidence shows that the average markup—the ratio of price to marginal cost—charged by firms in the economy has increased since 1990. That rise in markups was consistent with the rise in economic profits as a share of GDP over the same time period. There are reasons to think that increased market power may have contributed to the growth slowdown, perhaps by limiting innovation or investment by firms that faced less competition. However, when it comes to accounting for productivity growth, the story becomes ambiguous. Some of the rise in markups and profits we see in the data may have been a consequence of our own shift in spending patterns toward firms with more market power, and not a result of individual firms increasing their market power. Moreover, these shifts in spending toward high-markup firms may have raised productivity growth, as we shifted resources toward firms with higher productivity on the margin. In that case, the rise in market power seen in the data isn't responsible for the growth slowdown and may in fact have kept it from being worse.

A last explanation for the slowdown in productivity growth is also a little puzzling. What I'll document is that along a number of dimensions, the reallocation of human and physical capital between different uses has slowed down. The movement of workers between different jobs, including the movement of workers to different physical locations, slowed down over the past few decades. Alongside this, both the arrival of new businesses and the closing of old ones slowed over the same time period. Different evidence shows that much of the productivity growth we see within industries is driven by reallo-cations, which can come from things like a worker moving to take a higher-paying job, new owners taking over a failing restaurant, or Best Buy acquiring old Circuit City locations. The data is clear that these kinds of reallocations happened less frequently over the past two decades, but there is no clear explanation for *why*. This decline in "dynamism," as it is called, occurred over the same time period as the growth slowdown, and it seems we could attribute some of the decline in productivity growth to it.

Put all these explanations together, and we can get a decent idea of why productivity growth slowed over the past two decades. Much of the slowdown is attributable to the shift into services, which is some-thing I'll argue is best seen as a resounding success. That said, things like a rise in market power and reduced dynamism may have played a role in the slowdown. Both would appear to be failures, in the sense that we all (or at least most of us) might be better off if they were reversed. So while not everything contributing to the productivity growth slowdown represented a success, the majority of the produc-tivity growth slowdown *was* attributable to success.

THE REALLOCATION FROM
GOODS TO SERVICES

7

The reallocation from goods to services was important to the productivity growth slowdown, and it represents a success. To understand the importance of the reallocation away from goods and toward services for productivity growth, think of traveling down a four-lane highway. You've got a fast lane on the left and a slow lane on the right. Your average speed over the course of a trip is determined by how much time you spend in one lane versus the other. If you get lucky and can stay in the left lane the whole time, your average speed will be much higher than that of someone who has to keep moving over into the slow lane.

Economy-wide productivity growth is a little like the average speed of the economy. There are industries that represent the fast lane, with high productivity growth of their own—these tend to be associated with producing goods. And then there are industries that represent the slow lane, with low productivity growth—these tend to be associated with producing services. The time we spend in each lane is dictated by how much labor or capital we put to work in each industry. What we've seen over the past few decades is that we've been merging from the fast lane into the slow lane as work shifts out of goods-producing industries and into service-producing industries. The case you might be most familiar with is manufacturing, which tends to experience rapid productivity growth. Manufacturing employed about 20% of the workforce in 1980, but as of 2017 employed only about 9% of the workforce.

Despite the shift out of goods and into services and the reduction in productivity growth, this doesn't mean that productivity was falling. Think of merging into the slow lane. It doesn't mean you start going backward, just that you are moving forward more slowly. To understand how important this lane change was for aggregate productivity growth, and hence the growth slowdown, we need to put some numbers on all this. For that, we have to calculate the average speed in each lane and then determine how much time we spent in each one. And since production is more complex than just the split between goods and services, we're going to do this for a mega-sized seventeen-lane economic superhighway.

To get the productivity, or speed, of each industry, we'll do the same kind of analysis as for real GDP per capita in chapter 4. That is, we'll look at the predicted growth rate of output in a given industry based just on increased use of physical and human capital. Then we'll compare that to the actual growth rate of output in the industry, and this residual growth will be the productivity growth of that industry, or the speed at which traffic is moving in that industry's lane.

Given all those productivity growth rates by industry, we can then add them up, weighting each by a measure of how much they contributed to economy-wide productivity growth. These weights represent how long we spent in each lane. The weight for any given industry is going to be the share of total GDP accounted for by that industry. This share is measured by dividing the *value-added* of an industry by total GDP. The value-added of an industry is its net contribution to the economy, defined as the value of its output minus the value of goods and services it purchased from other industries. Thus the weight each industry gets in calculating economy-wide productivity growth depends on how much it "adds value" to the goods and services it uses in production, not just on its raw output.

THE SHIFT BETWEEN INDUSTRIES

Before we start, I should be more clear about what exactly I mean by *industry*. This is an arbitrary division of economic activity based on the kinds of things produced, how they are sold, and to whom they are sold. It helps to think of an industry from the bottom up. Let's say you own a furniture store, but you don't make furniture; you sell only to individuals, not to other furniture stores. Then your store falls under the industry of wholesale and retail trade. This distinguishes your firm from a furniture manufacturer, who sells only to stores like yours, not directly to the public. That manufacturer falls into the manufacturing industry.

Going through and classifying every single economic activity into one industry or another—and to the sub-sub-subindustries that make up each industry—is the kind of thing that could make you want to gouge out your eyeballs. The important point is that the high-level industries I'll talk about here are a rough guide to the type of economic activity being done in the United States, and they are not definitive. There are a handful of systems of classifying economic activity out there, and all have mutated over time as goods and services came and went.

With that throat clearing out of the way, what has happened to the industry composition of real GDP in the United States over time? Figure 7.1 plots the value-added share of GDP for four selected industries (out of seventeen total). The most pronounced feature of the figure is the steady decline of manufacturing's share of GDP from around 23% in 1970 to about 12.5% in 2015. Along the way, the decline was at times more rapid, and at times it slowed or reversed, but the dominant trend is downward.

This contrasts with the rise of the shares in the three service-related industries I chose to include in the figure. Health and social work is made up almost entirely of the health-care industry. This industry doubled its value-added share of GDP from around 4% in 1970 to around 8% in 2015. You might wonder why this number is not larger, but remember that this is the share of value-added in GDP, not the share of personal expenditures by individuals out of their own income. We'll get to that alternative way of looking at how spending has changed over time in the next chapter. For now, we can just note that health care grew as a fraction of GDP.

Both professional services (e.g., CPAs, architects, advertising agen-

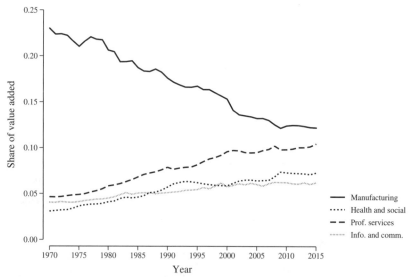

Figure 7.1. Value-added share of GDP for selected industries
Note: Data is from the KLEMS database. Shares were calculated by the author using current price value-added in each year. The exact ISIC (International Standard Industrial Classification) codes used are *C* for manufacturing, *Q* for health and social, *M-N* for professional services, and *J* for information and communication.

cies) and information and communication (e.g., publishing, TV production, computer programming) also rose as a share of GDP during the same time. Professional services went from around 5% to 10% of the economy, and information and communication grew from about 4% to 6%. In combination, these three industries, along with several other smaller service-related industries, are the mirror image of the drop in manufacturing. Note that the data in figure 7.1 doesn't say that the actual production of manufacturing was falling over time, only manufacturing's value-added share of GDP. From 1970 to 2015 the growth rate of value-added from manufacturing was positive; it just didn't grow as fast as professional services, health care, or information and communication.

THE EFFECT ON AGGREGATE PRODUCTIVITY GROWTH

Figure 7.1 told us that we spent less time in the manufacturing lane in 2015 than in 2000 or 1980, and more time in the health-care, professional services, and information and communication lanes. If each of those industry lanes had a different productivity growth rate, then switching lanes would have changed productivity growth. In particular, if manufacturing (and other goods-producing industries) tended to have higher productivity growth, and the other industries (including other service-producing industries) tended to have lower productivity growth, then moving from goods to services would be responsible for some of the slowdown in productivity growth.

And that, to a large extent, is what did happen. Table 7.1 shows, in the first column, the annualized growth rate of productivity from 2000 to 2015 for all seventeen industries. As I noted earlier, the classification of industries is a bit arbitrary, but it is not hard to think of them as either goods or services producing. Agriculture (0.91%), mining (3.02%), and manufacturing (1.36%) are all obvious goods-producing industries. If you scan down the column, you'll also see that their individual productivity growth rates are among the highest in the table. The only other industry with such high productivity growth over this period is information and communication (3.03%).

You might also think of real estate (0.89%) as related to goods, but this is a bit of a trick in the classification. Real estate here refers to the flow of services related to the housing stock. Think of renting an apartment. When you rent, you are buying a service from a company that happens to own the building. If you are a homeowner, then implicitly you are buying a service from yourself. In contrast, the construction industry is engaged in building *new* houses, and those houses qualify as goods (note, though, that construction has one of the worst productivity growth rates, –1.70%, of all industries).

From the other side, services tend to have low productivity growth rates. Wholesale and retail trade (0.73%), professional services (0.27%), education (0.36%), and finance (0.09%) all have relatively low rates, while accommodation and food service (–0.31%), public administration (–0.36%), and health care (–0.23%) all have negative productivity growth rates. In general, it appears that service-producing industries had lower productivity growth than goods-producing industries.

The productivity growth rates in table 7.1 are annualized averages

CHAPTER SEVEN

Table 7.1 Decomposing productivity growth, by industry

Industry	Productivity growth, 2000–2015	Value-added share of GDP (%)			
		1980	1990	2000	2015
Agriculture	0.91	2.19	1.63	0.97	0.98
Mining	3.02	3.22	1.50	1.09	1.84
Manufacturing	1.36	20.63	17.60	15.32	12.20
Utilities	−2.12	2.35	2.73	2.03	1.85
Construction	−1.70	4.65	4.18	4.55	4.11
Wholesale and retail trade	0.73	13.63	12.70	13.01	12.08
Transportation	−0.28	4.29	3.60	3.63	3.35
Accommodation and food service	−0.31	2.31	2.58	2.83	2.95
Information and communication	3.03	4.50	5.11	5.77	6.22
Finance and insurance	0.09	4.84	5.89	7.39	7.27
Real estate	0.89	9.99	10.68	10.89	12.13
Professional services	0.27	5.83	7.89	9.60	10.45
Public administration	−0.36	13.76	14.06	12.47	12.84
Education	0.36	0.63	0.70	0.85	1.14
Health and social work	−0.23	4.10	5.71	5.87	7.30
Arts and entertainment	0.39	0.64	0.83	0.98	1.04
Other services	−1.37	2.44	2.62	2.76	2.26

Note: Data is from the KLEMS database. Shares using current price value-added in each noted year were calculated by the author. Annualized productivity growth was calculated using the KLEMS series on value-added total factor productivity.

from 2000 to 2015, but to get the aggregate productivity growth rate, we need to take the productivity growth rate of each industry for one year (e.g., from 2003 to 2004), weight that by the value-added share in the initial year (2003), and then add up across all industries. That will give us the productivity growth rate in that one year (2003). We can do this for each year, and then string those aggregate productivity growth rates together to find the annualized aggregate growth rate from 2000 to 2015. This calculation is tedious, but it allows us to take into account the facts that the value-added share of each industry changed over time and that the productivity growth rate of each industry may have changed over time as well.

I'll spare you any more detail, but see the appendix if you'd like to bore yourself with the calculations. What is important for our purposes here is the final answer. Based on the industry-level data from the BEA database that lies behind figure 7.1 and table 7.1, the growth rate of aggregate productivity was 0.4% per year. If you have been paying close attention, you'll catch that this is *not* the same growth rate for aggregate productivity that I reported for the period 2000–2016 in table 4.2, which was 1.26% per year.

One reason for the discrepancy is that the industry-level data uses slightly different assumptions than I did to measure physical and human capital. I prefer the data I used in table 4.2 because it allows me to track productivity growth farther back in time (to 1950), at the cost of not being able to break things down by industry. In table 7.1, we can do careful industry-level accounting, but at the cost of not being able to go back as far in time (certain data goes back only to 2000). A second reason is that in table 4.2 I allowed for the idea that capital accumulation depends in part on GDP growth itself (remember the tomato garden), while the industry-level accounting in table 7.1 does not. It would be nice if everything agreed, but it is not crucial for what we're going to do here, which is to see how much the growth rate of productivity changed because of the shift between goods and services.

THE EFFECT OF REALLOCATION
ON PRODUCTIVITY GROWTH

For the whole economy, productivity growth fell by 0.25 percentage points from the twentieth century to the twenty-first century (from 1.51% to 1.26%). But how much of that was due to the shift from high-productivity-growth goods industries toward low-productivity-growth service industries?

Just to establish that the shift occurred, let's take a look at the last four columns of table 7.1. You can see how the actual value-added shares changed from 1980 to 2015. The numbers on the decline in manufacturing's share and the rise in professional services, health care, and information and communications are what you saw in figure 7.1. For the other industries, there are similar patterns for goods- versus service-producing industries. Goods-producing agriculture and mining declined in value-added share. Services like finance, education, arts, and accommodation and food service all increased in value-added share.

Using this information, we want to calculate what productivity growth would have been had the shift into services not occurred. To do this, we need to calculate another weighted average of industry-specific productivity growth rates, but holding the value-added shares constant rather than letting them change. Let's start by using the 2000 value-added shares and assuming that these shares stayed the same from 2000 to 2015. In this case, the productivity growth rate would have been 0.5% per year, or 0.1% higher than the actual productivity growth rate. It may not seem like a big difference, but that is a 25% increase in the productivity growth rate. The reason for the difference is that the weight on high-productivity-growth goods-producing industries is held at the 2000 value-added shares, rather than letting them decline over time. Productivity growth would have been higher if it hadn't been for the shift away from goods and into services.

We can also take this kind of calculation farther back in time. If we go back to 1990, the weights on the high-productivity-growth industries are even larger and the weights on services even lower. The implied growth rate of productivity from 2000 to 2015, using the 1990 value-added shares as weights, is 0.51%, just about the same as using the 2000 weights. But if we go back to 1980 weights, when goods production accounted for even more of GDP, the implied growth rate of productivity this century would have been 0.6%, or 0.2 percentage points higher than actual productivity growth.

The point is that the allocation of our resources across industries matters a lot for the rate of productivity growth. During the twentieth century, the weights on high-productivity industries were much higher, and so productivity growth was higher as well. There is no convenient way to report the weights on all industries for the entire twentieth century, as they changed year by year. But if you take the 1980 value-added shares as representative, then the little exercise I just did suggests that the shift into services during the twenty-first century shaved about 0.2 percentage points off of productivity growth. Recall that the actual drop in productivity growth was 0.25 percentage points, so the shift into services could account for almost all of the drop in productivity growth that is behind the growth slowdown.

This calculation has a lot of uncertainty around it, and that has a lot to do with trying to compare the entire twentieth century to the twenty-first. I think the 1980 weights are a good representation of the industrial structure during the period of the twentieth century we want to compare to, but one could make a reasonable argument for an alternative. In addition, my counterfactual calculations assume that the productivity growth rates themselves would be unaffected by holding the value-added shares constant over time. That is probably incorrect, as an industry's productivity growth rate may respond to the growth of the industry's own value-added over time. These counterfactuals should not be considered a concrete statement about what would have occurred, but they give us a guide as to how relevant the switch to services was for productivity growth.

THE SHIFT TOWARD SERVICES

Before we get to an explanation for why the shift into services occurred, I want to offer a little extra information on what lay behind the shift itself. Figure 7.1 plotted the share of total GDP accounted for by the value-added of four industries. That value-added share for an industry depended on two things. The first is the real value-added production of an industry. It isn't quite accurate to think of real value-added production as the raw output of an industry. If we were talking about the shoe industry, then the real gross output would be the raw number of shoes produced. But value-added requires that we subtract the real value of the intermediate inputs, like leather, that the shoe industry used. Real value-added in production is thus something a little more subtle than the raw output, but for our purposes, it is fine to have in mind raw production.

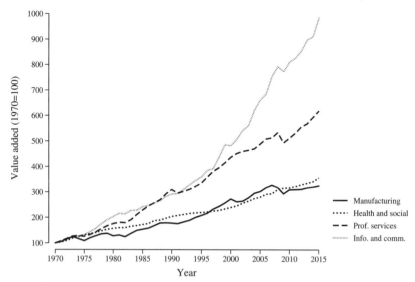

Figure 7.2. Value-added, indexed to 1970, for selected industries
Note: Data is from the KLEMS database. Shares were calculated by the author using KLEMS value-added in each year. The exact ISIC codes used are *C* for manufacturing, *Q* for health and social, *M-N* for professional services, and *J* for information and communication.

Figure 7.2 plots the level of real value-added production for the same four industries as in figure 7.1. As comparing that real value-added across industries is difficult, I've indexed all of them to equal 100 in the year 1970, so the figure allows you to see how much their real value-added grew over time. What stands out is the acceleration of production in information and communications, which produced ten times more value-added in 2015 than in 1970. Professional services were not that far behind, producing about six times more value-added in 2015 than in 1970. Both manufacturing and health care produced more in 2015 than in 1970, but the increase was more muted than in information and professional services. Manufacturing produced about three times as much, and health care a little more than three times as much in 2015 compared to 1970.

All of these industries were producing more real value-added over time, but certain services like information and communications or professional services were growing much faster. Part of the reason for the decline in the value-added share of manufacturing, therefore, was not because manufacturing produced less, but because it did not keep pace with the increase in some service industries.

The second thing that influenced the value-added shares of industries over time was their relative price. Again, we have to be careful here. The relative price of the value-added of the shoe industry is not the same thing as the price of a shoe, but for our purposes, it probably isn't a terrible approximation.

Figure 7.3 plots the price level of value-added for each industry, again indexed so that the price level is 100 in 1970. Here the first thing that stands out is the rapid increase in price of the health-care industry, which increased by a factor of 11 from 1970 to 2015. This increase in price explains why health care's share of value-added in GDP increased so much over time, even though as we saw in figure 7.2, its actual amount of value-added produced did not grow as fast as that of other industries. Professional services also saw a signifi-

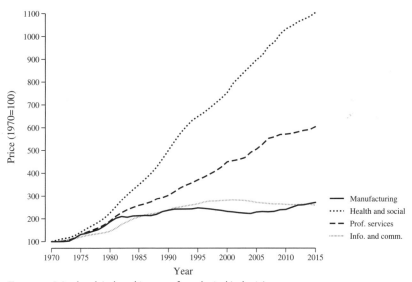

Figure 7.3. Price level, indexed to 1970, for selected industries
Note: Data is from the KLEMS database. Price index was calculated by the author using KLEMS price data in each year. The exact ISIC codes used are *C* for manufacturing, *Q* for health and social, *M-N* for professional services, and *J* for information and communication.

cant increase in price, by a factor of about 6, and this combined with the increase in real value-added to generate the gain in value-added *share* for that industry.

Figure 7.3 also shows that the price level of manufacturing rose, but not by nearly as much as that in the other industries. The combination of a mild increase in real value-added output and a mild increase in price combined to make the share of manufacturing in GDP fall over time. It was not that we produced fewer manufactured goods but that relative to other industries, production did not go up by as much as it did in those industries, and just as important, manufactured goods got cheaper over time relative to services.

As we saw already, these shifts had a significant effect on aggregate productivity growth. What I'm going to show next is that the shifts we just saw in figures 7.2 and 7.3 are what we'd expect to see as an economy becomes rich, and they are the consequences of success, not failure.

BAUMOL'S COST DISEASE

To explain why the shift into services occurred, why that shift was associated with lower productivity growth, and why it represents a success, I'm going to talk about the work of an economist named William Baumol.

Over the course of nearly seven decades of scholarship, Baumol contributed to many areas of economics, but perhaps the ideas he is most known for relate to the fundamental differences between service production and goods production. The origin of these ideas can be traced to two articles he published back in the mid-1960s. Both articles are what you might call "old-style" economics, explaining concepts with words rather than a series of equations (OK, there were some equations but not many). It makes the articles intelligible to almost anyone with some rudimentary economics training, although at times the lingo can get a little thick as well. Baumol stayed active until very recently (he passed away in 2017), publishing several more-accessible versions of his ideas for the public.

THE IMPORTANCE OF TIME

In his two original articles Baumol laid out his ideas about what makes services so different from goods. The quotes that follow are all from his 1967 article, which I find most relevant for our purposes here. To start, Baumol divided economic activity up in the following way:

The basic source of differentiation resides in the role played by labor in the activity. In some cases labor is primarily an instrument—an incidental requisite for the attainment of the final product, while in other fields of endeavor, for all practical purposes the labor is itself the end product.

For the first case, labor as an instrument, you can read "goods." Baumol uses the example of an air conditioner. Just by looking at an AC unit, or using it, there is no way to assess how much labor went into producing it—nor do we really care. The labor that went into producing it is incidental from the perspective of a consumer of the product. The same goes for cars, houses, refrigerators, laptops, and smartphones.

Contrast that to the following:

On the other hand there are a number of services in which the labor is an end in itself, in which quality is judged directly in terms of amount of labor. Teaching is a clear-cut example. . . . An even more extreme example is one I have offered in another context: live performance. A half hour horn quintet calls for the expenditure of 2½ man hours in its performance, and any attempt to increase productivity here is likely to be viewed with concern by critics and audience alike.

For most services, labor is the very essence of the product. If you go hear the horn quintet, as Baumol suggests, then you are buying the half hour of each player's time. At many restaurants, you are purchasing not just the food, but the time and attention of a waiter. For the service industries that are growing over time, like education, health care, and professional services, you are almost always purchasing people's time or attention as opposed to any tangible good.

If you go to the doctor, you want the doctor to spend some time with you, explaining why your back hurts and what your treatment options are. You want and need the doctor's attention to your condition, and there is no substitute for that expert time and attention. If you go to an hour-long yoga class because your doctor told you it would help your back, then you want sixty minutes of yoga instruction, and the instructor's attention on your form so that you don't hurt yourself again and can get the most relief from your back pain. If yoga doesn't work and the doctor screws up surgery on your back, then you'll call a lawyer to sue, and what you are buying is the lawyer's time and attention, which will be apparent because the lawyer will bill you in great detail for time, not for a specific product. Compare that to a good like an AC unit. The people working at the AC factory are probably lovely, but I don't want, or need, to spend any time with them every time I try to cool down my house.

For Baumol, the instrumental role of labor explains why productivity is high and, more important, can grow very quickly for the first kind of production (goods) but is low and grows slowly in the second kind (services). In producing goods, you can "do more with less," meaning that a company could invent ways to get more AC units or cars or laptops out of its existing labor force, or it could invent ways to get the same number of units by using a smaller labor force. The time spent by the workers isn't what matters to the consumer, so firms can shed workers or raise output per worker as much as possible without damaging the demand for their goods. They have every incentive to decrease the labor used, as doing so lowers their own costs.

But for services, you cannot "do more with less." No one wants to see the half-hour horn quintet played in only twelve minutes, or hear the quintet play two separate pieces at the same time for the whole half hour. You can't give a one-hour yoga class in less than sixty minutes. You can't achieve the same level of attention and service at a nice restaurant by halving the number of waiters. It takes a half hour to get my eyes checked by my optometrist; getting out of there in fifteen minutes would mean she checked only one eye. The time and attention of the workers in these industries are what we as consumers value, so if firms cut back on that time or attention, then demand for their service will suffer.

The difference in the role of labor in goods and services, and the implication of this for productivity growth, is not some absolute law of the universe. Yes, there are ways to increase productivity in some services by cutting back the labor used without changing demand much. A yoga instructor could add more students to the class. Online courses allow university professors to teach more people in the same amount of time. Remote medicine can free up a doctor's time to meet with more patients in a given day. But note that even these examples will run into issues at some point. Too many people in a yoga class and the instructor cannot observe and correct everyone's form. On-line courses have a similar problem, in that the professor cannot offer individual feedback to every single student. Remote medicine works to the extent that a doctor does not need to make an actual physical examination. The scope of productivity improvement in many services is constrained by limits on the actual time and attention span of the providers.

This was Baumol's first key insight. Compared to goods production, the productivity growth of services is going to be relatively low. And we saw exactly that in the data in the previous chapter on the productivity growth rate across different industries in the past fifteen years.

THE COST DISEASE

The difference in productivity growth between goods and services led to Baumol's second insight, which he named the *cost disease* of services. Every time a firm gets more productive—meaning that it can produce more output with fewer inputs (e.g., the time of its workers)—its costs go down. Because goods-producing firms can achieve higher productivity growth than service-producing firms, the cost of producing goods falls faster than the cost of producing services. This means that the relative cost of goods keeps getting smaller and smaller as compared to services. That means that the relative cost of services must be getting higher over time as compared to goods.

In a market economy, it should be the case that prices and costs move together. So Baumol's cost disease of services should show up as the relative price of goods getting lower and lower when compared to that of services. And this is in fact what we see in the data.

Figure 8.1 plots a price index for each of eight types of products. There are three products I would consider clear services: higher education, health care, and food service. There are three that I would

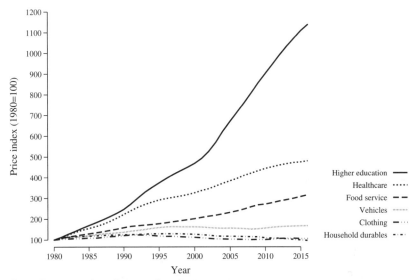

Figure 8.1. Price indexes by type of product

Note: Data is from the Bureau of Economic Analysis personal consumption expenditure table 2.4.4. The author made the calculations to index all price indexes to 100 in 1980.

consider clear goods: vehicles, clothing, and household durables (e.g., a dishwasher).

The distinct trajectories of the services and goods are quite apparent and entirely consistent with Baumol's theory. The growth of prices in higher education and health care far outstrip any other product, and even prices in food service are growing much faster than the prices of any of the goods plotted in the figure. The differences are huge, and likely something you are well aware of, in particular if you've been to the hospital or had a child go through college recently. Higher education prices went up by a factor of almost 12 in 2016 compared to 1980, while health-care costs were higher by a factor of almost 5. But even food service had prices three times higher in 2015 than in 1980. For two of the goods plotted, clothing and household durables, the data shows that their prices have remained flat over time, whereas for vehicles, there was only slight growth in their price.

Note that none of these statements is about the *absolute* cost of these goods. General inflation in prices has occurred in all products since 1980, so that the absolute number of dollars you had to spend on a car, a dishwasher, tuition, or an emergency-room visit were all higher in 2016 than in 1980. But in relative terms, the price of goods was close to flat while the price of services rose. Baumol's "cost disease" is clear in the data.

WE DEMAND LOW-PRODUCTIVITY SERVICES

Baumol's argument for why services tend to be low productivity and have low productivity growth seems reasonable. And his prediction that this means the price of services would rise relative to goods is borne out in the data. But that doesn't tell us why it is that more and more economic activity shifted into service industries with low productivity growth and out of goods-producing industries with high productivity growth, as we saw in the previous chapter. Baumol speculated about that in the same 1967 paper. His terminology gets a little hard to understand, so I'm going to put this argument into my own words.

If the demand for services is income elastic, and the demand for goods is income inelastic, then productivity growth in any industry will translate into a greater share of spending on services. *Income elastic* means that if you currently spend half of your income on goods and half on services, then you'll spend more than half on services if I give you an extra $100. Income inelastic is just the mirror image of this for goods. If I give you an extra $100, then you'll spend less than half of this on goods, which has to follow if you spend more than half on new services. Over time, this means the fraction of your income that you spend on services grows as your income grows. And this is exactly what we see. Think of Bill Gates. His income is thousands of times larger than mine. Yes, he has a bigger house, more refrigerators, and nicer cars, but his spending on goods is not thousands of times more than mine. In contrast, the fraction of his income that he spends on services (e.g., travel, restaurants, legal services, business services, personal assistants) is way, *way* larger than mine. As people get richer, Baumol suggested, the mix of their spending changes and shifts toward services.

Because our demand for goods and services works this way, as productivity in goods keeps growing, this makes us feel richer—we can produce more with less—and we use those savings to buy more services. Workers then move into the service sector to provide them, even though services were not the source of the productivity gain in the first place. This doesn't mean we consume fewer goods; while workers are leaving those industries, the remaining workers are more productive, so we can still enjoy the same number of goods (or even more goods) than we did in the past. But we can also enjoy more services than before, even though the productivity in services may not have grown.

An extreme example of this logic would be if goods and services were perfect complements. Let's say that we all want to consume one hour of yoga for every head of lettuce we eat. To begin with, let's assume that it takes one hour of work to grow one head of lettuce, and it obviously takes one hour of work to provide one hour of yoga. If we've got twenty hours of labor to provide, we'll use it to consume ten heads of lettuce and ten hours of yoga. Now, let's say we get more productive at making lettuce (a good), so now it only takes half an hour to produce one head of lettuce. We could get twenty heads of lettuce from our ten hours of lettuce work and still consume ten hours of yoga. But we don't like the asymmetry, given our preferences. So we switch some of our hours of work over to yoga and away from lettuce production, even though lettuce production just got more productive and yoga production didn't improve at all. To get equal consumption of lettuce and yoga, we'd end up using 13.3 hours on yoga, and 6.67 hours on lettuce production (which would give us 13.3 lettuce heads). We get more of both yoga and lettuce, even though we moved labor out of the industry with productivity growth and into an industry with stagnant productivity.

This logic is why you have to be very careful about making any kind of value judgments about the continued shift into services, and so about the productivity and growth slowdowns that are a result of that. Slow productivity growth in services is due to the time- and attention-intense nature of services and does not necessarily represent a failure of our technological know-how or aptitude. The shift into services is a consequence of our incredible success at making goods, not a sign of some failure or problem with the economy.

Knowing what we know about Baumol's cost disease and the shift into services, we can see how plans to reinvent or restructure health care and education—two very income-elastic services—may not result in their share of economic activity declining. Let's say that we came up with a set of miracle health-care policies that not only arrested the growth in health-care costs but actually lowered health-care costs for consumers by thousands of dollars per person. To be concrete, let's say that each and every person in the country would be able to get exactly the same health care they do today, but for $5,000 less per year, and then each person received that $5,000 in cash.

This seems a little ridiculous, but think of the stories about $50 emergency-room Band-Aids, or $40 aspirins, or hundreds of thousands of dollars for a two-day stay in a hospital. It sure seems like we could, given some kind of innovation in how we deliver health care, lower costs by thousands of dollars per person. That would be a lot like a onetime boost to productivity in health care. And it seems like that would go a long way toward lowering the share of GDP that is spent on health care and might lead to workers flowing out of health care and back into higher-productivity industries.

But here is the question Baumol thought to ask: what would people spend that extra $5,000 on? They could use it toward a new car or a major appliance, both manufactured goods. That would raise demand for those products and might pull workers into those industries, increasing the share of GDP accounted for by manufacturing. But they might spend that extra $5,000 to take a well-deserved vacation, spending it on tourism and hospitality services. Or they might decide to spend that money sending their kids to a better (or more expensive?) school, or putting them in day care full-time rather than part-time. Or maybe they send one of their kids to community college who might not otherwise have gone. Perhaps they use the $5,000 to send someone back to get a master's degree so he or she can get a promotion at work.

Some of the $5,000 might even be spent on even more health services. If health care were cheaper, individuals might undertake procedures to permanently deal with chronic problems rather than only alleviating symptoms. Maybe they'd get their kids full orthodontic treatment rather than partial work that straightened only one tooth. The $5,000 could easily be spent on visits to specialists rather than general practitioners, or to see a physical therapist, or to hire a nurse to look in on an elderly relative.

Services—and education and health services in particular—are income elastic. This means that a huge part of the money people would get back from any innovation in health care would be plowed right back into health care, education, and other services. What does that do? It increases demand for those services, which pulls more workers into those industries. The amount of spending on health care and education would still represent a significant fraction of GDP, and perhaps an even larger one. We would certainly be better off if we could raise productivity in health care, but it would likely be a onetime drop in the price of health care, and then the price would continue to grow relative to goods over time, because that's how our preferences for different types of products work.

THE LONG-RUN POWER OF PREFERENCES

In the end, that reallocation of economic activity away from goods production and into services comes down to our success. We've gotten so productive at making goods that this has freed up our money to spend on services. And because services have difficulty improving productivity as compared to goods, this means that we are merging from a fast lane into a slow lane of productivity growth. This effect has become more pronounced in the past two decades, but it is not just a recent phenomenon. Remember, Baumol wrote about these effects back in the 1960s, when goods production was still a much larger part of economic activity. Even then he could see these forces at work.

To give you some idea of how long this reallocation has been going on, we can go back in the data to just after World War II and plot the share of total personal consumption expenditures that are accounted

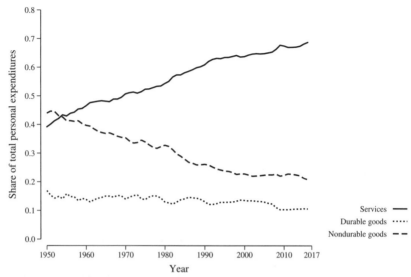

Figure 8.2. Share of goods and services in real GDP over time
Note: Data is from the Bureau of Economic Analysis personal consumption expenditure table 2.3.5. Shares of total expenditures were calculated by the author.

for by goods and services. For goods, I've divided the data up into durable (e.g., dishwashers, cars) and nondurable goods (e.g., food, clothes). Figure 8.2 plots the shares back to 1950. There are two things to note here. First, even in 1950 services accounted for a significant fraction of expenditures, about 40%. By 2017, the share of expenditures on services had climbed to around 70%.

Second, the share of spending on nondurable goods was very high in 1950, also at around 40% of total spending. That nondurable share then declined over time, halving to about 20% by 2017. In contrast, the fall in the share of spending on durable goods was not as dramatic. It started at about 16% and then declined to 11%. What drove the overall shift out of goods and toward services was a drop in our spending on day-to-day nondurable goods.

The shift into services that accounted for a portion of the growth slowdown was not a feature unique to the twenty-first century. It has been going on since 1950 (and even before) and that reinforces Baumol's point that this represents a long-standing difference in our preferences for services (income elastic) and goods (income inelastic). What changed in 2000 was that the share of economic activity had reached such a high level that the drag on productivity growth from this shift finally become tangible.

But keep in mind that we reached this point only because of our continued success during the twentieth century in increasing productivity in goods production. The decline in the share of spending on nondurable goods represents our achievement in making those goods available at such cheap prices that we no longer have to spend a large portion of our income on them. This allowed us to consume more goods and more services, and although this in turn led to rising relative prices for services and an increase in their share of total spending, we still have increased consumption of both types of products.

ACCOUNTING FOR SUCCESS

Before moving on, it seems worth summarizing where the explanation for the growth slowdown stands at this point in the book and to remind you of where I'm headed next. The growth rate of real GDP per capita fell from 2.25% per year in the twentieth century to 1% per year in the twenty-first, a drop of 1.25 percentage points. Of that, 0.80 percentage points, and perhaps as many as 1.11 percentage points, could be chalked up to the drop in the growth rate of human capital per person. The demographic shifts behind this represented a success for two reasons: rising living standards that affected choices toward fewer kids, as well as increased opportunities and reproductive rights for women, which allowed them to have more control over their choices.

Turning to productivity growth, the previous two chapters showed that the shift away from goods production into services could account for up to 0.2 percentage points of the growth slowdown. This shift was, in turn, driven by an immense increase in material living standards. Combined, the consequences of our success can account for about at least 1 percentage point of the 1.25 percentage point drop in growth, or 80% of the entire slowdown. That leaves only a small amount of the growth slowdown left to explain, and that small amount may be even smaller if we allow a larger role for the drop in human capital growth.

What I'm going to do for the remainder of the book is work through a number of explanations for the growth slowdown that would most likely be termed *failures* (e.g., overregulation, rising market power of firms) and show why they account for, at best, only a limited part of the slowdown. As a reminder, the argument here is not that these apparent failures are in fact successes or should be applauded or encouraged. They are failures from the perspective of people's actual well-being and economic security, but they did not play a major role in creating the growth slowdown. In the end, though, I'll come back to why that should give us some optimism about our ability to deal with these failures.

MARKET POWER AND PRODUCTIVITY

An economic phenomenon often put forward as an explanation for the growth slowdown is an increase in the market power of firms. This has manifested in several different trends, including a rise in the share of output that is paid out in economic profits, a matching fall in wages as a share of total output, an increased markup of prices charged by firms over their costs, and increased concentration of firms within many industries. Over the course of the next few chapters I'll provide or discuss evidence for all of these to make the case that market power did increase over the past few decades. This market power, for several reasons we'll get into, messed with the allocation of labor and capital across firms, with possible consequences for productivity growth. But it turns out that those consequences are not quite what you'd think, and even though increased market power represents a distinct failure in the sense of distorting allocations in the economy, it explained little of the growth slowdown itself.

MEASURING MARKET POWER

Before getting into the connections of market power and the growth slowdown, let's start by establishing that market power grew in the first place. The most straightforward way to do this is to look at the share of GDP that was paid out as economic profits over time. But looking at those economic profits is not easy, because they are not the same thing as reported accounting profits, and so we have to back them out from the data.

To make sense of that, let's back up a little and think again about accounting for GDP. What we did a few chapters ago was focus on GDP from the production side, and that meant we accounted for GDP as a combination of physical capital, human capital, and productivity. But we can also focus on GDP from the income side by asking who got paid for providing all that capital and seeing whether there was anything left over after making those payments.

One part of GDP is therefore accounted for by employee compensation, which is, for all intents and purposes, the payments made to people who provide human capital. That compensation consists of direct wages as well as the benefits that employees might get as part of employment, like health insurance or 401(k) matching. A second part of GDP is accounted for by payments to the owners of physical capital, which includes things like the rent paid to owners of real estate or the dividends paid to shareholders, who own the physical capital of firms.

The combination of employee compensation and payments to physical capital owners, though, does not account for all of GDP. If a firm takes the money that is earned by selling all the goods and services produced in a given year, and subtracts the pay of its employees and compensation to the owners of capital, there is money left over. That leftover money is considered an *economic* profit. It is earnings over and above what was necessary to pay for the inputs used in production. As such, it is a way of measuring the market power of firms. The ability to charge more for your product than it costs to produce it is the definition of market power. It doesn't matter where that market power came from (e.g., blocking competitors from opening or producing a unique good); if a firm can charge more than its costs, it has some market power. The economic profits are the crude evidence of market power.

Figuring out the size of economic profits is very difficult, however, because they are not something that firms report. Firms report *accounting* profits, and those are essentially a combination of the payments to physical capital and the economic profits. To find economic profits, one approach is to come up with an estimate of the unreported payments to physical capital and subtract those from the accounting profits.

That approach was taken in a paper by Simcha Barkai, who took on the task of calculating the implied payments to physical capital being made by businesses. The basic idea isn't too complicated. We have measures of the actual capital stock used by businesses. For some of that capital, we see explicit transactions in which someone makes a payment for using the capital. Rental payments on a warehouse and interest payments on a loan used to buy a bulldozer are two examples. If we know these, we can figure out the rate of return on this capital, then assume that this rate of return is being paid on all capital in the economy. The exact methodology requires a little more subtlety, as it has to account for the possible inflation in the value of capital as well as depreciation in capital, but this is the right idea.

The data to do this is all publicly available, and figure 9.1 plots my own calculation using Barkai's methodology of physical capital payments as a share of output, as well as economic profits as a share of output. One important note is that *output* here is only the output produced by corporate businesses; it excludes output produced by public entities (e.g., local, state, and federal government). Hence the figure doesn't show economic profits as a share of GDP but economic profits as a share of corporate business revenues. Even so, the overall pattern should still give us an idea of how market power has changed over time. The figure isn't an exact replica of Barkai's work, as I didn't allow for separate capital types in my calculations (e.g., structures versus equipment), but my results are very similar to his.

All that said, there is a lot going on in figure 9.1. Focus first on 1980, when the share of economic profits was around zero. This occurred in large part because interest rates—and so the implied payments being made to rent capital—were sky-high. From 1980 on, though, the share of economic profits climbed, reaching about 17% by 2016. It is this rise, punctuated by a number of fluctuations, that leads to the conclusion that market power rose over time. Economic profits and market power appear to be much higher in the twenty-first century than they were in the late twentieth.

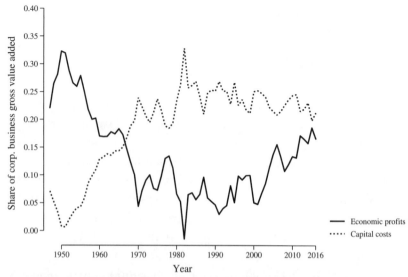

Figure 9.1. Share of capital payments and economic profits in GDP over time
Note: The two series were calculated by the author using data from the Bureau of Economic Analysis on the value of fixed private assets, gross value-added by corporate businesses, compensation of employees by corporate businesses, taxes on production by corporate businesses, and depreciation of capital by corporate businesses. The nominal interest rate used in the calculation is the Moody's Aaa corporate bond rate. The calculation follows Barkai (2017); see the appendix for details.

However, if you go backward from 1980, you'll see that the same calculation shows the economic profit share was around 20% in 1960 and 30% in 1950. This occurred in part because interest rates in those decades were very low, and so the implied payments necessary to physical capital were very low as well. Saying that economic profits in the twenty-first century are larger than in the whole twentieth century, then, is too strong a statement. It is true that they are larger now than they have been since the 1970s or early 1980s.

MARKUPS AND MARKET POWER

There is a different way to conceive of and measure market power. Rather than focusing on total economic profits, we could instead focus on the price charged by firms relative to their costs. And focusing on that allows us to think a little more about what market power means, which will be useful over the next two chapters.

Think about buying a coffee at a shop you go to on a regular basis. There is a maximum price that you'd pay for that coffee, and that price depends on the quality of the coffee itself, the convenience of the location, and how pleasant the staff is to you. There is also a minimum price that the coffee shop will accept to cover its costs. The actual price that you pay for the coffee lies somewhere between those two, because if it didn't, then one of you would refuse to participate in the transaction. In a crude way, market power is a measure of how close the coffee shop can set the actual price to the maximum you'll pay.

Every firm has some market power, but it varies according to preferences and the ability of other firms to offer similar products. The coffee shop may have some market power because it is right on your way to work, making it convenient, or possibly because it uses some particular Ethiopian beans you like, or because the barista knows your regular order. You pay something more than the cost of making a cup of coffee for all those features.

In comparison to the coffee shop, the gas station near my house has only a small amount of market power. There is nothing special about the product—gasoline—and since I pay at the pump, I don't even care whether the staff is friendly. The gas station does have the advantage in being on a corner right on my way home, which saves me from having to make a couple of lefts to get gas across the street. Because of this slight advantage, I'll stop at my regular gas station even if it charges a few cents more per gallon than the one across the road. But because it wouldn't take much to get me to switch stations, my station has very little market power, and I pay close to the minimum necessary to keep it in business.

At the other end of the scale of market power, consider a firm like Apple. The minimum that Apple could charge for an iPhone X is the marginal cost of producing one, and that is probably $150–$200. But Apple sells them for $1,000, well above the cost of producing one, and people are still buying them by the millions. Apple is able to charge an amount close to the maximum people are willing to pay, and this implies that the company has a lot of market power. The source of that market power is a combination of clever engineering, savvy marketing, and the cost of switching systems from iOS to Android.

A reasonable way to measure market power, then, is to compare the actual price paid to the lowest price a firm will accept, or its marginal cost. Economists call this ratio a *markup*. If your coffee shop charged $3.60 for a coffee, and it cost the shop $3 to make the coffee, then the markup is 3.6 / 3 = 1.2. The markup for an iPhone X is much higher, as $1,000 / $200 = 5. For the gas station, if a gallon of gas is $2.50, and the marginal cost of gas to the station is about $2.45, the markup would be only 2.50 / 2.45 = 1.02. The markup gives us a simple index of how much market power each firm has.

Jan De Loecker and Jan Eeckhout went back through data from publicly traded firms (i.e., those listed on the stock market) from 1950 to 2014 and calculated the markup charged by each over time. As you might imagine, this isn't as straightforward as my simple examples suggest, given that most of these firms produce a whole range of goods, and it is hard to track all those individual prices as well as the minimum amount a firm would take for each product. They used some very simple assumptions about firms—including that firms try to minimize the costs incurred during production—which allowed them to calculate the values they needed from the financial data of the firm. They calculated a single markup for each firm, which we can think of as an amalgam of all the individual markups that firms are charging. Regardless, the firm-level markups are an indication of how much market power those firms have in general.

What they found is that from 1950 to 1980 the average markup across all firms was about 1.18. But starting in 1980, the average markup started to rise almost without interruption. By 2014, the average markup was 1.67. This increase was driven to some extent by a general rise in the markup across all firms, but in particular by a few firms moving to very high markups. From 1950 to 1980, the 10% of firms with the highest markups averaged about a 1.50, below the average of all firms in 2014. In contrast, in 2014 the top 10% of firms with the highest markups averaged markups over 2.5. The increase in average markup was driven mainly by these firms at the top end. De Loecker and Eeckhout's findings are corroborated by work from Germán Gutiérrez and Thomas Philippon that used some different data sources and a different methodology. Additional work by De Loecker and Eeckhout shows that the increase in markups was not just a US phenomenon; it also took place in Europe and Canada.

Comparing the calculation of the economic profit share in figure 9.1 with the calculations from De Loecker and Eeckhout, you can see that they are consistent for the period from 1980 to today. Both indicate that market power for firms rose over time. But for the 1950s and 1960s the economic profit share indicated high market power, whereas the markups indicate that market power was low. There are a few possible reasons for this discrepancy, which include the possibility that I (and Barkai) or De Loecker and Eeckhout are using assumptions that are not quite right for that time period. Keeping that in mind, though, the common story from 1980 to today is that market power increased.

One last way to confirm that market power increased is to look at what firms were doing with the money they earned. The shareholders of firms are the owners of the physical capital and claimants on the economic profits. Gutiérrez and Philippon looked at the total payouts made by firms, where those payouts are the combination of dividends (direct payments to shareholders) and share buybacks (which are implicit payments to shareholders by raising share prices). They found that total payouts made by firms were equal to 2%–3% of assets during the 1970s. Following that, though, payouts rose to around 4% of assets in the early 2000s and closer to 6% of assets in 2016. Most of that increase, they documented, was driven by an increase in share buybacks. Despite that, dividend payments also became larger, which De Loecker and Eeckhout documented as well. Dividend payments today are about four times higher than they were in the 1960s and 1970s.

The increase in dividends and share buybacks could be evidence that firms increased either their capital stocks (requiring more payments to capital owners) or their market power (and were paying out their economic profits to shareholders). I go through this in much more detail in the next chapter, but Gutiérrez and Philippon documented that investment by firms in new capital fell over the past few decades, and so the payments to capital are almost certainly lower today than in the past. This implies that most of the payouts to shareholders represent economic profits. On the whole, the evidence points toward increased market power in the economy from the late twentieth century to today.

THE PARADOX OF HIGHER
MARKUPS AND PRODUCTIVITY

It feels as if increased market power *must* explain at least some of the growth slowdown. Basic economic theory tells us that when firms have market power, whether a single firm with a monopoly or several firms in an oligopoly, they restrict the amount of goods produced. The markup firms charge generates an economic profit for them but leaves consumers paying higher prices for fewer products.

All else being equal, we'd expect that an increase in market power would raise the markup charged, increase economic profits, and reduce the amount produced even further. And by itself, this reduction in the amount produced would put a drag on real GDP growth. But in reality not everything is held equal, of course, and when market power increases across many firms at once, or when we shift our spending from low-markup to high-markup firms, the implications for growth in real GDP are no longer so clear.

To think through the implications of increased market power for aggregate productivity growth, I'm going to rely on logic spelled out in work by Susanto Basu and John Fernald, which was then extended and expanded on by David Baqaee and Emmanuel Farhi. The first point to consider is that the effect of a rise in market power across all, or most, firms may be quite different from a rise in market power in one. If market power rises in a given product market—for example, a single health-care company takes over all the hospitals in a given town—then, yes, we would expect a company to restrict output. If it does, then it needs fewer workers and capital. The health-care company might lay off some nurses, doctors, or administrative staff.

If we are just thinking about this single product market, then we're all done. We need not think about the question of what happens to all those laid-off workers or unused capital. But if market power increased across many product markets, then in each one, workers are being laid off and capital is going unused. And if this is widespread enough, these changes would not be small enough to ignore. In the labor market or capital market, it would show up as a significant decline in demand, and both wages and the rental rate for capital would fall. And if the cost of inputs falls, then we'd expect that even firms with market power would hire more workers and invest in more capital. If the supplies of labor and capital are insensitive to the wage or rental rate, then we'd expect all that labor and capital to end up employed again by all these firms.

With all or most of the labor and capital still employed, we'd get a similar level of output as before the increase in market power. A widespread rise in market power would not necessarily lower output, or lower it by much, but it would result in a shift of output away from workers and capital, toward economic profits. The main result of increased market power would show up not as a growth slowdown but as a change in who gets paid.

The second point to consider is that our measures of market power at the aggregate level may have increased because our spending shifted toward products with a lot of market power, and not because each individual firm raised its markup. Baqaee and Farhi further dug into the markup data from Gutiérrez and Philippon and found that this appears to be the case. Although there were plenty of changes in the individual markups firms charge, many of them actually fell over the past twenty years. What explained the overall rise in markups from 1.18 to 1.67 was that spending shifted away from firms with low markups and toward firms with high markups. Which high-markup firms did we shift our spending to? Well, a lot of service firms, including those involved in communications, technology, health care, and education. In short, the rise in economic profits and markups we see at the aggregate level is part of the overall shift toward services we discussed a few chapters ago.

Here's where things get a little weird. Baqaee and Farhi show that the shift toward high-markup firms was *good* for productivity growth.

Whatever the source of a high markup, it indicates a product that is very valuable relative to its marginal cost. If we take the inputs required to produce a low-markup product and use them to instead produce a high-markup product, then we have raised the value of what we produce. As this increase in value came from reallocating our existing inputs toward a different use, rather than from accumulating new physical or human capital, the shift in spending toward high-markup firms shows up as an increase in productivity growth.

You might wonder how we can afford to shift into high-markup products. How can we pay higher prices? There are two things to keep in mind. The first is that, as we have seen, major shifts in spending occur as a result of becoming more productive and therefore richer. The second is that the people earning the economic profits from high-markup goods are consumers as well. When we shift toward buying their products, their income goes up and they spend it on goods and services. The increase in market power changed the distribution of income, but it did not slow down growth.

That caveat aside, how important was the shift into high-markup goods for productivity growth? Baqaee and Farhi calculate that about half of observed growth in productivity in the twenty-first century can be attributed to the shift toward high-markup firms and markets. That means that without the shift, productivity growth would have been even lower, and the growth slowdown would have been worse. Increased market power is not a meaningful explanation for the growth slowdown.

Don't confuse that statement with a claim that we should be complacent about the market power of high-markup industries. We could still be better off if we reduced market power in those industries, in the sense that we'd get even more output if we allowed competitors into their markets. Think of it as running a race. The farther along the course we go, the higher real GDP per capita is, and so our pace is the growth rate. Up ahead of us is another runner, and that runner represents an economy at maximum productivity, one in which all the industries have competition in them and are maximizing output. Market power means we got a slow start and are behind, but we're running at the same pace, and so we never catch up.

The shift into high-markup industries does a few things in this analogy. We start running a little faster because we shift into higher-value production. But the lead runner accelerates even more than us. We're going faster, but we're falling farther behind maximum productivity. Faster productivity growth but a wider gap between actual and maximum productivity are both consequences of an increase in market power. So the incentive to address market power and close that gap to maximum productivity can be greater now than several decades ago, even if we did not see a significant effect of increased market power on the growth rate.

MARKET POWER AND THE
DECLINE IN INVESTMENT

From the aggregate perspective, increased market power did not lead to a slowdown in productivity growth and may in fact have increased it. But if we dig down into what individual firms were doing, it is possible to find some evidence that they were changing their behavior toward investment both in capital and in research and development. In particular, increased market power was associated with less investment in both, consistent with the basic theory that firms with market power restrict output in favor of keeping their prices above costs. This will create more ambiguity about the relationship of market power and the growth slowdown.

THE FALL IN INVESTMENT RATES

In the previous chapter I cited work by Germán Gutiérrez and Thomas Philippon that documented the rise in payouts to shareholders over time as part of the evidence regarding the rise in market power. That is only part of their research, though, and these authors documented that rising market power was a substantial part of the explanation for lower investment in capital over the past few decades as well.

To measure the rate of investment, Gutiérrez and Philippon looked at how much net investment firms make relative to their operating surplus. Both of those terms require some definition. *Net investment* is spending on new physical capital goods minus the loss of capital due to depreciation. If net investment is positive, firms are adding to the capital stock. If

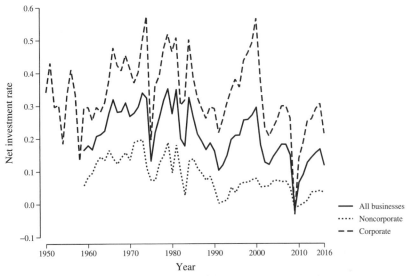

Figure 10.1. Net investment rate over time
Note: Data is from the Federal Reserve System. Net investment rates were calculated by
the author from data on net capital formation divided by operating surplus.

net investment is negative, the capital stock is getting smaller. In the
aggregate data, we do not see net investment become negative, although it may be for some firms in any given year. The other definition we need is for *operating surplus*. This is the combination of payments to capital and economic profits that I discussed a few chapters
ago. Technically, operating surplus also includes an adjustment for
indirect taxes paid—such as sales taxes—but in practice this does
not make much of a difference, so we can think of operating surplus
as the sum of payments to capital and economic profits. It is the total
amount that firms have available to invest.

The data that Gutiérrez and Philippon use for this is all publicly
available, so I've re-created and expanded on the basic figures they
report in their paper. Figure 10.1 plots this net investment rate for
three different groups from 1950 to 2016. What is labeled "All businesses" in the figure includes data for all nonfinancial businesses,
whether they are incorporated or not. The "Corporate" and "Noncorporate" lines break this total down into those categories to reveal the

differences between the groups. Before 1960 only the corporate set of companies was kept track of, so that is why this series runs back to 1950 while the others do not.

Looking at the figure, you can see first a lot of variation on an annual basis, but in general the three series move together. Second, it is clear that the noncorporate businesses do less investment from their operating surplus at all times compared to corporate businesses. There isn't much to make of this, as these are distinct types of companies. An example of a noncorporate business would be a law firm, which is unlikely to be investing a lot in physical capital the way, say, the corporate business GE might.

For our purposes, what is most relevant was the shift downward in the net investment rate that took place across all three series starting in about 2000. If you look at the corporate data, the net investment rate hovered around 30%–40% for the period 1950–2000, with a dip in the early 1990s. That run-up of corporate investment in the later 1990s was largely due to massive investments in computers. But following 2000, the average rate of net investment by corporations fell to around 20%–25%, even ignoring the sharp drop in investment occasioned by the financial crisis in 2008 and 2009.

A similar pattern played out for the noncorporate businesses, which had net investment rates of around 10% from 1960 to 1990. Their investment slipped to around 5% after that, with no distinct change in 2000. Regardless, their investment behavior is quite different now than it was thirty or forty years ago. Combining the corporate and noncorporate investment rates gives us the overall net investment rate. This averaged about 25% until 1990, dipped, and then experienced a surge in the late 1990s thanks to the corporate sector's investment in computing power. But since 2000, the net investment rate across all businesses has dipped to 10%–15%, again ignoring the significant drop during the financial crisis. This overall dip in investment rate is consistent with the earlier data on how the aggregate capital stock started to grow more slowly during the twenty-first century, which explains a small part of the growth slowdown.

IS IT WORTH INVESTING?

We have to be careful here, because investment and growth are linked in several ways, as I started to explain in chapter 4 with the tomato plants. It gets a little weirder than that, though, as it turns out. Consider your tomato plants: If you thought that next year there would be a drought, perhaps because of a long-run forecast or something you read in an almanac, then you would probably eat more of your tomatoes and save fewer of them to plant next year. Why bother if the crop will just fail anyway?

A similar logic is at work with investment. If firms believe that future growth will be weak, then they will rationally decide to lower their investment spending so that they are not stuck with excess capacity. We have to take seriously the possibility that the decline in investment spending by firms was driven by predictions of future growth.

To do this, I follow Gutiérrez and Philippon and calculate a Q ratio for firms, sometimes called Tobin's Q, after the economist James Tobin, a Nobel Prize winner who first outlined the theory behind it in 1969. The Q ratio measures the market value of a firm relative to the current cost of its existing capital stock. When the Q ratio is greater than 1, this means that shareholders believe that the firm's future is more valuable than its present, so to speak. In this case, it makes sense for firms to have positive net investment, as such investment delivers more than $1 in market value for every $1 of the firm's spending on new capital. When the Q ratio is less than 1, the opposite occurs. The future looks worse than the present to shareholders, and so it makes sense for the firm to run down existing capital stock, which leads to negative net investment.

For the set of corporate businesses, I used data on the market value of their equity and the replacement cost of their current capital stock to calculate what I'll call a "simple" Q ratio. It's simple because it doesn't get too sophisticated about calculating the firm's market value. In contrast, Gutiérrez and Philippon take into account a firm's existing financial assets, liabilities, and inventories as part of a firm's market value when they calculate a "complex" Q ratio.

Both the simple and complex Q ratios are plotted in figure 10.2,

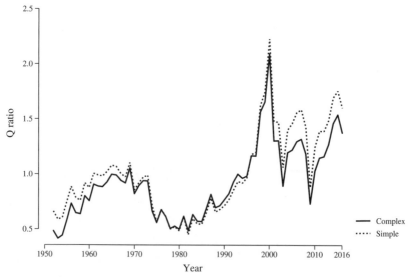

Figure 10.2. Q ratio over time
Note: Data is from the Federal Reserve System. The Q ratios were calculated by the author using data on the value of equities, liabilities, financial assets, inventories, and nonfinancial assets. See the appendix for specific formulas.

and you can see that they do not diverge by much. What you can also see is the pattern over time and how the period of the growth slowdown compares to the past. In the 1950s and 1960s the Q ratio was less than 1, or just about 1, and this is at a time when from figure 10.1 we know that the net investment rate was running quite high. The Q ratio plunged in the 1980s and early 1990s, before accelerating like crazy in the late 1990s. That acceleration coincided with the big run-up in the net investment rate we saw in figure 10.1. Since that peak around 2.0 of the Q ratio, it has fallen, to around 1.5 in my simple conception of it or to about 1.25 in the complex conception of it. Regardless, the Q ratio remained much higher during the 2000s than its historical norm. Yes, it plunged during the worst of the financial crisis, but that reversed almost immediately. The Q ratio in 2015 was higher than in any other year except for 1999 in this entire figure.

The implication of figure 10.2 is that the decline in net investment observed in the past twenty years was due not to a decline in the expected future performance of firms but to something else. Firms appear to have massive market value relative to the replacement cost of their capital during the past few decades, but that has not generated any significant investment, which we would have expected. Before turning to some explanations for that, it is worth thinking about how much investment we are "missing" given a decline in the net investment rate.

Gutiérrez and Philippon look at the relationship of the Q ratio and net investment over the period from 1990 to 2001, and then extrapolate from that what net investment should have been from 2001 to 2015 if the earlier relationship had continued to hold. They then compare the actual net investment to that hypothetical. What they find is that net investment was below their expectation, given the Q ratio, in every year after 2001. If they accumulate the shortfalls, they find that by 2015 the forgone investment was equivalent to 10% of the existing capital stock. That's big enough to warrant further investigation, even though we know that a decline in physical capital accumulation was not a major source of the growth slowdown.

THE CONCENTRATION OF FIRMS

One of the main explanations for slower investment that Gutiérrez and Philippon zero in on is the concentration of firms. By *concentration*, I mean the fact that a shrinking number of very large firms dominate employment and economic activity. You can see this in statistics from the US Census work on businesses. Figure 10.3 plots the fraction of total employment that is associated with firms that have five hundred or more employees, as well as the fraction of total employment from firms that have fewer than five hundred employees. In 1990, roughly 54% of employment was in relatively small firms, but then this started trending downward, hitting 50% around 2000 and about 47% by 2015. The mirror image of this held for large firms, where the fraction of employment rose from around 46% in 1990 to almost 53% in 2015.

The shift toward very large firms came at the expense of all the categories below them. That is, firms that employed only 1–4 workers went from employing about 5.5% of all workers in 1990 to 4.7% in 2015. Firms that employed 5–9 workers went from 6.7% to 5.3% in the same

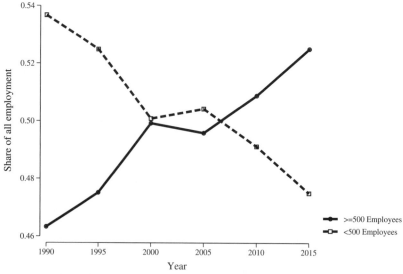

Figure 10.3. Share of employment by size of firm

Note: Data is from the US Census Bureau. Shares were calculated by the author using the reported data on number of firms in a given group and the total number of firms.

period. Similar declines hold for firms that employed 10–19 workers (from 8.1% to 6.7%) and 20–99 workers (19% to 16.6%). The only category of firms that stayed about the same was those employing between 100 and 499 workers, which employed about 14% of all workers the entire time period.

Although it is not necessarily true that the concentration of employment into fewer, larger firms implied an increase in market power, it is consistent with the increase in market power we saw in the data on markups and economic profits. And when Gutiérrez and Philippon looked more closely at the data on investment, they found that the industries that have concentrated the most displayed the biggest drops in net investment.

FEWER FIRMS AND LESS INVESTMENT

To nail this relationship down, Gutiérrez and Philippon looked at both firm-level and industry-level data on net investment, Q ratios, and measures of industry concentration, as well as institutional ownership (e.g., pension funds holding stock in a company). The method they use here is to run linear regressions of net investment on the Q ratio, industry concentration, institutional ownership, and other controls for firm or industry characteristics. And as I just used the words *linear regression*, there is a good chance that your eyes started to glaze over and you got sleepy. Let me take a shot at explaining what is going on here, as there is nothing mysterious about regressions, and they are not some kind of murky black box that researchers use to hide what they are doing. If you are quite sure that you want to know nothing about regressions, then feel free to skip ahead a few paragraphs to where I talk about the results.

The concept of regressions is straightforward, even if most statistics and economics professors often fail to make that clear. When you "control" for something in a regression, what you are doing is dividing up all the observations—in this case, firms—into little subgroups based on those controls. For example, if you control for the age and assets of firms, then that means you create one subgroup of firms that are all five years old and have between $50 million and $100 million in assets. Then there is another subgroup of firms that are five years old but have $100 million to $150 million in assets. And another subgroup that is six years old and has $50 million to $100 million in assets, and so on and so on. *Within* each subgroup, you then look at how institutional ownership and net investment, for example, are related. Last, you do a weighted average of all those subgroup relationships you just found to figure out the overall relationship of institutional ownership and net investment, where the weights depend on how many firms were in a given subgroup. It's not complicated, just tedious.

When Gutiérrez and Philippon regressed net investment by firms on total number of firms in their industry (to measure concentration), controlling for firm-level Q ratio, firm age, and firm assets, they first broke everything up into subgroups in which all the firms looked similar in Q ratio, age, and assets. Because inside each subgroup the firms have these similar characteristics, we know that it isn't Q ratio, age, or assets that drive any differences in their net investment rates. However, when they compared these firms' net investment rates to how many total firms are in their industry, they found that firms with fewer competitors invest less. And that holds up across all the sub-groups that they formed using data on Q ratios, age, assets, and a whole host of other controls that are not worth listing here.

Gutiérrez and Philippon found that two things are consistent in explaining the drop in net investment: the extent of institutional ownership of a firm's shares and the concentration of firms in the same industry. The larger the fraction of shares that are owned by institutions, the lower net investment is. The more concentrated an industry is into a few larger firms—and the greater the market power of any individual firm is assumed to be—the lower net investment is. This holds regardless of the fact that the authors account for the role of firm-specific characteristics in their analysis. Yes, firms that have a very low Q ratio of their own do not invest much. But firms with a very low Q ratio that also do not have many competitors invest even less. Firms that have low Q ratios that also have a lot of institutional ownership invest even less.

These two explanations are the only ones that consistently show up as important to the decline in net investment rate. The ability to access debt markets, reliance on bank loans, and changes in investor attitudes toward risk do not appear to matter. Neither does the amount of regulation faced by an industry, or firms' foreign activities, or uncertainty about sales growth. Any or all of those may matter to a specific firm or a specific industry at a given time, but none of those factors matters across all industries or all firms. In contrast, institutional ownership and the concentration of firms in an industry matter for the entire population of firms and industries.

Furthermore, this effect of market power on muting investment in physical capital spills over into investing in innovation through research and development. For the same set of data, Gutiérrez and Philippon looked at determinants of R&D spending relative to assets. They found, similar to the results for net investment, that more institutional ownership is associated with less R&D spending. In addition, the more concentrated an industry, the lower is R&D spending, again consistent with the net investment data. Now, the connection from R&D spending to innovation, and from innovation to productivity, is fuzzy. Remember that productivity captures more than just technology. But the decline in R&D spending is another example of how market power lowers the investments, broadly conceived, that firms make to becoming more productive.

Overall, the effect of institutional ownership on investment in both physical capital and R&D is open to speculation. It would not be hard, though, to believe that institutional shareholders press the firms' management to focus more on the short term and more on increasing share buybacks or dividends, rather than on investing in new capital. In contrast, Gutiérrez and Philippon's finding that industry concentration is related to lower net investment in both capital and R&D is consistent with the data on markups and economic profits. When the producers in an industry are concentrated into a few large firms, they are generally able to command more market power. If those firms have more market power, they may not see much of an incentive to invest, as their customer base is locked in.

The evidence here on firms seems clear, but even so, the connection of this to the aggregate growth slowdown turns out to be tenuous. Recall from chapter 4 that the change in physical capital growth was not a major contributor to the growth slowdown, at least compared to the change in human capital growth and productivity growth. It may well be that market power lowered firms' investment rates, but by itself that does not appear to have been a significant source of the growth slowdown. Even if the effect on investment was larger, that would offset the positive effects on productivity growth discussed in the previous chapter, leaving us with an ambiguous connection between market power and the growth slowdown.

THE NECESSITY OF MARKET POWER

11 Over the past few chapters we've seen that market power for firms increased and, for the most part, this coincided with the growth slowdown. However, tying the two phenomena together has proved difficult. Productivity growth turns out to have an ambiguous relationship to market power; an increase in market power from the aggregate perspective may be good for productivity because it means that more resources are being put to use by firms or industries that produce high-value goods and services. We just saw that in industries that became more concentrated, investment in both physical capital and R&D fell, although it isn't clear from an economy-wide perspective that this was significant in accounting for the growth slowdown.

But while market power may not have played a major role in our past, perhaps it can have an effect on our future. Continued increases in market power could lead to slower innovation and so slower productivity growth. In contrast, if we were able to reduce the market power of firms, this could maybe lead to more innovation and offset some of the growth slowdown.

That last paragraph contained a lot of conditional words: *could, perhaps,* and *maybe.* This is not just because we're talking about the future, but because the relationship of market power to innovation and growth is subtle and complex, getting at the very heart of why economies grow at all. To see this, we need to appreciate that the markup a firm can charge over its costs is the result of both supply and demand.

Market power and a large markup could reflect limits on supply, as when consolidation in the health-care sector means that there is only one hospital in a certain city at which to get a specific surgery. But market power and a large markup can also arise because there is a product that we happen to enjoy and are willing to pay a premium to obtain. This can be as simple as a coffee shop that you like to visit or the one I spent a lot of time at writing this book. The shop charges well over marginal cost for coffee (and food, for that matter). It isn't because the coffee shop slapped a patent on coffee drinking and sued everyone else out of business. It is because it provides a product— coffee, space, atmosphere—that you and I value relative to the alternative of buying lukewarm coffee out of an urn at a gas station.

Hence we need to think harder about the source of market power before we can address whether it will lead to slower growth in the future and whether reducing it would be good or bad for growth. As I'll try to explain here, market power is what generates the incentives to innovate in the first place. Without some market power, there would be no growth. This means that the answer to the growth slowdown is not to eliminate market power and markups, but to find the sweet spot for market power that provides optimal incentives for investment and innovation. To explain what I mean, I need to make a quick detour through the intellectual history of economic growth.

REWARDING NONRIVAL IDEAS

The modern understanding of the role of market power in economic growth can be traced back to two papers by Paul Romer that appeared in the late 1980s and early 1990s. It was because of those papers that Romer was just awarded a Nobel Prize in 2018, alongside William Nordhaus. In them, he described how to incorporate innovative activity into standard models of economic growth of the time, which did not consider why innovation happened at all. Although parts of both papers are very technical, the opening half of his 1990 paper is readable by anyone with some interest in economics, and what I present here is very much a summary of that paper.

What Romer focused on was the difference between standard inputs to production like physical and human capital and nonstandard inputs like ideas, blueprints, recipes, and technologies that we use to organize and control the standard inputs. Standard inputs are what economists call *rival* goods, which just means that if an input is being used here, then it cannot be used over there at the same time. My laptop is a rival input. When I am typing this paragraph, you cannot use it to check your email. If someone is using a bulldozer—a piece of physical capital—to level a roadbed in Houston, it cannot be simultaneously used to level a roadbed in Dallas. This rival property holds for human capital, too, particularly your time. If you are stuck in a meeting at work, you cannot also be getting anything productive done at your desk.

The nonstandard inputs, though, are *nonrival*. You can use a nonrival idea, or blueprint, or recipe, or technology in any number of places at once, and it does not diminish the ability of anyone else to use it. Software is a great example of a nonrival technology. Even though you cannot use my laptop when I'm using it, you can use the same word-processing program that I am using, at the same time, and neither of us would notice a difference. Do you remember that cake I used to explain productivity growth? Well, the recipe for that cake is nonrival. If I decide to bake a cake using that recipe, you can bake a cake using the exact same recipe, at the same time, in an entirely different kitchen. Things like the design of a product, or the blueprint for a house, or even the organization chart of a company are examples of nonrival inputs to production. They can be used by any number of people at once without limiting the ability of anyone else to use them.

This nonrival property makes nonstandard inputs the key to growth. Every time we come up with a new idea or technology, it can spread to everyone or every firm without making it less effective. An idea that raises production by 10% at one firm can raise production by 10% at another firm, too. That idea can raise total production by 10%. This is different from the standard inputs. If you give one firm enough capital to raise production by 10%, then you cannot use that capital at another firm at all. So the increase in physical capital does not raise the total output of all firms by 10%, but maybe by only 3% or 4%. In our discussion of accounting for growth, I provided some elasticities for physical and human capital to use as weights. Those elasticities were both less than 1—that is, 0.35 for physical capital and 0.65 for human capital—which is because of the rival nature of the standard inputs. Because rival inputs cannot be shared, the percentage increase in output doesn't equal the percentage increase in an input. Given that the standard inputs also tend to depreciate over time, it eventually becomes impossible to accumulate them fast enough to keep ahead of the depreciation, meaning that economic growth would end up disappearing if we didn't have more and more non-rival ideas and plans, something Robert Solow figured out back in 1956, in a paper that is the foundation of nearly all theories of economic growth.

Romer built on Solow's work by not only noting that nonrival inputs were different than rival inputs but also asking why anyone would bother to dream up these nonstandard ideas and plans in the first place. We have established that they can be copied without diminishing their use for other people or firms. This means that if you put some effort into innovation, others could use your design or idea or recipe or plans to compete with you. And if others are going to compete away your business, why bother to innovate in the first place? What Romer made clear was that these ideas and plans have to be made *excludable*, meaning that the innovators have to acquire the ability to prevent others from using them. In Romer's original articles, he zeroed in on patents as one way that we create excludable ideas. But other options exist. Coca-Cola, for example, has no patent on its formula. Instead, it is excludable because the formula is kept in a locked safe somewhere in Atlanta. Other nonrival ideas are best thought of as skills embedded in individuals. The ideas and plans that go into open-heart surgery are nonrival, but the ability to use those ideas and plans is excludable, limited to a small set of highly trained surgeons.

Whatever the source of excludability—patents, secrecy, training—the end result is the same: market power. By acting as the exclusive provider (or one of a few) of an idea, plan, or skill, the owner can charge a price above the actual marginal cost of their product, a markup. One of the best examples is software. The marginal cost of producing Microsoft Word is, for all intents and purposes, zero. You just need to copy the program from one computer to another. But Microsoft charges you much more than zero for Word because it is the exclusive provider of that product. And it is the exclusive provider of Word because it owns patents and copyrights protecting the code and brand.

What Romer established was that market power is *required* for innovation, because the markups it produces are the compensation for the time and effort put into innovating in the first place. Microsoft's markup on Word pays for the coding and testing that were necessary to produce the product. Another of the most commonly cited examples is pharmaceuticals, for which the high price of any given drug is justified by the amount of money the firm put into researching and developing the new drug, even if producing it turns out to be quite cheap. Even the owner of your local coffee shop used the prospect of charging a markup to justify putting all that work into creating the environment you enjoy so much. Without markups, there is no incentive to invest in R&D, whether as official as people in labs with white coats or as informal as the coffee shop's owner picking good music to play. Without R&D, there are no nonrival innovations. And without nonrival innovations, there is no productivity growth.

SO NOW MARKET POWER IS A GOOD THING?

How can this theory be consistent with evidence that increased market power was associated with lower investment and innovation? The answer is that the theory I described says that *some* market power is necessary, but it doesn't tell us what the optimal amount of market power is. For that, I'll lean on some work that centers on the research of Philippe Aghion and Peter Howitt. Those two, along with a number of coauthors they worked with over time, had the same underlying concept as Romer, but they thought harder about the nature of competition among firms. In particular, they looked into how innovation is used to grab customers and market share away from existing competitors. In their work, they take seriously the turnover among firms and workers as firms compete. Aghion and Howitt refer to their theory as "Schumpeterian," as it involves the idea of creative destruction — the replacement of old firms with new ones — originally described by Joseph Schumpeter.

To see their logic, it is easiest to think of the extreme cases first. If there is intense competition within an industry, perhaps because it is hard to exclude others from copying one firm's ideas, or because a firm's product (e.g., gasoline) is something people don't have strong preferences about, there is little incentive to innovate. If a firm does innovate, someone will copy that firm, and competitors will eat away whatever markup the firm can charge in a short time. Or even if no one copies the firm, its customers are very price sensitive and so the firm cannot charge a very high markup without driving them away. Either way, it isn't worth the trouble to innovate in this setting.

In contrast, if there is no competition within an industry, the firm or firms that do exist have little incentive to innovate, either. Whether because of some regulatory barrier (e.g., a cable company, hospitals) or because people have strong preferences (e.g., Apple fans), a firm's customer base is insensitive to price, and it is almost impossible for another firm to steal business. Perhaps more important, there is little additional market for the firm to soak up. In this case, there is again almost no incentive to innovate, as the firm has little to gain in terms of new customers. Think of the single hospital in a small town. Everyone already uses that hospital, so innovations that might improve service would gain the hospital very little.

In between these extremes, Aghion and Howitt tell us there is a sweet spot at which firms have just enough market power to reward them for innovating but not so much that they do not feel the pressure of staying ahead of competitors. In a paper with Nicholas Bloom, Richard Blundell, and Rachel Griffith, they showed evidence to this effect. The authors calculated patent activity (a proxy for innovation) within industries over time. They also computed something called the Lerner index for each industry, which is just another way of measuring the markup charged in each. When they compared patent activity against the markup, they found a clear hill shape. Patent activity was very low among industries with very low markups (i.e., lots of competition), and patent activity was also very low among industries with very high markups (i.e., very little competition). Peak patenting activity took place among firms with an intermediate level of markups.

ON THE WRONG SIDE OF THE HILL

When we look at the data from the past few decades and see that increased market power is associated with less innovation, it is consistent with the theory of economic growth I just described. Recall the evidence from Gutiérrez and Philippon on net investment and R&D spending that showed it was lower as an industry became more concentrated. The interpretation is that we have moved past the sweet spot and are now in the range where firms have "too much" market power. Even though they are able to charge huge markups, they do not face enough competition to induce them to innovate or invest as fast as before.

The implication is that by reining in the market power of firms and lowering their markups, it would be possible to increase the growth rate of productivity. But how much less market power should there be? And should it be lower for all firms and industries, or are there just some for which it is too high? Here's where we run into a significant problem, because market power is the result of supply and demand. For each and every product and service, we'd have to go back and figure out the optimal amount of market power that maximizes innovation and growth. For some firms, their markup represents our desire and demand for their product, and we would not want to eliminate that if it meant the firm might shut down. But for some firms, the markup might represent a restriction of supply, perhaps because they colluded with would-be competitors to carve up different markets. In that case, we would want to act to cut down their market power. But there is no single answer, and the fact that the average markup is higher—1.67 today versus 1.18 in 1980—doesn't tell us that all, or any, industries and firms have markups that are higher than optimal.

That said, there are several areas that seem to bear a closer look in terms of advancing market power beyond what is optimal in a general sense. Intellectual property rights are a prime example. As noted earlier, all those nonrival ideas need to be made excludable for their innovators and inventors to reap some benefits from them and to create incentives to innovate in the first place. Intellectual property rights (IPRs), which cover patents, copyrights, and the like, is the catchall term for the legal structures that create that excludability. But IPRs have expanded in the past several decades. In 1976, copyrights were extended to the life of an author plus fifty years, where before they could last a maximum of fifty-six years. In 1998, that was extended to the life of an author plus seventy years. This is a great benefit to the heirs of an author, but it doesn't do much to supply a living author with any great incentive to write.

Patent law has changed in a similar manner. In 1982 a new federal court was established with control over patent cases, and this led to a distinct change in what was considered patentable. In general, the standards were lowered, which allowed firms to patent things like software and business models. For example, you may know that Amazon patented "one-click" ordering in 1999. Whatever your gut feeling about the need for IPRs to protect innovation, this one is hard to defend. One-click ordering is a convenience that is obvious and simple to implement for any firm. It is roughly equivalent to patenting the idea "be nice to your customers." The European Union refused to patent it. Did this patent provide the excludability for an innovation that Amazon would otherwise have refused to make? Or did this patent just help Amazon shut out some potential competitors back in the days before it was Amazon as we know it today, when it was just an online bookseller with aspirations to something more?

The group of "patent troll" firms is something of a textbook example of IPRs creating market power with no benefits. These firms buy up patents and run around suing companies for infringement, mostly hoping to get some sort of settlement, while their targets hope to avoid actual litigation. They provide a useful benchmark for evaluating other firms. Do we think the rise in market power and markups over time is because firms are acting more and more like patent trolls, or because they have distinct innovations that are worth protecting?

You wouldn't call Apple a patent troll. Or would you? Apple sued Samsung in 2011 because Samsung produced a smartphone that was a rectangle with rounded edges and had a grid of app icons on the main screen. That case went on for years, with Apple awarded $1 billion, later knocked down to $548 million and then $399 million during retrial. In late 2017 a federal judge decided that there would need to be another retrial. Whatever the decision, does this represent a necessary action by Apple to defend the innovation of rounded edges and gridded icons, or was it an attempt by the firm to kneecap a potential competitor? Would Apple have gone out of business without those patents?

Partly on the basis of such examples, Michelle Boldrin and David Levine have argued for the abolition of IPRs. Their argument is that nonrival ideas are excludable through either training (e.g., as with a surgeon) or the tacit knowledge required to use them (e.g., manufacturing a car). In the case of Apple, they might argue that its intellectual property was protected by Apple's own brand, marketing, customer service, and better software, and that the patents themselves were just a way of extorting payments from Samsung.

A different example in support of their case against IPRs is Tesla, the electric car company, which gave away all of its patents. You could go out and build yourself an exact replica of a Tesla right now if you wanted to. To Boldrin and Levine's point, though, while in theory you could build your own Tesla, in reality you can't. You don't have the requisite knowledge, training, and capital to reproduce a Tesla in your own garage. That tacit knowledge and specialized equipment mean that the nonrival idea of a Tesla is effectively excludable, even with no legal protections in place.

That illustrates, I think, the need to think of IPRs and market power on a case-by-case basis. For Tesla, IPRs are unnecessary for the reasons Boldrin and Levine suggest. But for other products, such as pharmaceuticals, the legal protection of a patent can be crucial. Many drugs that have been developed—and are sold at large markups as firms recover the costs of R&D and Food and Drug Administration approval—are in fact quite simple to cook up. This is why generics become available the day those drugs lose patent protection and are often sold at a fraction of the branded price. Without IPRs, those generics would be available within days of the new drug being released, knocking the markup down for the innovating firm and eliminating the incentive for it to do more innovation on the next drug. The tough question with IPRs for pharmaceuticals, as with any kind of product, is how affordable you want current drugs or ideas to be relative to future drugs or ideas.

PUTTING LIMITS ON MARKET POWER

Intellectual property rights represent a legal means of creating market power, and so a markup. But the legal system also has a method for challenging and removing market power, known as antitrust enforcement. Antitrust law goes back to the Sherman Act, passed in 1890, and is often seen as a response to monopolies like Standard Oil that operated at the time. This act, along with some subsequent additions, gave the federal government the ability to block certain actions or break up firms if they were deemed to be anticompetitive.

The legal history of the Sherman Act and its enforcement is beyond the scope of this book, but much of it deals with the very questions that we're wrestling with here. What constitutes "too much" market power? When has a firm engaged in behavior that is anticompetitive versus just being good at what it does? As in the case of IPRs, there is no clear answer to these questions. However, also like the trend toward stronger IPRs, we can see that there has been a trend in the amount of antitrust enforcement over time.

Figure 11.1 plots the number of cases taken on by the Department of Justice's antitrust division over time. The division classifies cases as one of three types. "Restraint of trade" refers to cases brought against firms or groups of firms under section 1 of the Sherman Act. In this category, firms are investigated for engaging in activities that are meant to drive others out of business. This might include something like a price-fixing agreement between firms. Under "monopoly" fall cases under section 2 of the Sherman Act, or those cases in which a firm has a monopoly and engages in actions that maintain a monopoly that does not result from a superior product or business acumen. The actions against Standard Oil and US Steel were made under section 2 of the Sherman Act, and more recent examples include the breakup of AT&T in the early 1980s and the case brought

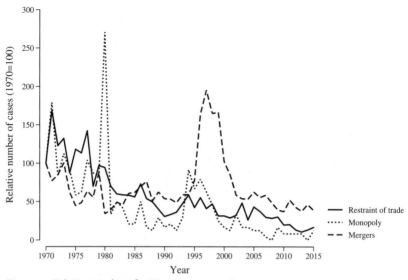

Figure 11.1. Relative number of antitrust cases over time
Note: Data is from the Department of Justice. Relative numbers of cases in the three series were calculated by the author.

against Microsoft in the 1990s. Finally are "mergers," cases brought under the Clayton Act, which prohibits businesses from buying assets from another business if doing so results in a monopoly or restraint of trade.

For each series, I normalized the number of cases to one hundred in 1970, as otherwise they are hard to compare. There are a few spikes, such as the surge in monopoly cases in 1980, or the cases against mergers in the late 1990s. But for all three series, the trend over time is downward. In 2016, the number of all three types of cases was less than half of what it was in 1970. For monopoly and restraint of trade, the number of cases was less than 20% of what it was in 1970. This is true despite the fact that the number of firms, as I show in more detail a little later in the book, has increased over time. Relative to the size of the economy and number of firms, antitrust cases have declined.

This decline in antitrust enforcement coincided with the rise in market power. That doesn't mean that fewer antitrust cases *caused* the rise in market power, or that that the rise in market power we saw in the data must necessarily be due to restraint of trade or monopoly. Figure 11.1 reveals that it *could* be that the increase in market power was due to firms' success at managing the legal system and restraining trade rather than success in introducing must-have products and services. This correlation is evidence that we should dig further into the relationship between antitrust enforcement and market power.

To the extent that increased IPRs and decreased antitrust enforcement led to the "wrong" kind of market power, we are past the sweet spot and market power was infringing on growth through restraining innovation and turnover between firms. It is plausible in this case to think of reforms—to IPRs and to antitrust enforcement—that could reduce market power and increase growth. But let me caution again that the case for reducing market power is not a case for eliminating market power. Without market power and the markups it provides we would lose the incentive to innovate altogether.

THE CONSEQUENCES OF MARKET POWER

The evidence from a few chapters ago showed that the market power of firms grew by a substantial amount from around 1980 to today. But drawing a clear line from that increase in market power to the growth slowdown is not possible. From a pure accounting perspective, a shift of labor and capital toward firms with high markups is good for productivity growth, as the products have high values relative to their costs. There was a decline in firms' net investment rate over the past few decades as well, and that decline was more severe in industries that had become more concentrated. However, the contribution of lower investment to the growth slowdown was never that large to begin with, so rising concentration can explain only a little. From a theoretical perspective, market power has an ambiguous relationship to innovation, with a sweet spot that maximizes incentives for firms and individuals. But both too much and too little market power can be damaging to innovation and also to growth.

As before, this does not mean that we should be indifferent to the increase in market power. This increase changed who reaped the benefits of the economic growth that did occur. Increased market power was associated with a smaller share of GDP flowing toward labor or the providers of physical capital, and a larger share to the claimants on the economic profits market power creates. In general, that meant the owners of firms. There are reasons to be wary of that, even if, relative to changes in demographics and the long-run shift into services, it did not explain why the growth rate of real GDP per capita fell.

REALLOCATIONS ACROSS FIRMS AND JOBS

The next topic to explore as a source of the growth slowdown is turnover of workers and capital between different firms, locations, or even jobs within firms. To get an idea of how this turnover can affect productivity, think of a local restaurant you know that for a long time was a so-so place to eat. It may have made enough money to stay afloat, but it didn't excite anyone. When that place finally closed down and got replaced by a new restaurant with a new chef and better service, it turned into a hot place to be and did a ton of business.

The same capital—the building, the walk-in refrigerator, the flat-top grill, the other kitchen equipment—got reallocated from one business to another, even if it didn't physically move. And if the new restaurant kept on the old waitstaff and cooks but gave them better recipes to use and held them to higher service standards, then the labor was reallocated as well.

This reallocation had an effect on productivity. Maybe not a big one from an aggregate perspective, given that we're talking about one restaurant in an economy with hundreds of thousands of restaurants, but it did have an effect. Productivity growth is growth in output beyond the growth accounted for by increased inputs. In this case, there were no new inputs—capital and labor were the same as before—so the increase in value-added created by new ownership of the restaurant showed up as productivity growth. The reallocation of labor and capital from one use to another can, in many cases, lead to gains in productivity.

These kinds of reallocations go on all the time. When the electronics chain Circuit City failed, Best Buy bought up many locations, and thus there was a reallocation of the capital and labor to a new firm. When some managers and salespeople break off from a company to open their own firm, that is a reallocation. If your company shifts you from one kind of job to another, that is a reallocation as well. Some of those reallocations may require you to relocate from one city to another, and those actual physical kinds of reallocations we'll focus on in more detail in the next chapter.

Not every reallocation increases productivity. There are plenty of restaurants that come under new management and somehow manage to be even worse than the ones they replaced. Maybe it turns out that you are not very good at the new job your company shifted you into. Maybe Best Buy made a mistake purchasing some of the Circuit City locations, and it will not be able to do any better. But for the most part, these reallocations should tend to increase productivity, given that firms would undertake the reallocations only if they had some expectation that it would increase their revenues relative to the costs of production.

It turns out that the rate of reallocations fell over the past few decades. This suggests that the productivity slowdown may be because there were fewer productivity-improving reallocations taking place. This connection is not necessarily true, of course. The rate of reallocation may have fallen because we got better at identifying which reallocations would lower productivity and then avoided those. But it seems unlikely that this is the entire reason for the fall in the reallocation rate, and so the decline is a plausible source of slower productivity growth.

LOOKING WITHIN INDUSTRIES

We can start by thinking about reallocations across establishments, like in the restaurant example. This includes the movement of capital and workers out of establishments that closed down (exited the market) and into establishments that opened up (entered the market), but it also includes the movement of capital and workers between existing establishments.

I need to pause here to be clear about what I mean by *establishment*. The different locations of a given firm are establishments. Each Starbucks you see is an establishment, even though they all are part of a larger firm. The separate manufacturing plants of Toyota USA—places like Georgetown, Kentucky, and Lafayette, Indiana—are establishments. When I talk about reallocations between establishments, that includes moving workers or capital between different locations—from Georgetown to Lafayette—even if they still work for the same firm. Workers and capital can also "move" if their establishment is bought out by another firm—if Honda bought the Georgetown plant, for example. Any time these inputs change establishments, there could be an effect on productivity, and that depends on whether the new establishment has higher or lower productivity than the old one. But don't get hung up on the physical location. An establishment can be "new" for a worker just because it has new management, like the waiters who kept working at your local restaurant.

Calculating the effect of reallocations between establishments is difficult, because you need data at the establishment level, meaning that you need to track the number of employees in each Starbucks in the United States, the amount of capital used in each one, and income statement information for each establishment so you can calculate their individual establishment value-added. With that information you can back out the productivity of an establishment to figure out if a reallocation increased or decreased productivity overall. Only in the past few decades has this kind of detail become available to researchers. What is available so far indicates that reallocations of inputs across establishments are quite important to productivity growth within industries.

Lucia Foster, John Haltiwanger, and Chad Syverson decomposed the productivity growth of a handful of manufacturing subindustries, focusing on those with very homogeneous products, such as concrete, plywood, and gasoline. The value of looking only at homogeneous products is that the authors didn't have to worry about differences in the quality or features of products. That would have been a headache if they were comparing, say, the production of a Toyota Highlander to the production of a Honda Pilot. For their purposes, concrete is concrete, to a large degree.

On average, across all the separate subindustries they studied, productivity grew by 5.13% every five years, or almost exactly 1% per year. What they then did was ask how fast productivity would have grown if there had been no reallocation of labor and capital between establishments. It turns out that growth would have been only 3.44% every five years, or about 0.6% per year. The reallocation of inputs accounted for about 40% of total productivity growth in these industries.

What Foster and her coauthors were also able to figure out was how important different aspects of reallocation were for growth. They found that nearly all the gap between 5.13% and 3.44% was due to the net entry of establishments. Productivity grew by 1.35% every five years because inputs were pulled into brand-new, higher-productivity establishments (e.g., a new plywood manufacturing facility) and pulled out of establishments that had relatively low productivity. In contrast, movements of inputs between existing establishments didn't contribute much at all to productivity growth.

The power of reallocation doesn't apply only to these manufacturing subindustries. Foster and Haltiwanger, along with a different coauthor, Cornell Krizan, did a similar study for the retail sector. They found that productivity growth in retail between 1987 and 1997 was 11.43%, or about 1.1% per year. Almost none of it was from existing establishments getting more productive. If it weren't for the shuffling of inputs between different retail establishments, including new firms taking over existing establishments, productivity growth in the whole retail industry would have been zero in those ten years.

Moreover, it wasn't inputs getting moved between existing establishments, like shifting staff from one location of a Whole Foods to another. It was a combination of new, high-productivity establishments entering the economy and old, low-productivity establishments exiting. Think of a new Whole Foods location hiring staff, or buying the shelving, from a Stop and Shop that shut down. It need not even involve different physical locations. If an OfficeMax moved into the storefront abandoned by a Barnes and Noble, that is an example of an entering establishment replacing an exiting establishment.

Why are those new establishments more productive than the exiting establishments? It may be that the new establishments use better management techniques that get more value-added out of existing inputs. Or it may be that the old establishment simply saw a shift in demand away from its products (e.g., a physical bookstore). Whatever the reason, the replacement of low-productivity retail locations with higher-productivity establishments was central to productivity growth in the whole retail industry.

We don't have detailed studies like this for every industry, so drawing broad conclusions is impossible. But the evidence suggests that reallocation effects are significant, even if they may not explain all of productivity growth, as they do in the retail industry. And they happen to be another example of why you should not confuse productivity growth with technological change. Sometimes productivity growth is just about better management or better organization.

TURNOVER IS SLOWING DOWN

The productivity boost we get from moving workers, capital, or both from a low-productivity establishment to a high-productivity establishment requires ... movement. We need establishments with low productivity to go out of business and be replaced by establishments with high productivity, whether that comes from existing high-productivity firms spreading out to new locations across the country or from brand-new firms with good ideas. We need workers to switch jobs from low-productivity establishments to high-productivity establishments, which might involve physically moving or staying put when the establishment gets a new owner.

Thanks to a series of papers by Ryan Decker, John Haltiwanger, Ron Jarmin, and Javier Miranda, we know that the speed at which these changes happen has declined over time. Using data series that, in many cases, they created from scratch using detailed information from the US Census, we can track the turnover of jobs and establishments in the whole economy.

Figure 12.1 plots the entry rate of establishments, which is the

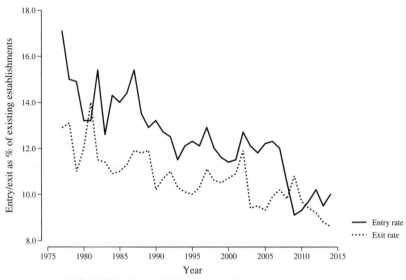

Figure 12.1. Establishment entry and exit rates over time
Note: Data is from the US Census Bureau Business Dynamics Statistics.

number of new establishments that open in a given year relative to the existing number of establishments. In 1976, this was about 17%, meaning that seventeen establishments opened for every hundred that already existed. In the same year, the exit rate was about 13%, or thirteen establishments of every hundred closed. Comparing those two rates, the number of establishments rose by a net 4% that year.

Over time, though, *both* the entry and the exit rates trended down. By 2000, the entry rate was only about 12%, and the exit rate about 11%. On net, the number of establishments was growing by only 1% per year. Relative to the existing base of establishments, fewer establishments were created and fewer went out of business in the 2000s and 2010s than in prior decades. This meant fewer opportunities for inputs to get turned over from low-productivity establishments to high-productivity establishments.

This is a good place to revisit the difference between growth rates, growth, and levels. The rate of establishment entry and exit fell over time. But that does not mean that there were fewer establishments in the economy, or even that we added or closed fewer than in the past.

Figure 12.2 shows the equivalent of establishment *growth* as opposed to growth rates. The darkest bars at the top show the total number of establishments that entered in a given year, which bounced around between 600,000 and 800,000 per year over the whole period, with a peak of about 820,000 new establishments in 2006. The lightest gray bars at the bottom show the number of establishments that exited the economy each year, which bounced around between about 500,000 and 700,000 most of the time. The biggest loss of establishments was 751,000, in 2002, and not during the financial crisis. The economy shed 723,000 establishments in 2009, during the worst of the recession.

The point of this figure is that there is a tremendous amount of turnover in establishments each and every year. Similarly, a high number of exiting establishments is not unique to recessions, and

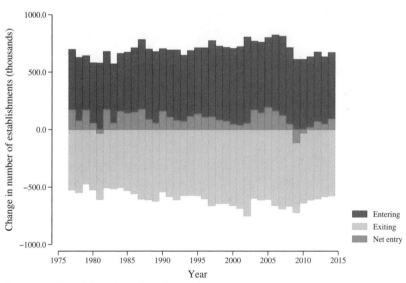

Figure 12.2. Growth in entry, exit, and net entry
Note: Data is from the US Census Bureau Business Dynamics Statistics. Absolute growth in entrants, exits, and net entry was calculated by the author.

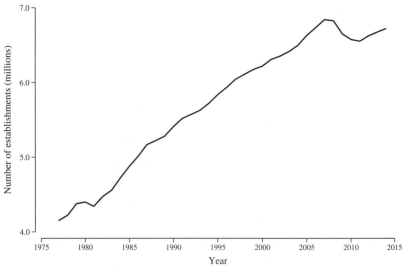

Figure 12.3. Number of establishments and firms
Note: Data is from the US Census Bureau Business Dynamics Statistics.

a high number of entering establishments is not unique to booms. The continual churn of establishments resulted in the net entry of establishments, shown in the figure in the medium gray bars. This net number is much smaller in scale than the number of entering or exiting establishments, as those two tend to cancel out. But it came out to about 100,000 net new establishments each year, with a high of 193,000 net new establishments in 2005 and a low of a net loss of establishments of 113,000 in 2009. Since the end of the recession, it appears that the net addition of establishments has been not quite as large as before, as the absolute amounts of entry and exit have been smaller than they were before 2009. Whether that is a permanent feature of the economy remains to be seen, but it is consistent with the lower rates of entry and exit we saw in figure 12.1.

If we step back to look at the level of the number of establishments, as in figure 12.3, we can see the end result of all this entry and exit. In 1976 there were a little over 4 million establishments in the United States, and this rose until it hit a peak of 6.8 million establishments in 2007. At this point the recession hit: the number of establishments exiting outpaced entries, and the number of establishments dropped to 6.55 million in 2011 before climbing again. The establishment data is a lot like the data on GDP. When you look at the growth rate, you can see a distinct change over time, but the growth and level data puts that in some perspective. Just as we are still adding billions to our GDP every year, despite a lower GDP growth rate, we are still turning over establishments in the economy every year and adding more, even though we are doing this at a lower rate than before.

Now, is the growth slowdown related to the decline in establishment growth? To the extent that we take seriously the evidence from the beginning of this chapter on the importance of net entry for productivity growth in some selected manufacturing industries and in the retail industry as a whole, then yes, it is. Although we are adding more establishments, the pace at which we are doing it has slowed down, which means that workers and capital are not shifting from low- to high-productivity establishments as fast as they once did. This pulls down productivity growth, which in turn pulls down the growth rate of GDP.

We have to be careful here. As I mentioned at the beginning of this chapter, we don't know for sure that slower turnover of establishments has lowered productivity growth. These figures tell us that entry and exit happened at a slower rate over time, but they don't tell us whether it is in fact low-productivity establishments that exited and high-productivity establishments that entered. That would make sense, as high-productivity establishments are also more likely to be profitable establishments, and it would be odd if firms left open unprofitable establishments or added establishments that were not profitable to begin with. It would be odd, but before I was an economist I worked for several large corporations, and I had plenty of bosses who made decisions that were anything but profit maximizing. So it's possible that the slower turnover of establishments was good for productivity growth, but it seems more likely that slower turnover was a drag on productivity growth. What I'll show you at the end of this chapter, though, is some evidence that in fact slower turnover of firms did contribute to slower productivity growth.

JOB TURNOVER SLOWED ALSO

The same kind of evidence, and a similar story, can be seen in data on the number of jobs created and destroyed year by year. This data is more refined than just counting the number of people employed. A firm that shuts down would result in a set of job "destructions." A new firm or establishment that opens up would result in a set of job "creations." But it is also more subtle than that. A person who transfers from the Seattle office to the Dallas office of a company would count as both a job destruction (in Seattle) and a job creation (in Dallas). Someone who doesn't even physically relocate could also represent this kind of combined destruction and creation if he or she changes positions within the same firm. And someone who quits a job to take a new one also counts as one job destruction and one job creation. The data tries to count all the labor market turnover going on, not just establishments closing and new establishments opening. And we want that kind of data, because productivity depends on people moving from low- to high-productivity jobs (or vice versa), regardless of why they moved or whether they still work for the same establishment.

Figure 12.4 plots job creation and destruction rates over time, similar to the rates for establishments. In 1976, the number of jobs created was equal to roughly 22% of the total existing number of jobs in the economy at that point, and the number of jobs destroyed was a little over 15%. This data is spikier than the establishment data, so you can see more of the business cycle represented over time. See the surge in job destruction during the early 1980s, around 2001, and in 2009, for example. The drops in job creation are visible during those same periods.

But overall, the rates tend to trend downward over time, just like the establishment rates did. Even ignoring the financial crisis, the job creation rate fell to about 14% in 2014 while the job destruction rate fell below 12%. This meant that there were fewer opportunities to swap a worker from a low- to a high-productivity job, which could account for part of the slowdown in productivity growth.

At the same time, this slowdown in the rates didn't necessarily mean that the economy created or destroyed fewer jobs than it did

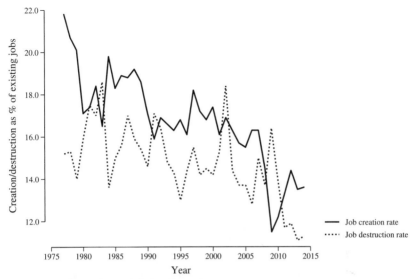

Figure 12.4. Job creation and destruction rates
Note: Data is from the US Census Bureau Business Dynamics Statistics.

before. Figure 12.5 shows something similar to what we looked at for establishments, only for jobs. The darkest gray bars indicate the number of jobs created, at about 15 million to 16 million new jobs every year. That's about 1.3 million jobs per month, or about 300,000 jobs per week. On the downside, the light gray bars at the bottom show the number of jobs destroyed. That averaged about 14 million per year, or about 1.16 million jobs a month or 270,000 jobs per week.

A lot of that job creating and destroying tends to net out to zero; a person quitting a job one place to take another shows up as a job destruction and a job creation but has no effect on the number of people working. But the pace of job creation tended to be faster than job destruction, and the medium gray bars in the middle of figure 12.5 show this net job creation. Every year, the economy added about 1.7 million jobs, but this fluctuated over the business cycle, as you can see. In 1983, 1991, 2002, 2009, and 2010 there was a net loss of jobs, with the decline in 2009 standing out, with a loss of 5.6 million. Since the recent recession, the economy has added between 2 million and 3 million jobs per year.

All this net job creation over time means that the total number of jobs tended to rise over time, too. Figure 12.6 plots this total. In 1976 there were about 65 million jobs in the economy, and that number rose, with only small pauses, all the way up to 2009, when the number of jobs topped out at nearly 120 million. The recession hit, and the number fell to just above 110 million. It has since climbed back toward 120 million, although we haven't reached the 2008 peak again.

Although the number of jobs is higher now, even with the recession, than it was in the 1970s or 1980s, the *rate* of job creation and destruction is lower than it was in those decades. The proportion of jobs that turn over every year is lower, which may be contributing to the slowdown in productivity growth, similar to what we saw with number of establishments. We might think that workers are interested in moving into higher-productivity jobs because those jobs are likely to pay higher wages. Even if there is no effect on wages, we might think that firms are interested in moving workers from low- to high-productivity jobs, as doing so should raise their profits. At best, all

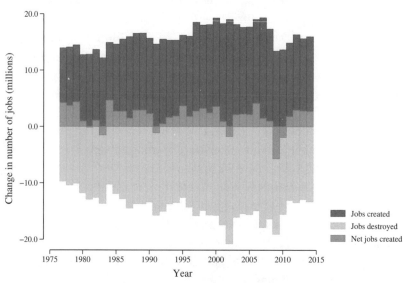

Figure 12.5. Growth in jobs created and destroyed over time
Note: Data is from the US Census Bureau Business Dynamics Statistics. Absolute growth in creations, destructions, and net jobs created was calculated by the author.

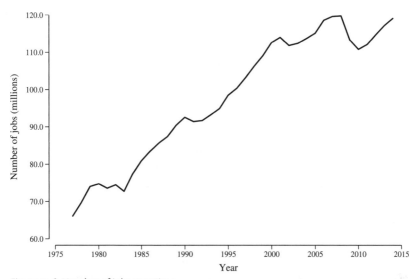

Figure 12.6. Number of jobs over time
Note: Data is from the US Census Bureau Business Dynamics Statistics.

the jobs being destroyed are low productivity and all the jobs being created are high productivity, and thus worker turnover is positive for productivity growth.

Of course, not every job created is more productive than every job destroyed; sometimes workers and firms make mistakes. But think of each instance of job creation or destruction as a chance at a productivity-improving move. With a slowdown in the job creation and destruction rates, this means that we're taking fewer chances at improving productivity by moving workers around. It's consistent with the slowdown in the rate of establishment entry and exit as well, which isn't too surprising. The turnover of establishments and the turnover of workers are tied together, almost by definition.

IS SLOWER TURNOVER A PROBLEM?

The evidence is clear that the turnover of firms and workers declined over the past few decades, particularly during the twenty-first century. While I've suggested that this had an impact on the productivity growth rate, I haven't done any calculations to show you the size of that impact. Doing that would be similar to what I did with respect to industries a few chapters ago, when we went over the switch from goods to services, but in this case it involves calculations that are a lot more tedious because we are talking about thousands of firms and millions of workers. I will spare you the deep dive into those kinds of numbers, and rely on more work by Decker, Haltiwanger, Jarmin, and Miranda. They estimated that from 1997 to 2014 the decline in turnover could have shaved about 0.1 to 0.15 percentage points each year off of the growth rate of productivity.

This means that the drop in the rate of reallocation could explain a meaningful amount of the productivity slowdown and thus contribute to an explanation for the growth slowdown. If you recall, 0.1 to 0.15 percentage points is not far from what I calculated as the effect of shifting from goods into services in chapter 7. These two phenomena interact to some extent, as the shift into services is a kind of reallocation itself, so they are not completely separate explanations. But while I explained the shift into services as a consequence of success, the drop in reallocation rates seems likely to be evidence of something going "wrong" in the economy.

However, despite the data showing that the reallocation rate slowed down, there is not a clear consensus as to why it slowed down. Part of this may be that the data I have presented here has been available for only few years, and we just have not had a chance to dig into it for long enough to draw clear connections. But I can lay out some ideas for what was driving the drop in reallocation. One idea is increased market power, as discussed in the previous few chapters. If existing firms are putting up regulatory or financial barriers to entry, then this could explain why the entry of new establishments slowed.

An alternative explanation is offered by Jan De Loecker and Jan Eeckhout, who provided the markup data I discussed a few chapters ago. They lay out a simple argument that as firms gain market power, their response to shocks—good or bad—becomes more muted. Think of a surprise shock to the price of an input. If there is a drop in the price of raw wood, for example, then we would expect furniture manufacturers to expand production, in part because they could charge lower prices. If the furniture industry is very competitive, then this expansion in production, and the associated expansion in employment and capital use, may be quite large. If the drop in price is large, it may make sense for firms to open new furniture-making establishments.

In contrast, if the furniture industry has a lot of market power, perhaps because of a concentration of manufacturers, then the response to the decline in wood prices may occur, but it will be smaller. There will be fewer new workers hired and less capital used. The price decline might not engender the building of any new establishments. In industries with a lot of market power, the incentive to adjust production—and reallocate the inputs necessary to do this—is smaller than in competitive industries.

There is some corroborating evidence here. Decker and coauthors looked at evidence on the shocks hitting firms, which would include things like the shock to the price of wood. They found that in the 2000s, the frequency and size of these shocks were about the same as in the 1990s. However, they calculated that the response of firms to these shocks, in terms of their employment, was 40% smaller in the 2000s than in the 1990s. Firms appeared to be less responsive to shocks, which is consistent with De Loecker and Eeckhout's explanation of the effect of market power, as well as being consistent with the drop in reallocation rates in general. This argument isn't locked down, however. The same authors find, in some of the work referenced earlier, that most of the decline in job reallocations is due to a drop in the entry and exit of young firms (five years or younger). There is less evidence that very large firms, which could be more credibly accused of having excessive market power, are behind the drop in reallocation rates.

An entirely different explanation for the slowdown in job and firm turnover is the same slowdown in population growth I discussed in chapter 5. In a recent paper, Hugo Hopenhayn, Julian Neira, and Rish Singhania describe how the aging population could drive these dynamics. If existing firms face some limits on how much they can expand their labor force (e.g., a grocery store can't employ more than twenty cashiers or twenty baggers to work twenty checkout lanes), then during times of rapid labor force growth, it will be easy for new firms to start up, as there are lots of workers available looking for jobs.

During the 1960s and 1970s, when the surge of baby boomers entered the labor force, lots of new firms entered to take advantage of that labor supply boom.

Of those firms that did start up during this boom, many survived the decades that followed, with ramifications for the entry and exit rates today. Once the growth rate of the labor force started to fall in the 1990s and accelerated during the twenty-first century, the existing set of firms was easily able to accommodate the new workers entering the market. New firms were not needed to absorb workers, and this helped push down the entry rate. With fewer new firms entering, the average age of firms increased. As older firms tend to be larger and exit at lower rates, this meant a concentration of employment into large, old firms as well as a drop in the overall exit rate. Hopenhayn, Neira, and Singhania calculate that the baby boom and subsequent decline in fertility can account for almost all changes in firm reallocation documented in this chapter. And as we established earlier, population aging reflects a success of living standards and family planning, meaning that the changes in firm turnover can be considered a consequence of success as well.

If these authors are right, then this only strengthens the case that the growth slowdown is best viewed as the—often unintended—consequence of success. But even if the true source of the drop in reallocation rates is an increase in firm market power, the contribution to the growth slowdown of slower reallocation is not very big compared to the direct effect of slower human capital growth and the shift into services. It is also possible that both of these stories are wrong, in that they assume that firms are the driving factor behind slower reallocation. It may be that workers themselves became less willing to move between jobs, an idea we'll take up in the next chapter.

THE DROP IN GEOGRAPHIC MOBILITY

13 In many cases the desire of a firm to reallocate a worker between jobs or establishments may involve a change in physical location, perhaps just across town or maybe across the country. In such a case, the ability and willingness of the worker to undertake that move become crucial. Firms may want to put more workers in Silicon Valley, but if people don't want to go or can't afford to move there, then this stops a productivity-improving reallocation. Even if firms are willing to bear the moving costs or subsidize housing, this might change their decision about whether such a move makes financial sense, even if absent those costs it would improve productivity.

Thus, part of the reason for the decline in job reallocations over time may be a decline in geographic mobility within the United States rather than a deliberate choice by firms to limit reallocation. The drop in mobility may be due to preferences, similar to how our preferences drove the shift away from goods production toward services. It may also be due to rising housing costs in cities that we'd expect to be an attractive destination because of their level of productivity. Either way, the decline in geographic mobility is a potential source of slower productivity growth over the past few decades.

THE DECLINE IN MOBILITY

Figure 13.1 plots two series of data. The bars show the raw number of people who reported living in a different location a year earlier. This does not tell us

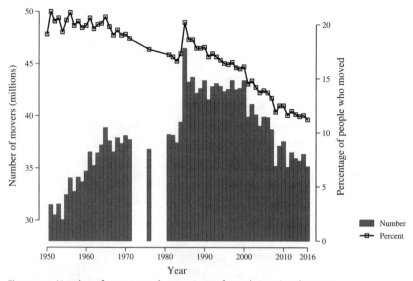

Figure 13.1. Number of movers, and percentage of people moving, by year
Note: Data is from the US Census Bureau. Percentage of people moving was calculated by the author.

whether they moved between cities or states. Someone who moved down the block would count in these numbers. But you can see that there is a steep increase in movers from around 1950 to the early 1980s, from 27 million movers to more than 45 million. The gaps in the figure are for a few years in the 1970s when the US Census Bureau did not ask this question on its regular survey. Regardless, once the number of movers hit its peak in the early 1980s, it began to decline slowly. It hung out around 42 million until the year 2000, and then the raw movement of people dropped to about 35 million by 2016.

This decline in the number of movers occurred at the same time that the size of the US population was rising. As a proportion of that population, therefore, the percentage of people who moved in a given year fell over time. That is plotted in figure 13.1 by the black line. In the 1950s, about 20% of the population moved at least down the block in any given year. Starting in the 1980s, as the absolute number of movers dropped, so did the movement rate. In 2016, the percentage of people who moved was down to about 11%.

The decline in overall movement showed up at all levels of analysis. Raven Molloy, Christopher Smith, and Abigail Wozniak compiled migration data from a variety of sources to document the amount of movement between different geographic areas. At all levels, starting in 1980, there was a decline in migration. In 1980, about 2.75% of all people moved to a different state in a given year. By 2000 this had fallen to 2.5%, and in 2010 it was down to below 2.0%. This downward trend also showed up across what are known as MSAs, or metropolitan statistical areas, which constitute large urban agglomerations. For example, Dallas/Fort Worth/Arlington is one MSA, and Washington/Arlington/Alexandria is another. Whereas in 1980 about 3.5% of all people moved from one MSA to another (which may or may not have involved leaving the state), this was down to less than 3% by 2010. In one of their sources, Molloy, Smith, and Wozniak found that the share of people who moved counties fell from 6% in 1980 to 3% by 2010. At whatever level we examine, there was less shuffling of people between locations within the United States over time.

CERTAIN PLACES ARE MORE PRODUCTIVE

This decline in mobility matters because there are distinct differences in the level of measured productivity between locations. A crude way of seeing this is to look at the size of real GDP per worker at the state level. Just as we can divide up economic activity into different industries, we can divide it up by where it is produced. The classification of where something is produced does get a little fuzzy, particularly for some services. For example, if a lawyer who is based in Chicago flies out to work with a client in Denver, where should that get counted? There isn't an obvious answer, but it is implausible that the differences we'll see across states are due just to recording errors by the BEA.

At the state level, I don't have enough data to calculate a residual productivity number, as detailed human capital and physical capital data is not available. In its place, we'll look at a cruder measure, gross state product (GSP) per worker, which is just like GDP per worker, except for a state rather than the whole country. Keep in mind that some of the differences in GSP per worker may be due to differences

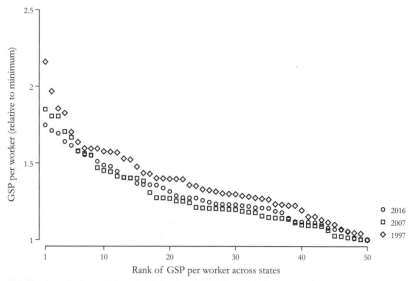

Figure 13.2. Relative GSP per worker across states, by rank
Note: Data on gross state product (GSP) and labor force is from the Bureau of Economic Analysis. GSP-per-worker ranking was calculated by the author.

in capital stocks, or in education and experience by state, but nevertheless I believe there is information here on how productive states are relative to one another.

Figure 13.2 plots the GSP per worker for each state, relative to the GSP per worker for the lowest state, in each of three years. The states are arranged along the horizontal axis by rank of GSP per worker, so each set of points slopes down. In all three years, the top-ranked state has a GSP per worker about two times higher than the minimum in the same year. There were about ten states in each year with a GSP per worker 1.5 times higher than the minimum. In 2016, twenty-nine states had a GSP per worker more than 1.25 times the minimum, down from 1997, when thirty-five states had a GSP per worker more than 1.25 times the minimum. In terms of the actual states, for 2016 the highest GSP-per-worker levels were found in Alaska, California, Connecticut, Delaware, Massachusetts, New York, North Dakota, Texas, and Washington. Most of those contain major metropolitan areas or, like Alaska and North Dakota, significant resource wealth. Among the lowest were Alabama, Arkansas, Arizona, Florida, Maine, Mississippi, Montana, South Carolina, and Vermont, with Idaho having the dubious honor of the lowest GSP per worker among the states.

The variation in output per worker is even more dramatic if we look across cities or, more precisely, across MSAs. Figure 13.3 plots the real GDP per worker for the 382 MSAs tracked by the BEA. The vertical axis plots the value of GDP per worker relative to the minimum, which happens to be the Lake Havasu–Kingman area of Arizona. The axis labels may look a little strange because I've plotted the values in what is often called a ratio (or log) scale. Each step up the axis implies the same proportional change in relative GDP per worker. Hence moving from 1 to 2 (doubling) looks the same as moving from 2 to 4 (doubling). This makes it easier to pick out the variation in the data, as otherwise the figure would be dominated by a few outliers.

Most cities lie in the range of 1 to 4, meaning some cities have GDP

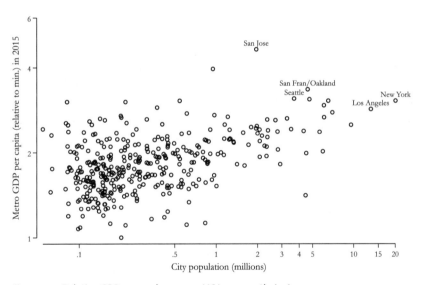

Figure 13.3. Relative GDP per worker across MSAs versus their size, 2015
Note: Data on labor force growth is from the Bureau of Labor Statistics, at the county level, which was matched by the author to MSA. Data on GDP and total population is from the Bureau of Economic Analysis Regional Accounts. Relative GDP per worker was calculated by the author. City size is measured by total population.

per worker four times higher than others. San Jose, which captures the rough area of Silicon Valley, is an outlier with a value of almost 5. But leaving aside San Jose, there is even more variation in output per worker across cities than there is across states.

A second fact about these MSAs becomes clear on the horizontal axis, which shows their size in millions of people. This is also plotted in a ratio scale, as again I don't want the figure to be dominated by huge outliers like New York City or Los Angeles. Several things come out of figure 13.3. First, most MSAs are small, between 100,000 (0.1 million) and 500,000 (0.5 million) people. In comparison, there are only two with more than 10 million people (LA and New York). More interesting, though, is the fact that the relative GDP per worker in an MSA has a positive relationship with its size. New York, with a value for GDP per worker close to 3, is about twice as productive as the mass of cities around 100,000 to 500,000 in size. Large urban agglomerations tend to be the most productive places in the economy.

A possibility implied by figure 13.3, as well as figure 13.2, is that we could raise GDP for the United States as a whole if workers moved from low-productivity states or MSAs to high-productivity states or MSAs. This isn't necessarily true, as we don't know what the *marginal* output of a worker—the effect on output of adding or subtracting one worker—is in each location, just the average output of all workers. If a worker from Lake Havasu, Arizona, moves to New York, there is no guarantee that he or she would instantly produce three times more output or be paid three times more in wages. As Enrico Moretti documented in his recent book, there is only a subset of urban areas where we might expect new workers to gain from a move. These select locations—Silicon Valley, the Research Triangle in North Carolina, Austin, Seattle, and New York, among others—are innovation centers, as compared to other urban areas that may be large but present fewer opportunities. Nevertheless, there does appear to be some scope for productivity gains from workers moving to at least a few select urban areas.

Yet it does not appear that people are moving from low-productivity states and MSAs to high-productivity ones. Figure 13.4 plots the percentage growth in MSA population from 2001 to 2015 against the rela-

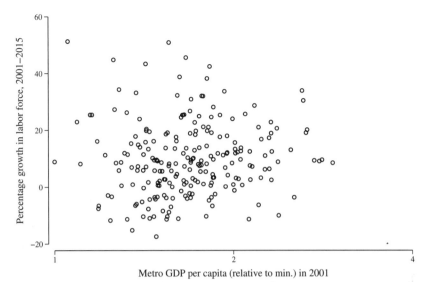

Figure 13.4. Growth in MSA labor force versus relative GDP per worker, 2001–2015
Note: Data on labor force growth is from the Bureau of Labor Statistics, at the county level, which was matched by the author to MSA. Data on GDP is from the Bureau of Economic Analysis Regional Accounts. Relative GDP per worker and growth rate of labor force were calculated by the author.

tive GDP per worker of the MSA in 2001. There is no discernible relationship, and that is an issue from a perspective of economic growth. Cities that have very high relative GDP per worker—and quite likely a higher marginal GDP per worker—were not growing any faster than cities with low relative GDP per worker. If there was a positive relationship in the figure, then this would mean more-productive cities were getting larger in size, which would have contributed to higher GDP per worker in the aggregate. From the perspective of economic growth, the best strategy is to make the big, productive cities even bigger.

On the basis of the data in figure 13.4, though, we were not reallocating workers toward these large, productive cities as fast as we could. Whether that is a significant explanation for the growth slowdown remains to be seen. I don't have comparable data to do something like figure 13.4 for the twentieth century, showing that there used to be a positive relationship. Perhaps we've never been very good at geographic reallocation. But other evidence seems to imply that we were better at it once. The very productive West Coast cities, like Los Angeles, San Francisco, and San Jose, were not always as large as they are today. They grew through enormous inflows of people over the course of the twentieth century, which suggests that people did flow toward productive places in large numbers at one time.

WHAT LIMITS GEOGRAPHIC REALLOCATION?

With the data and caveats in mind, we can ask why people are not moving away from low-productivity locations and toward high-productivity ones. One answer may be similar in spirit to the shift from goods to services: it's all about our own preferences about where to live. A second may be barriers in high-productivity locations that keep people from moving in, which in a loose way would be similar to the story of market power by firms limiting the entry of possible competitors.

Let's tackle the first explanation, which we might call an unintended consequence of cheap air-conditioning. It is no secret that the population of the United States has been moving south and west over time, gaining warm winters and letting the air-conditioning take care of the hot summers.

Take a look at figure 13.5, which plots the growth rate of the labor force—not population—in MSAs against their average January temperature. In contrast to figure 13.4, there is a more obvious positive relationship. I've highlighted Florida and Arizona, as they are the prototypical Sunbelt states to have gained population over time as people retired. But the figure shows that workers, not just retirees, flowed toward cities that have warm winter temperatures. Some, or even many, of those workers flowed toward those cities because of retirees, to work in health care or other service industries. Regardless of the reason, the geographic reallocation of labor within the US appears driven in part by weather, not by level of productivity. This puts a drag on productivity growth because while people are moving to cities in the South, those cities are not the most productive ones. There are 32 cities that have an average January temperature above 65 degrees, mostly in Florida and Arizona. These cities have a

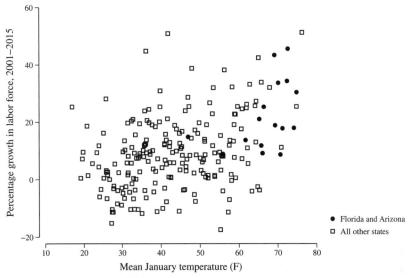

Figure 13.5. Growth in MSA labor force versus mean January temperature
Note: Data on labor force growth is from the Bureau of Labor Statistics, at the county level, which was matched by the author to MSA. January temperatures are from the Centers for Disease Control and Prevention.

productivity level, on average, about 1.7 times the minimum (located in Arizona, if you'll recall). In contrast, there are 172 cities that have an average January temperature below 40 degrees, and their average productivity is more than twice the minimum. Moving south moved people toward lower-productivity locations.

On net, this was bad for aggregate growth. This may be an effect that dissipates over time, however. As noted in figure 13.3, it is larger cities that are more productive. To the extent that this reflects a causal relationship of density on productivity, as the cities in the South get larger, they'll also get more productive. The large size and high productivity of places like Chicago and New York is not exclusive to those specific physical locations. If places like Miami, Atlanta, Dallas, Houston, Austin, and Phoenix continue to become more productive as they grow, then the flow of people into them will cease to be a drag on productivity growth and could even enhance it. For the past few decades, though, the preference for warm winters pulled people toward low-productivity cities, much like the preference for services pushed people toward low-productivity industries.

THE PROFITS OF HOUSING

The second explanation for limited geographic reallocation sounds like the effects of market power on job turnover. Large cities with high productivity don't have a lot of competitors, and that is especially true once we factor in people's preferences for weather, amenities, and being close to family. If you want to live in the Pacific Northwest but also want to move to a city with high productivity and lots of high-wage jobs, then you are kind of stuck choosing Seattle. The more people who have these specific preferences and want to move there, the greater the demand for housing. That demand could be answered by an increase in the supply of housing, which could keep the price of housing from rising much. Or if there were restrictions on growth in the housing stock, higher demand could lead to rising house prices while limiting the actual inflow of people. In the latter case, higher house prices might be enough to convince you not to move to Seattle, despite your preferences. You, and the broader economy, could miss out on a chance for a reallocation toward a higher-productivity job.

If this situation reminds us of the market power of firms, then we should be able to see some evidence for it in the same way as before. We can follow the same process as in chapter 9, using the methodology in Simcha Barkai's work, to calculate economic profits of housing as a share of the value-added from housing. This will help us see, in a crude sense, if increased demand for housing in the economy was associated with higher prices for homes or an expansion of housing supply.

Before we get to the calculation, let me pause to explain how housing contributes to GDP. Start by thinking about an apartment building. When you pay rent to live in an apartment, that rent is counted as part of GDP, because you are purchasing the service of having a roof and four walls. For homeowners, there is no transaction that takes place, because it would be silly to write yourself a rent check every month. But the BEA imputes the rent that you would pay if you did write yourself that check and adds that to GDP, because even though you own the house, you are receiving the real service of having a roof and four walls as well. There is a different argument about whether we even want GDP to measure implicit transactions, but that isn't the point here. An additional note is that I'm not talking about the construction of new homes, which is a totally different economic activity. All we're interested in here is the flow of GDP coming from existing housing. About 12% of total GDP in any given year comes from the implicit rents homeowners pay to themselves.

Just like total GDP can be divided up into payments to labor, payments to capital, and economic profits, we can divide up the GDP from housing into those payments as well. But this takes a little work, because as I explained a few chapters ago, the BEA cannot track the breakdown of payments to capital and economic profits. In short, I'm going to use the exact same methodology as in Barkai's work from chapter 9 but apply the logic to the housing sector. An important assumption I'll make is that there are zero payments to labor coming from housing value-added. What I mean is that labor plays a very small role in "producing" the flow of value-added that you get from housing. Yes, you might rake your leaves or fix a leaky faucet yourself as part of living in your home, but this is a trivial part of the flow of value you get compared to the value-added provided by the house itself.

That means I need to divide up the GDP from housing only into payments to capital and economic profits. As before, to do this I'll need some information on the nominal rate of return that housing earns, and for that I'll use the average thirty-year mortgage rate. I'll also need information on housing inflation and depreciation, which I'll back out from the data. But all I'm trying to get here is how much of the value-added of housing should be seen as a payment for the actual capital in the house versus how much of the value-added is an economic profit. That economic profit represents earnings—in particular to homeowners—that are over and above what is strictly necessary to pay for the housing services they receive. One way to view

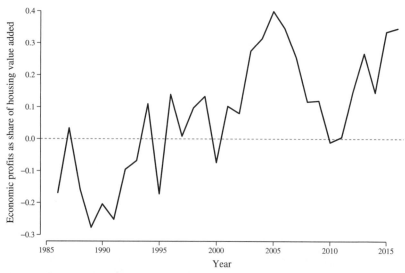

Figure 13.6. Economic profits as a share of housing value-added, 1985–2016
Note: The series was calculated by the author using data from the Bureau of Economic Analysis on the value of residential assets, gross value-added from housing services, and depreciation of residential capital. The nominal interest rate used in the calculation is the average thirty-year mortgage rate. The calculation follows Barkai (2017); see the appendix for details.

these economic profits is as representing the earnings that accrue to owners for being smart or lucky enough to own a home in a city that faces an increase in demand for housing.

The results of this calculation can be found in figure 13.6, which shows the economic profit from 1985 to 2016. In the mid-1980s, the profit share was negative, indicating that homeowners were losing value from their property. The required rate of return on their capital appeared higher than the actual flow of value-added they received. At that point in time, interest rates and mortgage rates were at historically high levels, around 11%–13%, implying a high required return.

Around 1995, economic profits were around 0% of housing value-added, but from that point forward the share rose, albeit with some massive fluctuations, as you can see around the time of the financial crisis. The rising trend, though, appears to hold across the roughly twenty years of data in the figure. By 2016, economic profits were calculated to account for about one-third of the value-added of housing, in part because the mortgage rate was at a historically low value of about 4%. During the early twenty-first century, owners of houses were enjoying sizable economic profits. Figure 13.6 applies to the aggregate economy, so you cannot draw any conclusions about specific housing markets, but this is consistent with the price of housing rising in cities that have both an increase in demand for homes (because they are productive) and limitations on construction (for whatever reason).

WHAT IS THE EFFECT ON PRODUCTIVITY GROWTH?

The slowdown in geographic reallocation is clear in the data, and the data on output per worker across MSAs and states suggests that this could have had an effect on productivity growth. We might attribute the slowdown in reallocation to restrictions on housing supply in productive places, something the aggregate data on the economic profits of housing is consistent with.

Even if you buy all that, though, how big of an effect on productivity could this have had? Some recent research by Chang-Tai Hsieh and Enrico Moretti attempts to calculate the effect of housing restrictions in very productive cities on productivity growth. There is no clean empirical way to estimate this; we do not have a bizarro Earth in which San Jose approved a series of fifty-story apartment buildings to compare to the actual Earth. So Hsieh and Moretti set up a model that allows for multiple cities, with workers who are free to move around between cities and who care about their real living standard, which is wage divided by the price of a house in the city they live in.

In the model, what matters for determining where people live is the elasticity of housing prices with respect to population. If the elasticity is high, then as people try to move into a city, the price of housing goes up a lot, lowers the real living standard in that city, and shuts down the inflow of people. This means that few people end up there, even if the city is very productive. This would also show up as increased economic profits for the existing owners of real estate in those cities. If the elasticity is low, however, then the opposite occurs, and people flow into the city without raising the housing price much, the living standard stays high, and therefore more people want to move in. In this case, the economic profits of housing would be low.

Hsieh and Moretti are able to draw on estimates of these elasticities from earlier work by Albert Saiz. His estimates are a function of not only regulations or zoning but also geography. San Francisco has a high elasticity in part because there is no undeveloped land in it, or near it, thanks to the Pacific Ocean. Dallas, in contrast, has low elasticity in part because there are almost no geographic limits to its expansion. On top of those geographic limits, San Francisco's elasticity is even higher because it tends to have more restrictions on building than Dallas does. Hsieh and Moretti take Saiz's elasticities and put them in their model, and then set all the other parameters in the model so that they can replicate, for all intents and purposes, figure 13.3, regarding MSA productivity and size.

Once they can reproduce the data in their model, they can start to play with it. The main result I focus on is where they look at what happens to real GDP per worker if they lower the house price elasticity in just three cities: San Jose, San Francisco, and New York. What they do is set the elasticity equal to the median of the elasticity for all cities, which means that the housing market elasticity in those three cities drops to that of a place like Richmond, Virginia. More workers decide to move into those three cities, implicitly because those three cities are allowing for a vast expansion in their current housing stock. But as those three cities are also very productive relative to almost all other cities, the expansion of housing enables the economy to produce more GDP. What Hsieh and Moretti calculate is that total GDP would have been 3.7% higher in 2009 if just these three cities had more elastic housing markets.

Hsieh and Moretti make this calculation considering a period of time from 1964 to 2009. But let's assume that it was just the rise in housing restrictions starting around 1990 that kept us from having that extra 3.7% higher GDP. Remember, that was when the economic profits of housing started rising. If we look only from 1990 to 2009, then the 3.7% loss of GDP would imply that growth was lower by about 0.18% per year. That would be a significant drop in the growth rate due to the drop in mobility, which may be driven by restrictions on housing in high-productivity locations.

However, there are reasons to believe that this might be an over-estimate. In their counterfactual calculation with higher growth, Hsieh and Moretti find that the New York MSA would be larger by about 318%, meaning that with less-restrictive housing it would have more than 80 million people rather than 20 million. For perspective, 80 million is almost one-quarter of the US population. I am willing to believe that more people would move to New York if housing prices were cheaper, but it seems implausible that even with an aggressive relaxation of housing restrictions, one-quarter of all Americans would move to the Big Apple. The effect on the growth rate from housing restrictions is almost certainly less than 0.18% per year.

Further, to really account for the growth slowdown, we'd want to see that the effect of housing restrictions became much worse starting around 2000. It isn't obvious that is the case. Economic profits of housing started rising in 1990. And while there were big housing profits in the 2000s, these fluctuated quite a bit given the financial crisis. Even if we allow that housing restrictions are a failure, that they lowered the growth rate of productivity by something like 0.1% per year, and did this only starting in the 2000s, this is still small relative to the combined effect of slower human capital growth and the shift into services. The decline in geographic mobility was not trivial, but it does not explain the growth slowdown.

DID THE GOVERNMENT
CAUSE THE SLOWDOWN?

At this point I've produced a lot of evidence regarding the sources of the growth slowdown, but I have not addressed several common scapegoats head-on. One of those is the government, which could have choked off economic growth through tax rates and regulation. A second is inequality, which might have changed our spending patterns and investment behavior to the detriment of broader economic growth. Finally, the impact of trade, and of Chinese trade in particular, is often presumed to have reduced economic growth through its influence on the manufacturing industry.

What I'll show in the next three chapters is that although all three of these had real effects on the economy, no effect was large enough to account plausibly for the growth slowdown. None of them had much of an effect on the growth rate at all, it turns out.

In this chapter I'll start with the government. It is common to hear that taxes and regulations strangle business activity, and so economic growth. If that is true, then just like anything else, taxes and regulation would have to affect physical capital accumulation, human capital accumulation, or productivity growth. Taxes, corporate or individual, could limit the savings people are willing to set aside or the investment that corporations are willing to make, thereby slowing down physical capital growth. Individual income taxes may decrease the time people put into the labor market, their willingness to participate in the labor market at all, or the level of training they are willing to invest in, thus lowering human capital growth. Taxes may make certain reallocations of workers between establishments not worthwhile from a firm's perspective, and regulations may limit or even prohibit firms from undertaking certain kinds of innovation or expansion. This could limit productivity growth.

All these effects make sense in theory, but they turn out to have very small consequences for economic growth in the data, with few exceptions. In general, it is very hard to find real effects of taxation and regulation on the aggregate growth rate of real GDP, even though there may be distinct effects on particular firms or individuals.

THE EVIDENCE ON TAXES

The prima facie evidence points to lower tax rates—corporate or individual—having no effect on the growth slowdown. There were two substantial tax cuts passed in 2001 and 2003 under George W. Bush, and yet it was around this time that the growth slowdown began. That doesn't bode well for the idea that the growth slowdown is a result of higher taxation. But it doesn't constitute firm evidence, as there were a lot of other things going on in the economy at the time of the tax changes. It could be that we just got very unlucky right around the time of the Bush tax cuts. But we can get some better evidence of the effect of these tax cuts by examining some research on the dividend tax cut that passed in 2003.

The lower dividend tax rate was proposed as a way of rewarding investment, and the argument was that it would induce a surge in investment spending and lead to a higher growth rate for physical capital, and hence a higher growth rate for GDP. Danny Yagan studied the effect of this tax cut. He did this by comparing what happened with S-corporations, which include partnerships and sole proprietorships that cannot pay dividends, and C-corporations, which issue shares and may pay dividends. With a cut in the dividend tax rate, we might expect that C-corporations would increase their investment spending relative to S-corporations. But Yagan found no effect on their investment spending at all.

But that doesn't mean there were no changes in response to the dividend tax cut. Raj Chetty and Emmanuel Saez looked at corporate behavior and found that, as we might expect, the payment of dividends went up. Further, companies that had not paid dividends before started paying them after the tax rate fell. The increase in dividends was most pronounced in firms that had large institutional ownership or executives that held a significant percentage of shares. The dividend tax cut lowered the effective tax rate for institutional owners and executives but did not increase investment in capital. And without that increase in capital, it is no surprise that there was no effect on the growth rate of GDP.

The experience of Kansas in the past few years is another instructive case. When Sam Brownback was elected governor in 2010, he pushed for and signed off on a massive experiment in tax cuts as a strategy for economic growth. Income tax rates were slashed, and the tax rate on pass-through business—which includes sole proprietorships and partnerships like law firms—was cut to zero. Additionally, four state agencies were cut and two thousand state employees let go, which was justified as limiting government interference in the economy of Kansas. The rationale for the tax cuts was the same as for the federal dividend tax cut. It was proposed that the cuts would jumpstart the Kansas economy as new businesses rushed to set up shop there to take advantage of the lower taxes and reduced regulation.

It didn't pan out that way. Total employment in Kansas was about 1.4 million in 2008 before the financial crisis and Brownback's changes. It was 1.4 million in 2017. Considering that the rest of the economy gained jobs from 2008 to 2017, this means that Kansas fell behind relative to the rest of the United States in terms of employment. The growth rate of GDP in Kansas was 1.98% per year from 2005 through 2010, before the election of Brownback and including the financial crisis. From 2011 to 2016, after the tax cuts were implemented, the growth rate of GDP was 0.91% per year, about half that of the previous period. For comparison, the growth rate of GDP from 2005 to 2010 in the whole United States was 0.76% per year, which includes the effects of the financial crisis, and then it was 2.16% per year from 2011 to 2016, almost double that. After Brownback's tax cuts, Kansas fell behind the rest of the United States in terms of economic growth. There was no jump-start.

The experience of Kansas is instructive but perhaps not universal. Ufuk Akcigit, John Grigsby, Tom Nicholas, and Stefanie Stantcheva examined the effect of corporate and personal taxation on innovation in the United States during the twentieth century. They found that there are statistically significant effects of tax rates on the location and amount of innovative activity—measured by patenting—across states. Corporations, in particular, appear to move their innovative activity from state to state in response to tax rates. The effects are weaker when there are agglomeration effects in innovation; the clear example of this is Silicon Valley, where firms have remained in a relatively high-tax state because the benefits of being close to one another outweigh the tax costs. Although all this may be true, it does not offer much of an explanation for the growth slowdown. There was no broad increase in taxes on corporations or individuals at the state level starting around the early 2000s that could have acted to lower innovation rates.

If we look at individuals, there is little evidence they respond much to tax rates. Under normal circumstances, we'd expect that as individual income tax rates get higher, workers will be less willing to provide more labor, which in our terms would decrease the stock of human capital in use. And although this is most likely true in theory, it again turns out that the empirical effect is small. There is a large body of research that has estimated how sensitive labor supply is to income. A review by Emmanuel Saez, Joel Slemrod, and Seth Giertz reported that the effect on labor supply, and so actual taxable income, is small. Labor supply, in particular the decision to participate in the labor market at all, appears to be driven in large part by age and family structure, which means that there is little scope for tax rates to change whether people work or not. One exception that crops up in some studies is for married women, who appear more sensitive to tax rates than other groups in terms of their labor market participation. But even that effect is not large in an empirical sense, and the shift of married women into or out of the labor force is not big enough to explain any significant share of the growth slowdown.

And as already mentioned, if individual income tax rates were going to offer a significant explanation for the growth slowdown, then there must have been a truly enormous tax rate hike in the early 2000s to drive people out of the labor force. But of course the exact opposite happened with the Bush tax cut of 2001, which lowered rates in most tax brackets by about 3% and created a new lower bracket of only 10%. There is no evidence that higher tax rates caused the growth slowdown.

THE EVIDENCE ON REGULATION

Compared to taxation, there is less clear evidence on the effect of regulations on economic growth. Part of the reason is that how to measure regulation isn't so obvious. One novel way of doing so was used by Nathan Goldschlag and Alex Tabarrok to look for a relationship between regulation and reallocation. They used measures of regulation at the industry level developed by Omar Al-Ubaydli and Patrick McLaughlin. These latter researchers used a text-analysis program to comb through all federal regulations and identify words like *shall* or *must* that are assumed to impose some regulatory burden on a company. They also trained the program to identify which industries the regulations apply to, so that one can see how the regulatory burden varies. For example, the waste-management industry has 97,326 terms like *must* or *shall* applied to it in regulations, but the courier and messenger industry has only 7,340. You can also see which agency issued the restriction; as you might guess, the Environmental Protection Agency is responsible for as many as the next two agencies (Internal Revenue Service and Occupational Safety and Health Administration) combined.

Goldschlag and Tabarrok took this regulation data and compared it to data on firm start-ups as well as job creation and job destruction by industry. I showed earlier that all three measures slowed over time, indicating less reallocation of workers between existing firms or from old firms to new firms. Goldschlag and Tabarrok were able to see whether the slowdown in reallocation within an industry was related to the level of regulation. In short, they found no relationship. Industries that are subject to higher levels of regulation or to more rapid growth in regulation did not see fewer firms starting up or lower rates of job turnover. There are even results, when looking at firms by size, that show more intense regulation being associated with more job creation and destruction, which we'd expect to be associated with higher productivity growth. The authors also separated regulations into industry-specific (e.g., rules related to treatment of wastewater at a coal plant) and general (e.g., rules governing minimum wage), and looked at whether those general regulations are related to the start-up of firms or the reallocation of workers. Again, they didn't find anything showing that they were.

Consistent with this evidence is data using the American Legislative Exchange Council's ALEC-Laffer ranking of state competitiveness. ALEC is a think tank and lobbying group that promotes limited government and free markets, according to its own promotional materials. Laffer refers to Arthur Laffer, of the eponymous curve that relates tax revenues to tax rates. ALEC and Laffer combined information on several measures of state economic policies to determine which states are the most competitive. The ranking is not always clear about what is meant by *competitive*, but the publications associated with the rankings (released every year) show this to be a combination of low taxation and light regulation. Some elements ALEC considers include personal and corporate tax rates, whether there is an inheritance tax, number of public employees, quality of the state legal system, whether or not it is a so-called right-to-work state (meaning that workers cannot be obligated to join a union), and whether there are tax or expenditure limits on the state government. So it isn't quite an index of regulation alone but an amalgam of taxes and regulations.

Regardless, the idea is that the ALEC-Laffer ranking indicates the best states for doing business, and if regulation (and taxation) are important, we'd expect to see that lower-ranked states have lower economic growth and/or a lower level of GDP per worker. In figure 14.1 I've plotted the level of GDP per worker, by state, against the state's ALEC-Laffer ranking. The GDP per worker numbers are all relative to the minimum state and are for 2016. The ALEC-Laffer ranking is from 2012. I used this earlier year because I wanted to allow for the possibility that if a state was just enacting policies that improved its ALEC-

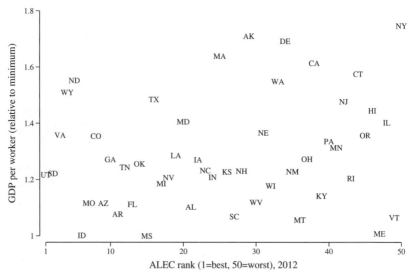

Figure 14.1. Level of GDP per worker versus ALEC ranking, by state
Note: GDP per worker is from the Bureau of Economic Analysis Regional Accounts, and ALEC is the source of the rankings. Rank in GDP per worker was calculated by the author.

Laffer rank, it might take a few years for that to show up as higher GDP per worker. The figure doesn't change much, though, if we use the ALEC-Laffer rank from 2016 or the GDP per worker from 2012.

What you can see is ... not much. If anything, there is a slight positive relationship, which means that states with lower ALEC-Laffer ranks produce more output per worker. New York, California, Connecticut, and New Jersey all rank quite low but are among the states with highest output per worker. Among the best-ranked states, places like North Dakota, Wyoming, and Texas all do well on GDP per worker, but all are also major oil and gas producers. States with high rankings but without such resources, like Utah, South Dakota, Idaho, Missouri, and Arizona, do much worse in terms of GDP per worker. There is no clear indication that scoring low on ALEC's index of regulation and taxation is associated with having low productivity.

It may be that the ALEC-Laffer ranking is more informative about the growth rate of GDP per worker, even if it doesn't show up in the level of GDP per worker. So in figure 14.2 I plotted the average growth rate of GDP per worker between 2012 and 2016 against the ALEC-Laffer ranking. Here you can see . . . again, not much. There is a lot of variation, with some states, like Alaska, having very low average growth rates. This is an effect of falling oil prices, which is why North Dakota and Louisiana also have such low growth rates. Even leaving aside those states, though, there is no evidence that states with higher rankings on the ALEC-Laffer index had higher growth rates in this period.

What we see again is that several states with very low ranks, like California and Washington, had very high growth rates in this period, higher than or equal to the growth rates of states with high ALEC rankings like Texas, Georgia, and Colorado. But across states, there is no tendency of the growth rate to go up or down as the ALEC-Laffer ranking increases. You should be a little more wary of these figures than of the text-analysis research. The lack of relationship I've shown you in the figures may be because the ALEC-Laffer ranking doesn't measure regulation or taxation well, not necessarily because regula-

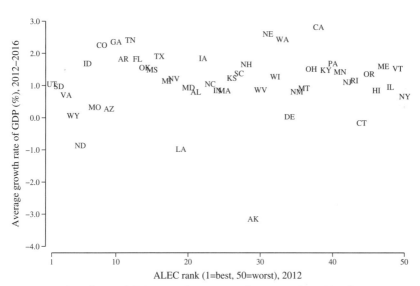

Figure 14.2. Growth rate of GDP per worker, 2012–2016, versus ALEC ranking, by state
Note: GDP per worker is from the Bureau of Economic Analysis Regional Accounts, and ALEC is the source of the rankings. Annualized growth rate in GDP per worker was calculated by the author.

tion and taxation don't have a noticeable effect on GDP per worker. But combined with the evidence from the Goldschlag and Tabarrok paper and on taxation, there is a consistent story that the government did not have a signification effect on the slowdown.

WHAT ABOUT HOUSING?

The omission so far has been the housing market, and I mentioned in the previous chapter that the frictions imposed by housing regulations may be part of the slowdown in geographic reallocation. The issue is that if housing regulations are tight in the most productive cities, then few workers can move into those cities to take advantage of their higher productivity.

Joseph Gyourko, Albert Saiz, and Anita Summers surveyed around two thousand cities in the United States to get information on the regulations governing real estate development. This included things such as whether local zoning boards must approve each project, whether state approval is necessary, whether there are defined density restrictions (e.g., large minimum lot sizes) or requirements for how much open space must remain within the city. From these individual data points, they created an index of real estate regulation. This index is normalized to be zero for the median city, with positive numbers indicating high levels of regulation and negative numbers indicating low levels of regulation. The numbers don't mean anything by themselves, but do allow the authors to compare one city to another.

What they found is that real estate regulations are tightest in the Northeast and Mid-Atlantic (e.g., Massachusetts, New Hampshire, New Jersey, Maryland) and along the West Coast in California and Washington. At the other end of the scale are states with the loosest restrictions, which tend to be in the Midwest and South (e.g., Alabama, Iowa, Indiana, Louisiana, Kansas). But these state-level differences hide the variation that occurs within states. Looking at the largest metro areas, the most restrictive real estate markets are in places such as Boston, Philadelphia, Seattle, San Francisco, and New York. In contrast, Cincinnati, St. Louis, Indianapolis, and Kansas City have some of the least restrictive regulations.

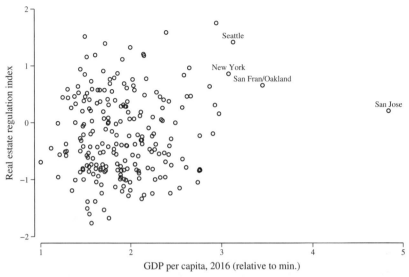

Figure 14.3. Real estate regulation and GDP per worker, 2016, by MSA
Note: GDP per worker is from the Bureau of Economic Analysis Regional Accounts, combined with Bureau of Labor Statistics data on labor force by MSA. Rank in GDP per worker was calculated by the author. Real estate regulation index is from Gyourko, Saiz, and Summers (2008).

The issue for economic growth is that heavy regulations tend to be in states and metro areas that are among the most productive places in the country. In figure 14.3 I've plotted the measure of real estate regulation in an MSA (recall that these are major metropolitan areas) against GDP per worker in 2016. As before, the GDP per worker is relative to the minimum of all MSAs. You can see that there is a rough positive relationship between the two, indicating that more-productive places also tend to have tighter regulations on housing.

The San Jose MSA, which includes Silicon Valley, is an outlier in terms of GDP per worker, as we saw before. It also happens to be above average (i.e., has an index value greater than 0) in terms of housing regulation. It may be surprising that San Jose does not rank even higher in terms of housing regulation, but one possible reason for this is that the housing regulation index is based on information from 2008, and since then it may have become more restrictive. Regardless, there is a tendency of very productive MSAs, like Seattle, New York, and the Bay Area, to have regulations much higher than the norm across the rest of the country.

As I mentioned in the chapter on housing, anything that limits the movement of people into more-productive locations would limit economic growth. This is a case where it is plausible that a reduction in regulation could have a meaningful effect on the growth rate of GDP. However, we don't have a similar real estate regulation index that goes back in time to around 1990, so we cannot say that it was an increase in real estate regulations that caused the growth slow-down. But of all the evidence regarding regulation and taxes, this is the most plausible link to the slowdown. Hsieh and Moretti's re-sults reported in the previous chapter, which found a drag on growth from housing restrictions, could perhaps be chalked up to local gov-ernment regulations limiting housing growth in high-productivity locations.

WHY AREN'T THERE BIG EFFECTS ON GROWTH?

Housing aside, there is not much evidence that taxes and regula-tion have an effect on economic growth. This doesn't mean they have no effect on economic growth, but whatever effect they have is too small to pick up in any meaningful way. This negligible relationship may seem surprising, but there is a plausible reason that taxes and regulation are a small part of the incentives for investment and inno-vation. To explain, let me reach back to the work we did a few chapters ago on competition, when I discussed how firms require some sort of markup to cover the fixed costs of innovation and investment. That was true, but it is only part of the story.

The motive for firms, which I believe is hard to argue with, is to generate net profits. And those net profits come from the interaction of three components: markup, tax rate, and scale. We've already dis-cussed markup in some depth. It captures the price relative to mar-ginal cost for each unit produced. Scale, however, captures how many units can be sold. Scale multiplied by markup provides total profits for a business. Even firms with small markups, like Walmart, can make massive total profits because their scale is so big. Finally, taxes are levied on the profits arising from markup and scale, leaving the firm with a net profit. You can think of regulations as something like an effective tax on profits, because of the costs of compliance. The tax rate matters for net profits, yes, but in relation to markup and scale, it may not be that important.

To see what I mean, consider New Zealand. The country has a representative parliament with a central bank that was a leader in adopting strict independence from political interference. Life expectancy is excellent, at eighty-two years, and the average amount of schooling is 12.5 years, about the same as in the United States. That will rise, though, over time, as about 81% of college-age New Zealanders do go to some sort of postsecondary school. The homicide rate is four times lower than in the United States. In short, it seems like a great place to live.

More important from the perspective of economic growth, New Zealand ranks first overall in the World Bank's *Doing Business* indicators. These evaluate each country in ten major categories (each of which has many subcomponents) related to business conditions. They include how easy it is to set up a new business (in which New Zealand ranks first), dealing with construction permits (third), registering property (first), and accessing credit (first). It ranks a little lower in enforcing contracts and resolving insolvency, but overall New Zealand still pulls out the top spot for having a pro-business environment. It is a model of quality economic institutions. Moreover, the explicit and implicit tax rates are quite low.

But there are no classes taught at business schools about how to break into the New Zealand market. There is not a continual stream of executives flying to Christchurch every day to try to negotiate *any* kind of deal to get into the New Zealand market. Why? Because New Zealand, with a population of about 4.8 million, has fewer people than the greater Atlanta area. It doesn't matter much that the effective tax rate and cost of regulation in New Zealand are low, because the scale of the economy is too small to make it worth investing in.

There has been a little outside investment in New Zealand. In total, according to the International Monetary Fund, foreign direct investment by all countries in New Zealand was about $2 billion in 2016.

But in the same year foreign direct investment in China was $170 billion, eighty-five times larger. This is despite the fact that China ranks 78th in the *Doing Business* indicators. It is 93rd in starting a business, 172nd in dealing with construction permits, and 119th in protecting minority investors. It is, of course, ruled by the Communist Party, with no democratic elections, and—despite a series of reforms that began in the late 1970s—continues to have an economy dominated by state-run enterprises. There are severe rules on capital flows in and out of the country that are designed to foster Chinese exports. The explicit and implicit taxes in China are enormous.

Yet there are 1.3 billion Chinese people, with a total GDP that is just about as big as that of the United States. Whatever the institutional limitations on investment within China, and whatever taxes levied by the Chinese government, it still makes sense for firms to make massive investments in the Chinese economy because it is just so huge. Even though Hollywood might make movies in New Zealand, it makes those movies for the Chinese market. MBA programs run classes focused on operating in the Chinese market. Even though China imposes a heavy tax on firms in the forms of regulations, rules for domestic ownership, and actual explicit corporate taxes, it still makes sense to invest. Scale matters.

The logic extends to the United States, where markups and scale seem more relevant than taxes and regulation in explaining the net profits firms can earn, and hence for the incentives they have to invest and innovate. Just think about where firms choose to expand and invest within the United States. Yes, places like California and New York rank low on the ALEC-Laffer index, but firms are desperate to get into those markets. Why? Because they are already huge economies in their own right, and scale matters. Across cities, the same dynamic holds. Firms want to invest in cities with big markets, and they do so even if it means facing higher tax rates or more regulation, because scale can dwarf the effects of both.

Think of Salt Lake City, which according to ALEC-Laffer is in the state with the most business-friendly environment, Utah. Let's say that the low taxes and light regulatory burden mean that your business keeps 95% of its raw profits (i.e., the effective tax rate is only 5%).

In contrast, let's assume that the high taxes and regulatory burden in the New York City area, in last place in the ALEC-Laffer ranking, means that you keep only 50% of your raw profits. Would you want to operate a business that served the Salt Lake City area or the New York area?

If the scale of the two markets were equal, you'd opt for Salt Lake City, because your net profits would be much higher. But of course scale isn't equal. Greater Salt Lake City has about 1 million people. Greater New York has about 20 million people. By raw numbers of people alone, serving twenty times the possible customers swamps whatever difference in taxes might be faced. Total profits in greater New York would be about ten times higher than in Salt Lake City, even with the difference in tax rates.

If you restricted yourself to just the boundaries of New York City (and ignored the areas of Long Island and New Jersey that are part of the metro area), with about 8.5 million people, your profits would still be four and half times larger than in the entire Salt Lake City region. If you operated just in Queens, with 2.4 million people, you'd still earn 25% more in profits than in Salt Lake City. And that holds just thinking about raw population numbers. In terms of total GDP, the New York City area is about forty times larger than the Salt Lake City area, which means that the scale of the profits you could earn is even more skewed in favor of New York. Scale matters, and that is a key reason we do not see any appreciable effect of regulation and taxation on economic growth.

PROFITS ARE NOT GROWTH

This is not all to say that taxes and regulations don't matter for the bottom line of firms—they do. Any firm would rather face a low tax and regulation burden over a high one. So you can understand why firms lobby hard for reductions in both. But the argument often made in support of those reductions is that they will automatically boost the GDP growth rate, and that is not the case.

It pays here to think hard again about what GDP measures. It is not an aggregate of the financial performance of firms; rather, it is an aggregate of the real value of goods and services produced. An example will help illustrate the difference. In late 2011, American Airlines filed for bankruptcy. In that year, American Airlines reported a net loss of $1.9 billion. The following year the company reported a net loss of $1.8 billion, and in 2013 it repeated the trick by losing $1.8 billion again. What does that tell us about American's contribution to real GDP? Nothing.

From the perspective of real GDP, all that matters are the passengers that American carried in those years. American Airlines flew about 86 million passengers per year in 2011, 2012, and 2013, all while in bankruptcy. The service of hauling millions of people from one place to another became part of the flow of real goods and services in each of those years, despite the fact that American was bleeding cash.

The implication of this is not that we should set all taxes to 100% or that regulations are costless to the economy. Without some profits, no firm would bother to operate at all. With an onerous enough set of regulations, no firm will find it worth the trouble of complying and so will shut down. But the evidence indicates that taxation and regulation did not have a significant effect on the ability of firms to produce real goods and services, and specifically there was no substantial shift in government policies around 2000 that could explain the growth slowdown.

DID INEQUALITY CAUSE THE SLOWDOWN?

From the Occupy Wall Street movement to Thomas Piketty's *Capital in the Twenty-First Century*, economic inequality has gathered a lot of attention over the previous decade. And given that this coincided with the growth slowdown, it is natural to wonder whether inequality was a material cause of the slowdown in any way. From the perspective of the growth slowdown, though, the best way to view the rise in inequality is as just another symptom of the increasing market power of firms that we've already discussed rather than a separate cause in and of itself. The increased profits accruing to firms thanks to their higher markups had to go to somebody, and in large part executives and financial professionals reaped those rewards.

That said, are there reasons to suspect that the increase in inequality exacerbated the growth slowdown? Stagnant incomes at the bottom of the distribution may have limited investment in education, slowing the growth of human capital. Increased concentration of income may have accelerated the shift away from goods, as more and more purchasing power accumulated with high-income individuals whose preferences skew toward services. But when we add up the numbers, it does not seem that these two effects were large enough to explain much of the growth slowdown.

THE CONCENTRATION OF INCOME

The basic story of the increase in inequality may be familiar, but I've reproduced some figures here to illustrate what happened over the past few decades. The data comes from a new set of distributional national accounts put together by Thomas Piketty, Emmanuel Saez, and Gabriel Zucman, who have gone through the tedious task of taking the national accounting data on GDP that we have been using and matching it up with individual tax and survey data to provide a comprehensive data set on how GDP is allocated. You'll recall that we've played with this kind of breakdown before, looking at how much of GDP was paid out as wages, payments to capital, and economic profits. What these authors have done is use the individual-level data to eliminate some of the uncertainty that goes into those kinds of breakdowns.

Figure 15.1 shows in raw terms how much of GDP was earned by four separate groups. The first, represented by the solid line, is the income earned by the 50% of individuals with the lowest incomes. Around 1960, they earned about 20% of all GDP, and that was true until about 1980, when that share started to fall. As of 2014, their share of national income was close to 10%. The next group, which includes individuals with income that runs from the 50th percentile (i.e., the median household) to the 90th percentile, earned about 45% of national income in 1960. There was a drop in this group over time to about 40%, but it was not quite as severe as for the bottom half.

While those two groups experienced declines in their shares of national income, the remaining two groups experienced rising shares, by necessity. The individuals between the top 10% and top 1% of income earned about 23% of national income in 1960, and by 2014 that had increased to 27%. More dramatic was the rise of the top 1% of all individuals, who earned 12.5% of national income in 1960 and 20% in 2014, meaning that the increase in their share was almost identical to the drop in share of the bottom half of individuals.

We can use further data from Piketty, Saez, and Zucman to break down where the increase in the income share of the top 1% came from. Figure 15.2 plots several components of the group's total income share over time. The top band of the figure shows reported labor income. Note that in 1960, compared to the rest of their income sources, labor income accounted for a small portion of top 1% income. That changed over the course of the following decades, so

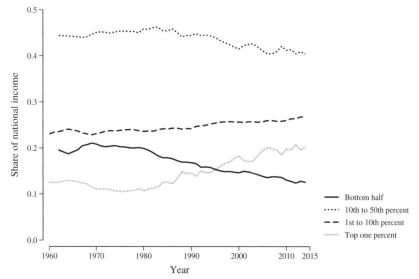

Figure 15.1. Distribution of national income, by percentiles
Note: Data is from Piketty, Saez, and Zucman (2016), with shares calculated by the author.

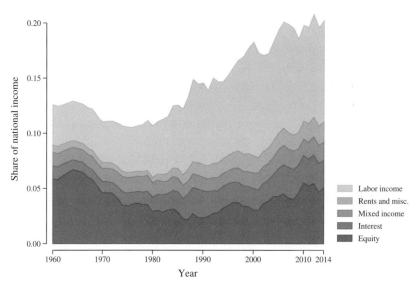

Figure 15.2. Sources of income for the top 1%
Note: Data is from Piketty, Saez, and Zucman (2016), with shares calculated by the author.

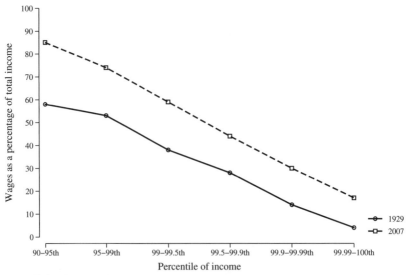

Figure 15.3. Labor income for the top 10% in 1929 and 2007
Note: Data is from Piketty (2013).

that much of the rise in their overall share represented an increase in labor income. That increase in labor income appears to have come at the expense of payments to equity, meaning dividends and similar payments. In 1960, the top 1% received about 46% of their total income from equity, but by 2014 that had fallen to 25%.

The evidence here shows that much of the increase in inequality came from an increase in the wages earned by the top 1%. This shift toward wage income as a source of top-end inequality represented a distinct change from inequality in the past. The Piketty, Saez, and Zucman data gives us some information on the top 1%, but Thomas Piketty's data from *Capital in the Twenty-First Century* provides more extensive insight into the fraction of income that is accounted for by capital (dividends, capital gains), labor (wages), and mixed income for subsets of the top 10%.

Figure 15.3 shows wages as a percentage of total income for different groups within the top 10% for both 1929 and 2007. For the people in the 90th through 95th percentiles of income, wages accounted for about 60% of their income in 1929, with capital and mixed income making up the rest. By 2007, that share had risen to 85%. Across all the percentiles of income, the role of wages went up over time, by about 20 percentage points for most categories. At the same time, there were distinct differences in the composition of income between the 90th or 95th percentile and those with the mind-boggling incomes of the top .01% of all earners. The people in the very top groups—think Warren Buffett—earned only about 18% of income from wages and the rest from capital income. The comparison to 1929 shows that the very top-earning individuals over the past century received the majority of their income from capital. But the role of wage income increased by a substantial amount for all groups.

The rise of wages as a source of top-end inequality reflected a rise in the role of "superstars" in the income distribution. The most obvious examples that might come to mind are athletes and actors. Piketty, Saez, and Zucman give data on the average income for groups of people by percentiles. In 2014, the top 10% had an average income of $303,857, whereas the top 5% had an income of $466,453. The minimum salary in Major League Baseball is around $500,000, so if you can make it to the big leagues, you'll be in the top 5%. The top 1% had an average income of $1,305,301 in 2014. The NBA rookie salary minimum is about $800,000, so you'd probably be a top 1% type if you could make it on a team. The actor Mark Hamill is reported to have made about $1 million for his role in *The Force Awakens*, so that alone probably snuck him into the top 1%, despite the fact that he appeared on screen for about thirty seconds and spoke no lines.

As you move up the distribution, the average jumps up. The average income of the top .1% was $6,021,708 in 2014. That means most of your favorite basketball and baseball players are somewhere around the top .1% of the income distribution. In Hollywood, Harrison Ford is reported to have earned between $10 million and $20 million for *The Force Awakens*, so he's in the upper end of that group. Finally, the top .01% of the income distribution earned about $28,121,142 in 2014. Guys like LeBron James and James Harden would be in this top group, along with a handful of NFL quarterbacks like Aaron Rodgers and Tom Brady. Actors like Tom Cruise, Brad Pitt, and Leonardo

DiCaprio can all land in the top .01% based on their earnings from just one movie, although it can be hard to parse out their salary from their share of the box office for each movie.

Although these examples of "superstars" from sports and movies help illustrate the income distribution, they are not the underlying source of the overall rise in inequality over the past few decades. More relevant was the expansion of what Piketty calls "supermanagers," in reference to top executives at large firms. Data from Jon Bakija, Adam Cole, and Bradley T. Heim shows their relative importance. Using individual tax returns from 2005, they found that about 41% of the top .1% of earners are executives of nonfinancial firms. Another 18.4% are finance professionals. By comparison, only 3.1% of the top .1% are in sports, media, and the arts combined. Another way of saying this is that for every mid-level NBA player like Trevor Ariza, Channing Frye, or Cole Aldrich who makes it into the top .1%, there are about twenty CEOs, CFOs, COOs, and hedge-fund managers in there with them.

The increase in income of these top executives and finance professionals explains two-thirds of the increased share of national income accounted for by the top .1% since 1993 (and more if we go back to 1979). The increased importance of wages within top-end income, and the rise in inequality overall, is driven by the salaries and other compensation (e.g., stock options) awarded to top executives and financial professionals.

DID INEQUALITY ACCELERATE THE SLOWDOWN?

All that said, there is no reason that a top 1% income share of 20% (as in 2014) is per se bad—or good—for economic growth. Nor is there any reason that the income share of executives or finance professionals would have a strict relationship to the growth rate of GDP. There is a vast literature studying the relationship of inequality (measured in a variety of ways) to the growth rate of GDP or its level across countries. But that literature has no definitive finding on the role inequality plays in growth, in part because it is almost impossible to separate the effect of inequality on growth from the coincident effect of growth on inequality.

If we are looking for an influence of the income distribution on growth, then we need to look at physical capital accumulation, human capital accumulation, and productivity growth. For physical capital, there is an old argument that inequality is good, because the very rich tend to save a greater fraction of their income than the very poor. Concentrated income thus leads to more savings and in turn more physical capital. Although it is true that savings rates tend to rise with income across families, there are a lot of links in the chain from that to an observable effect of inequality on physical capital accumulation. From the perspective of the growth slowdown, those links appear to have failed. Inequality rose over the past few decades at the same time that the growth rate of physical capital fell. We just saw that it was executives of firms who accounted for most of the rise in inequality, but if those executives had some greater propensity to save and invest than others, it did not show up in the data we looked at earlier regarding investment spending by firms. Recall the data from chapter 10 showing that the investment rate of firms has fallen in the past few years.

Trying to assess the impact of inequality on the acquisition of human capital is far more difficult. There is a large literature discussing the effect of human capital on individual wages, and thus on inequality, but that is not what we are interested in. Instead, what matters for growth is whether there is an effect of inequality on the acquisition of human capital. Just one of the possible ways this could work is through the effect of parental income on college enrollment. The National Center for Education Statistics reported that between 2000 and 2013, about 80% of kids with family incomes in the top 20% attended college right after high school, whereas only 50% of kids with family incomes in the bottom 20% did so. But even if we could use information like that to parse out the effect of an increase in inequality on college enrollment rates, we'd still need to think about the effect of inequality on college completion rates, and on high school graduation rates, and on high school equivalence rates, and on young childhood outcomes associated with all those things, and so on and so on. Trying to dig into all that is beyond the scope of this book.

Let's attack this instead with some simplistic calculations. In 2015, about 25% of individuals age 25–34 in the United States had completed a bachelor's degree, 11% had completed an advanced degree, and another 29% had completed some college (which includes associate degrees as well as people who didn't complete undergraduate degrees), for a total of 66% who had some college or more. These people were born between 1981 and 1990, so this is the first cohort of people whose education decisions were made during the period when inequality began to rise. If we assumed that inequality had a significant effect on education decisions, then we would guess that without the rise in inequality, more of this age cohort would have gone to college or completed college.

How big of an effect could this have had? Let's say that, if not for the rise in inequality, 65% of this group would have either completed a four-year degree or received an advanced degree, and another 15% would have gotten an associate's degree. And let's say that the remaining 20% would all have completed high school. This would mean that the average education of that cohort would have been about 14.9 years, as opposed to the 13.7 years shown by the actual data.

If that group of 43 million 25- to 34-year-olds had this extra education, then the average years of education for the entire workforce of individuals age 25–65 would have been higher by about 0.30 years of education. The effect is small because the younger cohort accounts for only about one-quarter of the work force, and so their increase in education isn't very visible in the aggregate. This in turn would mean that the entire stock of human capital, which depends on how we translate years of education into a number comparable across individuals, would have been higher by about 2.3%. That's nothing to sneeze at. But if the human capital stock were higher by 2.3% in 2016 than it otherwise would have been, this would have added only about 0.14% per year to the growth rate from 2000 to 2016, during the period of the slowdown.

Recall from chapter 5 that the rate of human capital growth fell by 1.11% in the twenty-first century compared to the twentieth. So even if inequality could be blamed for the drop in education acquisition, at best it would explain perhaps one-eighth of the drop in human capital growth. And let me remind you that my example here is a massive overstatement of the possible effect of inequality on education acquisition. So the true effect of inequality on human capital is much likely smaller than the 0.14% I just cited.

INEQUALITY AND THE SHIFT TO SERVICES

Leaving aside human capital, another possible effect of inequality is on the composition of demand. As we saw earlier, as the country became richer, on average, expenditures on services rose faster than expenditures on goods. That general relationship also appears to hold across households or individuals, as richer ones tend to spend a greater share of their income on services than poor ones. Note that I said *share* and not *dollars*. High-income individuals spend more, in absolute terms, on goods than low-income individuals do, but as a share of their income goods account for a smaller proportion.

With the expenditure share of goods falling with income, a concentration of income at the top end would result in a lower share of expenditure on goods in the aggregate. As we saw a few chapters ago, the shift from goods to services was a big contributor to slower growth in productivity, as those service industries tend to have low productivity levels and do not experience rapid productivity growth. The question is how much of the shift toward services was due to rising inequality, as opposed to just the overall long-run trend. Some back-of-the-envelope calculations show that it did not have a big effect. Timo Boppart calculated the expenditure share of goods for different income groups in the US and found that the top fifth of earners spent 10 percentage points less on goods compared to the bottom fifth of earners across time.

I'm going to try to give the inequality explanation the benefit of the doubt here. We know that the top 10% of earners had about 38% of all income in 1990 but about 47% in 2014. So let's assume that those top 10% of earners spent 25% of their income on goods in 2014, a little less than Boppart's data on the top 20% of earners. And let's assume that the bottom 90% of earners spent 40% of their income on goods, which is close to the average for the very poorest people in Boppart's analysis. Based on this and the income share of 47% for the top 10% in 2014, the overall expenditure share of goods was 33% (47% times 25%

plus 53% times 40%). That's a little higher than what I showed using aggregate data, but it is not a bad approximation given that we are using an entirely different data set.

Now, if inequality had not gone up, and the income share of the top 10% were only 38%, as it was in 1990, what would we expect the expenditure share of goods to be? It would be 34% (38% times 25% plus 62% times 40%), only 1 percentage point higher. The expenditure share of goods fell by a total of about 5 to 7 percentage points between 1990 and 2014, depending on whether we look at the aggregate data or at Boppart's data. At best, then, the increase in inequality could have accounted for one-fifth of the shift into services and away from goods. But remember, I've rigged this to be as favorable as possible to the inequality story, so the actual effect is going to be smaller. Therefore I would say inequality exacerbated the shift out of goods production, but it is a minor part of the overall picture. The general rise in living standards is far more important.

In combination, the effects of rising inequality on human capital and the shift into services are marginal. The rise in inequality is not, per se, a source of the growth slowdown. It does, however, corroborate the story that there was a significant rise in market power by firms over this period, as we see more income flowing to executives associated with those firms.

DID CHINA CAUSE THE SLOWDOWN?

16

There is temptation to assign blame for the growth slowdown to trade, and particularly the increase in imports from China. The timing looks right. China began to increase its exports starting in the 1980s, but it was in 2001 that China became a full member of the World Trade Organization, and at that point tariffs on Chinese imports to the US fell to match the low rates that applied to other members. This lines up with our placement of the origin of the growth slowdown around the turn of the century.

There are ways to link China to the growth slowdown. Some make sense and some do not. I'll show first that the simple increase in imports we experienced over time, whether from China or Mexico or wherever, does not have any necessary connection to the level of GDP or growth rate. The common argument asserting that imports have a direct negative effect on the United States' GDP is based on a misinterpretation of an accounting identity.

That said, this doesn't imply there was no effect of trade at all. There is solid research that links the introduction of Chinese imports to significant declines in employment within manufacturing industries and beyond. That could, in theory, have contributed to the growth slowdown, either through shrinking the stock of human capital if workers did not find new employment or by accelerating the shift in workers toward lower-productivity-growth industries. And while it looks like those things occurred, the size of the effect of China, and trade in general, looks too small to account for the growth slowdown in any appreciable way.

IMPORTS ARE NOT THE ISSUE

Let's take care of the misinterpretation problem first, because it creeps up all the time once the topic turns to international trade. Imports do not, in a mechanical way, lower growth. First, as you know from having made it this far in the book, there is a big difference between growth in GDP, the growth rate of GDP, and the level of GDP. In almost every case, when someone says that imports lower growth, what he or she is trying to say is that imports lower the level of GDP. However, even using the correct terms, this statement is still wrong.

People often make this mistake because they get caught up in the national income accounting identity they learned in an introductory economics course. I am going to violate my "no equation" pledge here and reproduce the offending identity so that you can see what I am talking about. The identity is usually written, with perhaps some variation in the exact lettering, as follows:

$$Y = C + I + G + X - M. \tag{16.1}$$

The Y is GDP. The C stands for consumption, the I for investment, and the G for government purchases. The X is exports, and the M is imports. The value of imports is subtracted on the right-hand side, and thus it becomes tempting to say that if imports are higher, it must be that Y, GDP, is lower. That's wrong because the right-hand side of this equation is just a way of accounting for GDP; it does not determine the size of GDP.

I'm going to fix the confusion by doing something simple: adding M to both sides. We've now got

$$Y + M = C + I + G + X. \tag{16.2}$$

This identity helps, because given the common way that people interpret a relationship like this, if they imagine that M goes up, they'll jump to the conclusion that one of the things on the right (C, I, G, or X) must have gone up as well. That is much closer to the truth. It also helps because it groups related terms together.

On the left is GDP (Y) plus imports (M). This is the total goods and services available to us in a given year. We produce our own real GDP, and we ship in a bunch of goods and services from other countries. On the right-hand side we have a way of categorizing the purchases of those goods and services. Consumption (C) is just goods and services that are either nondurable, like food, or durable, like a couch, but not used to produce any other goods. Investment (I) is better referred to as "capital purchases," as these are goods and services that are used as capital, meaning they assist in producing more goods and services in the future, like a drill press or an office computer. The third term is government (G), which refers to all the goods and services, like tanks and paper clips, purchased by federal, state, and local governments. Finally, exports (X) are best referred to as "foreign purchases"; they are goods and services that noncitizens buy.

Think of the $Y + M$ term as a giant pile of goods and services. We all show up and start purchasing the stuff from this pile, which you can think of as sorting goods and services into four different, smaller piles. The first pile is consumption goods, the second is capital purchases, the third is government purchases, and the final pile is stuff that foreigners purchase. An increase in imports means that there is a bigger pile of stuff to purchase. But there is no necessary mechanical effect of having more imports on the size of our own production, GDP.

Figure 16.1 plots the size of the giant pile of goods and services over time, with 1950 set equal to 100. This looks a lot like a plot of the level of real GDP per capita over time, and that is because it is real GDP per capita plus the amount that we import, which you can see is a small but growing amount. We divide that giant pile of stuff into the four piles of purchases; those are plotted in figure 16.2.

It is easy to see that the absolute purchases in each of the four categories rose over time. What isn't as clear from the figure is how the proportions changed over time. Consumption purchases took up the largest share, making up about 60% of the whole pile in any given

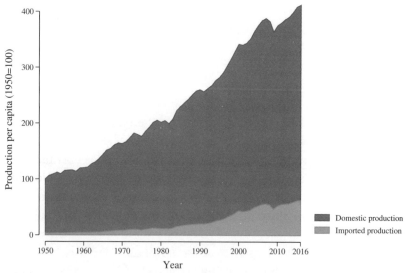

Figure 16.1. Production per capita available for purchase, over time
Note: Data is from the Bureau of Economic Analysis.

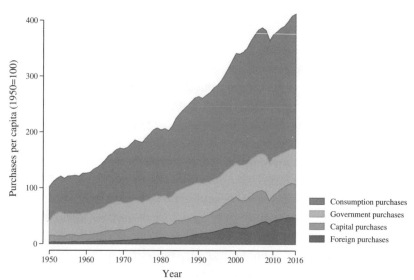

Figure 16.2. Categories of purchased production per capita
Note: Data is from the Bureau of Economic Analysis.

year. Government purchases declined as a fraction of the total pile, from about 30% in 1950 to about 18% in 2016. Capital purchases rose over time, from about 12% in 1950 to about 18% in 2016. Finally, foreign purchases took up only 2% of the pile in 1950 and increased to nearly 10% by 2016.

This is all just accounting. Yes, imports increased over time. Yes, exports increased over time but not by as much as imports. However, all that tells us is that the pile of stuff we've got available (GDP plus imports) increased in size, and most of it was purchased for use here rather than being purchased for use in a foreign country. Nothing about a higher growth rate in imports meant that, by definition, the growth rate of GDP must be lower.

REAL EFFECTS OF TRADE

Now that we've gotten the mechanical, and wrong, conception of the relationship between GDP and imports out of the way, we can turn to plausible connections of trade and growth. As we saw before, we can account for the growth of GDP through the growth in physical and human capital stocks or through growth in productivity. So in terms of trade, we want to think about how it may have acted on those inputs to producing GDP. The inputs most obviously involved here are the stock of human capital (if trade with China pushed people out of the labor force) and productivity (if trade reallocated workers toward low-productivity-growth industries).

Let's start with the effect on the number of employed workers. Imports (from China or any other country) in an industry either put domestic competitors out of business or shrink their market. Either way, there is a loss of employment in those industries that are exposed to trade. Now, if these workers reallocate into other industries and firms without much of a delay, the overall effect of this import penetration will probably be positive. Consumers gain from having access to cheaper imported goods in the stores, and displaced workers are reallocated, perhaps to an even more productive industry. Everyone wins.

I'm not going to spend time measuring the gains that accrue from lower prices for consumer goods. That leads us down a path of trying to compare the implicit utility gains for consumers with the costs to workers who are displaced. We're more interested here in the effect of trade with China on the inputs to producing domestic GDP. Here, and this perhaps will not be surprising at all, there is little evidence that workers displaced by trade are moving into other industries or firms. This is consistent with all the data seen earlier on the slowdown in worker turnover between firms and industries, and with the lack of geographic mobility. For workers in industries affected by import competition, the workers who have lost their jobs are not being re-allocated to either new industries or new locations.

David Autor, David Dorn, and Gordon Hanson provided a recent overview of the empirical literature on this subject. The first thing they discuss is that industries that faced greater competition from China did in fact see larger drops in employment. This is not as easy to establish as you might think. To start, you need to decide how to measure "competition from China." This is done by using import penetration, the share of total expenditure within the US in a narrow industry accounted for by Chinese imports. For example, for women's nonathletic footwear, roughly 100% of total expenditure is on imports from China. That constitutes a lot of competition from China for any potential American producer. In contrast, for automotive trimmings (e.g., leather car seats), close to 0% of expenditure is used on imports from China, so there is little competition. Despite China's entry, there is a lot of variation in the narrow industries that were affected. China produces a lot of things, but it does not produce everything.

If we look at the change in employment in an industry and im-port penetration, there is a negative relationship; industries like women's nonathletic footwear saw bigger percentage drops in em-ployment than did automotive trimmings. But this leads to a second issue, which is whether the imports from China *caused* the decline in employment, or whether both of those things were driven by some outside force. For example, it is possible that the firms in women's nonathletic footwear were poorly run and going to lose market share no matter what happened with China, and that China just happened to take advantage of their ineptitude. A lot of work in this literature has gone into analyzing this issue, and Autor, Dorn, and Hanson explain the main line of attack. The idea is that by looking at import penetration of the same industries in other countries (e.g., France, the United Kingdom), we can infer how much change in employment was due to China pushing firms out versus China getting pulled in. In short, if we see that import penetration is large in an industry in these other countries as well, then it was probably China's entry, and not domestic industry problems, that explains the loss of employment. And when the authors used this in their analysis, it looked as if the employment losses were strongly related to China's entry. For every extra percentage point of import penetration in an industry (e.g., going from 51% to 52%) there was a loss of 1.3% of employment in the same industry.

Industries that faced competition from China did in fact lose employment, but we still need to see what happened to those displaced workers. Remember, if they were shuffled into different firms and industries without too much trouble, it would indicate little negative effect of trade on production and growth. But as Autor, Dorn, and Hanson show, the evidence is that many of these workers fell out of the labor force, and any reallocation that did happen was very slow. You can see this in work that looks at variation across regions, in particular commuting zones, which are clusters of counties that appear to share a common labor market. You can think of commuting zones as similar to the MSAs we've discussed, but they can also include rural areas without a major city. Regardless, these commuting zones differ in how exposed they were to trade with China, depending on the types of industries they had. For example, furniture manufacturers in certain commuting zones in North Carolina and Tennessee saw a lot of competition from China, whereas certain commuting zones in Alabama or South Carolina that produce cars did not.

Across all the commuting zones, the finding was that for each additional $1,000 in imports per domestic worker, the unemployment rate went up by 0.2 percentage points (e.g., from 5% to 5.2%) and the percentage of working-age people not in the labor force went up by about 0.5 percentage points (e.g., from 15% to 15.5%). To give you a better sense of the possible impact, the most exposed commuting zones saw an increase of about $4,300 in imports per worker, meaning that trade increased the unemployment rate by 1 percentage point and the percentage of workers out of the labor force by about 2.4 percentage points.

A further intriguing result of this research is that there was no significant effect of increased exposure to trade on the population size of these commuting zones. That is, in response to competition and loss of jobs, people did not leave these places. The combination of all these results shows that the reallocation effects we'd expect to mitigate the costs of trade did not manifest. People did not move out of commuting zones that experienced losses from trade but rather stayed unemployed or exited the labor force.

THE CONTRIBUTION TO THE GROWTH SLOWDOWN

By pushing some workers out of the workforce, or making them unemployed, increased trade with China limited the growth of the human capital stock. The estimated effects from Autor, Dorn, and Hanson suggest that between 1990 and 2000, trade lowered manufacturing employment by 548,000, and between 2000 and 2007 by another 982,000. In total, we could attribute about 1.53 million lost manufacturing jobs to trade. For comparison, between 2000 and 2007 the total number of manufacturing jobs fell by around 3.5 million, so that trade could account for about 43% of that decline. Over the longer period from 1990 to 2007, Autor, Dorn, and Hanson calculate that trade accounted for about 21% of the decline in manufacturing employment. Over either period, trade with China had a significant effect on manufacturing employment.

In addition, these direct losses also led to indirect losses of employment in these commuting zones. Across the United States, increased trade from 1990 to 2007 lowered the percentage of people in the labor force, regardless of industry, by about 1 percentage point. The labor force participation rate was about 66% in 2007, so it would have been 67% without trade. Rather than 153 million workers in the labor force in 2007, there would have been 155 million. Trade with China also raised the unemployment rate by about 0.37 percentage points. In 2007, the unemployment rate was 5.0%, so it would have been 4.63% without that trade. Thus, rather than having 145.3 million employed workers in 2007, we would have had 147.8 million. That's an increase in the number of employees of 1.7%. Ignoring the fact that the workers displaced by trade do not have the same exact level of skills or hours worked as everyone else in the economy, the human capital stock could have been higher by as much as 1.7% without the impact of additional trade with China.

Is that a big effect? Remember that this difference is accumulated over the course of seventeen years from 1990 to 2007. The effect of trade with China meant that the growth rate of the human capital stock was smaller by about 0.1 percentage points per year. Compared to the effects of population aging that we discussed earlier, this is not a major effect.

You would be right to wonder whether this effect gets larger when we take into account the effect of increased trade with all countries, not just with China. Autor, Dorn, and Hanson consider this as well, and find not only no effect of trade on employment, but in some cases positive effects of trade on employment (in particular with Mexico and other Central American nations). So if we were to incorporate the entire effect of trade, we'd most likely find that it had a positive but negligible effect on growth in human capital.

Leaving aside the stock of human capital, the employment effects of trade with China could influence productivity through the allocation of workers between industries. What Autor, Dorn, and Hanson show is that China lowered manufacturing employment and, to a lesser extent, employment in other industries. The distinct effect on manufacturing means that China contributed to the decline in the share of employment in that industry and the share of manufacturing in total GDP. Recall from chapter 7 that manufacturing's share of GDP fell from about 17.6% in 1990 to 12.2% by 2015, and relative to many other industries that expanded their share, manufacturing had relatively high productivity growth. By shifting economic activity out of manufacturing, trade would have lowered weighted average productivity growth and contributed to the growth slowdown.

How big was this effect? There isn't a direct way to use Autor, Dorn, and Hanson's numbers, because they looked at employment in manufacturing, and we want to look at the share of manufacturing value-added in GDP. But we can work out some back-of-the-envelope calculations to see whether trade could have had a big effect. If we take Autor, Dorn, and Hanson's numbers seriously, let's say that with a different trade policy we could have had 1.53 million extra manufacturing workers in 2015. In reality, there were about 12.3 million manufacturing workers that year, so our hypothetical trade policy would have raised manufacturing employment by about 12%.

With more manufacturing workers, the production of manufactured goods would have been higher as well, accounting for a larger percentage of GDP. Ignoring the fact that simply raising manufacturing employment by 12% would not by itself raise production by 12%—remember those elasticities we talked about in chapter 4—let's assume that manufacturing production does go up by 12% in response. This would mean that manufacturing's value-added share of GDP would rise as well. How much it goes up depends on where those 1.53 million extra workers come from. If they would otherwise have been in high-productivity industries, this could be bad for real GDP. But let's make this as optimistic as possible and assume that the extra 1.53 million workers were all unemployed, and so adding them as manufacturing workers represents a pure gain to real GDP. From the data in chapter 7 we know that manufacturing's share of value-added was 12.2% (I know, there is a lot of the number 12 floating around). With our assumption of extra manufacturing workers producing extra GDP, the value-added share could rise all the way to 13.4%.

As we saw in chapter 7 as well, because manufacturing has higher productivity growth than the average industry, at about 1.36%, a bigger value-added share for manufacturing would increase productivity growth. The additional manufacturing workers would raise it by 0.016% (.0136 times the difference between the shares 0.134 and 0.122). Now, to be thorough, we'd also have to account for the fact that productivity growth would fall by a little because the remainder of the economy had a lower value-added share. But again, let's keep things optimistic and ignore this.

The result is that replacing the manufacturing workers lost to trade would increase productivity growth by about 0.016%. For reference, productivity growth according to the industry-level calculations from chapter 7 was 0.4% per year. In short, our little experiment would have almost no effect on aggregate productivity growth rate. And the implication is that the effects of trade with China estimated by Autor, Dorn, and Hanson cannot offer an explanation for the growth slowdown.

Although the effect of Chinese trade was real in terms of replacing US manufacturing firms and employment—and that had real, negative impacts on those workers and their communities—in terms of the growth slowdown, the impact of Chinese trade was not large. The growth slowdown would have happened even if China had never become a major exporter, as the US was already in the middle of a long-run shift away from goods production toward services production. China accelerated this in a small way but was not responsible for it.

THE FUTURE OF GROWTH

Now that we've covered all of the plausible sources of the growth slowdown, it might help if I go back and lay out how much of the slowdown can be attributed to each. These numbers were scattered around the book in various places, but let's look at them all in one place. Table 17.1 breaks down how we went from growth of 2.25% per year in the twentieth century to 1.0% per year in the twenty-first. Each row shows the effect on the growth rate from a given source.

The drop in family size and population aging, for example, lowered the growth rate by about 0.80 percentage points all by itself, far and away the largest contributor to the growth slowdown. The shift from goods to services took off another 0.20 percentage points, at least. My point about success leading to the slowdown was built on those two explanations, which together account for three-quarters of the drop in the growth rate.

Beneath those, the two biggest explanations for the growth slowdown were the declines in the reallocation of workers and firms, which could explain about 0.15 percentage points. The drop in geographic mobility could account for another 0.10 percentage points, although that might be an aggressive estimate. Finally, the contributions of taxation and regulation, increased inequality, and trade with China were each about 0, as we saw in the previous few chapters.

The drops in reallocation and mobility have the

Table 17.1 Accounting for the growth slowdown,
twentieth to twenty-first century

Growth rate (%)	Explanation
2.25	Average growth from 1950 to 2000
	SUCCESSES
−0.80	The effects of smaller family sizes and aging
−0.20	The shift from goods to services
	POSSIBLE FAILURES
−0.15	The decline in reallocation of workers and firms
−0.10	The decline in geographic mobility
≈ 0	Taxation and regulation
≈ 0	The increase in inequality
≈ 0	Trade with China
= 1.00	Average growth from 2000 to 2016

flavor of failures. But a plausible explanation for the drop in reallocation—increased market power—may itself be a symptom of population aging or the shift from goods into services driven by higher living standards. And while there were reasons to suspect that the drop in geographic mobility could be tied to more onerous housing regulations, the effect on growth rate may be overstated. What this all means is that the table could well be understating the influence of success on the growth slowdown.

Either way, table 17.1 will appear off if you compare it to the original accounting in chapter 4. Here, the effect of human capital is smaller than in chapter 4, and the combined influences on productivity are bigger. That probably reflects again that the shift into services, the drop in reallocation, and the decline in mobility are all intertwined and interact with one another. The combined effect of those three is likely smaller, whereas the effect of smaller family sizes and population aging is likely larger than what I've shown here. Regardless, there is little scope to argue that the failures in table 17.1 can account for a majority of the growth slowdown.

WHAT ARE YOU PREPARED TO DO?

In chapters 5 and 8 I provided some specific arguments for why population aging and the shift into services should be seen as successes. Here, let me take a step back and give you a broader way of thinking about all this. Ask yourself this question: what would you sacrifice to reverse the growth slowdown?

Start with the demographic shift that led to an aging population and a reduction in the number of workers per person in the twenty-first century. It accounts for a huge portion of the growth slowdown and was the result of falling fertility rates. In general, lower fertility rates are associated with higher living standards. Would you sacrifice the level of living standards and go back to the real GDP per capita of 1930 or 1920 to generate more rapid population growth?

Remember, associated with the drop in family size was an increase in the age of marriage, higher female labor force participation, higher education levels, better household technologies, and improved reproductive rights for women. Which of those would you be willing to sacrifice to jump-start growth? Would you restrict the ability of women to work or roll back access to contraception? Would you accept thousands of unplanned births every year to add a few tenths of a percentage point to the growth rate of real GDP per capita?

I don't see how the answer to those questions could be yes, but even if it were, it isn't clear that doing this would have a demonstrable effect on the growth rate any time soon. Remember, the current growth slowdown is the consequence of decisions in family size that took place going back to the 1940s. If you did manage to engineer another baby boom, you'd have to endure two decades of *below*-average growth in real GDP per capita while all those new kids grew up to working age. If you somehow managed to deliver on the rollback of rights and living standards necessary to generate massive fertility rates, it would be around 2050 before you started to see any appreciable effect on the growth rate.

If the sacrifices necessary to reverse the effects of population aging don't seem worth it, then perhaps you'd do something to shift more production back into goods rather than services? One simple way to boost employment in goods-producing industries would be to get rid of a bunch of our goods. If you imploded, say, half of the existing housing stock—refrigerators, toilets, and all—and half of the existing stock of factories and office buildings, with all their internal capital included, then imagine the boom in demand for new goods that you'd create. It would necessitate a massive shift of labor into construction and manufacturing to reproduce those factories, office buildings, houses, computers, furniture, and appliances that go into them. To make sure that all that manufacturing is done within the US, you'd have to make sure that foreign companies could not sell their durable goods here. Which you might be willing to do, but this would mean that their price, in terms of the amount of labor and capital we have to use to produce them, would be much higher than it is today. Again, if you were willing to sacrifice the level of productivity and living standards we enjoy today, then you could probably raise the growth rate of real GDP per capita.

As an aside, we know something like this can work because we've seen it before. After World War II, both Germany and Japan had some of the highest growth rates of GDP per capita ever recorded, and that high growth lasted for close to two decades. It was largely because much of their capital and durable-goods stock had been incinerated by firebombing. Is a higher growth rate so important that you'd replicate that level of destruction to achieve it?

Perhaps that example seems a bit hyperbolic, but consider the case of China over the past few decades. China's high growth rate was driven in part by its lower living standard relative to that in the United States. Earlier in the book, I mentioned that China's GDP per capita was only about 25% of that in the United States. To make that more tangible, consider these facts. Around 2000, when China's growth rate was more than 6% per year, fewer than one in three Chinese had access to a flush toilet, and one in four had no access to a clean source of drinking water. Today, there are about seventy televisions in the US for every hundred people, but in China there are twenty-nine.

In the United States there are about eighty-seven mobile phones for every hundred people, while in China there are about forty-seven. There are about eighty road vehicles (e.g., cars, vans, trucks, buses) for every hundred people in the US, but in China there are only about fifty. The point is that we should not be surprised that China's growth rate is high. It is trying to catch up to the material living standards we already enjoy in the United States. Would you give up your TV, your phone, your car, and your toilet to ensure that the growth rate of GDP per capita was higher?

If you are not willing to abandon decades of development to raise the growth rate by a percentage point or so, then almost by definition the changes embedded in that development are a success. The growth slowdown is a consequence—even if unintended—of choices we made across decades of rising living standards.

SUCCESS, NOT PERFECTION

The claim that slow growth is an outcome of success does not mean that things cannot get better. Throughout the book, I've shown that many economic problems turned out to have little effect on economic growth. But that doesn't mean these problems don't exist, or that addressing them is not warranted or possible.

Economic profits increased in the previous two decades as a share of GDP at the expense of payments to workers or owners of physical capital. That the increased economic profits went almost exclusively toward higher dividends and share buybacks, as opposed to increased investment or innovation, raises valid questions about the rules and regulations that allowed this to happen, even though it had an ambiguous effect on productivity growth. In fact, the lack of a significant effect of higher economic profits on growth should make us even more willing to question this redistribution, as it is hard to see which benefits it created for the economy as a whole.

In chapter 11 I outlined a few examples of how increased market power may be the result of tighter intellectual property rights and a decline in the enforcement of antitrust laws. And while I discussed how some market power is necessary to create incentives for growth, there is a strong argument to be made that we have gone too far in allowing market power to accrue. Brink Lindsey and Steven Teles, in their recent book *The Captured Economy*, provide a more detailed examination of the specific ways in which intellectual property rights and the regulatory environment have created market power, as well as several possible remedies. These remedies are worth exploring, because they speak to who benefits from growth in the economy.

This debate is valuable even though the effect of the remedies on the growth rate may be ambiguous. If we did rein in market power in some industries or for some firms, the ultimate effect on the growth rate might not be that large. Any increase in the growth rate that this generated should be considered a bonus, not the primary goal.

A similar view is useful with respect to several other issues. Trade generated severe consequences for certain regions and workers and contributed a little to the shift into services. Changes in trade policy, specific trade deals, and assistance programs could alleviate the economic damage done to those regions and workers or exacerbate it, depending on the particulars. But as the evidence showed, there is little reason to suspect that increased trade had much of an effect on the growth slowdown itself. Hence the debate on trade should focus on whether, and how, the winners from trade might compensate the losers, and any effect on the growth rate is going to be of secondary importance.

The current constellation of government spending, regulation, and taxation benefits some and hurts others. But as we saw, there is little evidence that shifts in these policies would have a significant effect on economic growth. Thus the arguments over the proper level of all three are best had in terms of their effects on different groups, as opposed to their effect on aggregate growth. In particular, claims that specific policies will "pay for themselves" in any capacity are fatuous. Government fiscal and regulatory policy is, to a large degree, about the division of the economic pie, not its size.

One plausible exception to this may be local government regulation of housing markets. We saw evidence in chapters 13 and 14 that restrictions limiting the supply of new housing, or making it prohibitively expensive, may have contributed to the decline in geographic mobility across the United States. Loosening those housing regulations could lead to a noticeable boost in the growth rate, although that does not mean changing those policies would be painless for everyone.

Taken all together, I think the right conclusion is that while we do not have a problem with growth, we may have a problem with distribution. Across all these areas—market power, trade, taxes and regulation, housing—there are serious implications for who actually gained from economic growth, even though there were not major effects on growth itself. This suggests that we should engage with these issues on the merits of their distributional consequences and put less weight on their supposed effect on the growth rate.

IMPORTING HUMAN CAPITAL

Whether it's because we wouldn't want to make the changes needed, or because the changes wouldn't have a big effect, the conclusion seems to be that there is no way to reverse the growth slowdown. But there is one exception that could have a direct, appreciable effect on economic growth: immigration.

The single biggest contributor to the growth slowdown was the drop in human capital growth due to population aging. Reversing that organically would require a distinct regression in living standards and individual rights, and it would take decades to pull off. Bringing in new workers as more and more retire, however, could offset much of the growth slowdown and in a short time frame.

We saw in chapter 5 that during the twenty-first century, the falling ratio of workers to population subtracted 0.35 percentage points from the growth rate. If we just wanted to reverse that, how much immigration would be necessary? We'd need the number of workers to grow at the same rate as population, which was about 0.7% per year over the past few years. This would require us to add about 1.05 million workers per year. The labor force has added only around 750,000 workers per year recently, so we would need to pull in about 255,000 additional working-age immigrants to stop the worker-to-population ratio from continuing to fall.

For most of the twenty-first century, the US has taken in about 1 million documented immigrants per year, so adding 255,000 more is certainly plausible. A century ago, the US absorbed 1.25 million immigrants in several years and regularly took in over 1 million annually. That took place during a time when the total US population was only around 100 million, meaning that these flows represented a much larger rate of immigration than the same 1.25 million would today, now that the population is over 325 million people. If we were willing to add even more immigrants, we could raise the growth rate by even more than 0.35 percentage points. Taking in 750,000 additional working-age immigrants every year would raise the growth rate by about 0.60%, offsetting almost half of the entire growth slowdown. And taking in 1.75 million immigrants today would still represent an immigration rate of about half of what we handled in the early 1900s.

The other question for human capital growth is about the kind of skills or education immigrants would bring with them. The effect on skill level depends on whether the immigrants tend to be more or less skilled than the current workforce. Ensuring that immigration adds to, or at least does not detract from, the average skill level is something well within our control. As it happens, recent immigrants to the US have tended to be better educated than the current US population. Data from the American Community Survey in 2015 shows that among all immigrants who arrived in the US from 2010 to 2015, about 40% had a bachelor's degree, higher than the percentage in the native population (about 30%). It is plausible that immigration will raise the average skill level of the workforce because we've already seen it happen.

A typical worry is that additional immigrants would not add to the workforce but replace existing workers. However, there is little evidence that this would be the case. Giovanni Peri, working with several coauthors, has shown in a wide variety of countries and contexts that immigration does not have a significant negative effect on employment for natives. Nor does it depress the wages of native workers, in part because immigration often makes the skills of natives—such as their language ability and familiarity with local markets—more valuable. And by increasing the scale of local markets, increased immigration often creates incentives for firms to expand or innovate, meaning that immigration tends to be a net positive for the receiving country, over and above the direct effect it has on growth in human capital. As a tool for offsetting the drag on growth caused by population aging, a modest amount of additional immigration is the best bet.

WHERE DO WE GO FROM HERE?

Explaining the growth slowdown is different from trying to forecast the growth rate in the future. It would probably be wise to avoid the latter, but nevertheless let me offer some tentative predictions about what to expect with respect to growth over the next few decades. You may not be surprised that I believe the growth rate will continue to be low relative to the twentieth century and may fall further as living standards continue to improve. I see no obvious reason that the growth rate would accelerate in the near future.

Take human capital first. At some point the demographic changes that have been pulling down the growth rate will subside, as the baby boom generation will not live forever. But that is still several decades into the future, so for the time being this drag on the growth rate will persist. As noted earlier, a significant increase in immigration—and skilled immigration, in particular—could offset this and bring the growth rate back to twentieth-century levels. Without that, though, there is no reason to suspect that the growth rate will recover as the result of an increase in the growth rate of human capital. Demographics just move too slowly to create any surprise in the growth rate.

If you recall from the work on human capital, there was also a persistent drag on growth from the decline in hours worked per employee over time. The average workweek, which was around seventy hours during the 1800s, fell to less than forty hours per week in the twentieth century and has continued to drop during the twenty-first. John Maynard Keynes, back in 1930, famously speculated about the possibilities of a fifteen-hour workweek as our demand for material goods reached satiation. This decline would represent another success, coming about as a result of a choice to "buy" ourselves shorter workweeks in response to productivity growth. Nevertheless, fewer hours worked would push down the growth rate of real GDP per capita even further, even as our actual well-being or happiness rose.

The logic behind the drop in hours is similar to that of the shift into services, and I'd expect that shift to persist. Given the available evidence, this would continue to push down the growth rate of aggregate productivity. But it is worth noting that perhaps the future of productivity growth in services is brighter than we'd guess just from extrapolating the data we have. It may be that it is only now that service industries are reaching the scale necessary to implement substantial productivity improvements, or maybe we've spent more time searching for productivity improvements in goods production because they seem like low-hanging fruit. There is even some recent research suggesting that low productivity growth in services may be an artifact of measurement error, not something fundamental to those industries. If any of this is true, then it would allow us to be more optimistic about the future growth rate of productivity, although it would still be unwise to assume anything.

I think a similar sentiment is warranted with respect to technological change in general. There are, without a doubt, an incredible number of new and improved technologies arriving every day. Self-driving cars, gene editing, low-cost solar panels, more efficient batteries, biofuel, quantum computers, 3-D printing of metals, artificial intelligence, and on and on and on. Any, or all, of these could generate profound changes in how we live and how we produce the goods and services that go into GDP. That said, it isn't obvious that we'll see profound effects on the growth rate of the economy. Many of those innovations make the production of goods more efficient, but that would only accelerate the shift into services. And there may be a larger question about whether we want to adopt or pursue these innovations at all. As Charles Jones suggested in a recent paper, given our current life expectancy and living standards, the risks inherent in any technology—to the environment, society, or our own health—may not be worth pursuing just to add a fraction of a percentage point to the growth rate.

In the end, I doubt that there will be any appreciable acceleration in the growth rate of real GDP per capita in the future. But as I've tried to explain throughout the book, you should not assume that this is a failure. The growth rate, by itself, should not be used to judge the progress or well-being of our economy and society. Economic growth is a function of our choices about how to spend our time, spend our money, and build our families, not something that is forced on us from outside. In the past, those choices happened to coincide with fast growth because we were building up our material living standard. As we achieved that success—not for all, but for most—the choices we made changed. And while those new choices did not promote rapid growth, that doesn't make them wrong. Slow growth, it turns out, is the optimal response to massive economic success.

APPENDIX: DATA AND METHODS

The notes in this appendix provide details on specific research cited, the data sources and calculations behind all the tables and figures in the book, and any additional calculations I made in the text. They also include expanded theoretical explanations, with equations, of some of the concepts I use and explain in the text.

General Information on Data in Figures and Tables

The raw data and code used to create all the figures and tables in the book are available online at https://growthecon.com/fully/. All the data I use is publicly available, and the analysis in this book is replicable by anyone with access to the statistics program Stata and a modicum of technical ability.

There were two main sources I used:

1. The Federal Reserve Economic Data (FRED) database, found at https://fred.stlouisfed.org. I accessed this using the "freduse" utility program in Stata. This database combines information from the main data sources of the US government, including the Bureau of Economic Analysis (BEA), Bureau of Labor Statistics (BLS), and US Census Bureau, among others. The value of using this service is that one can not only replicate the figures and tables found in the book but also update them over time as FRED adds new months, quarters, and years of data. In the rest of the appendix, I list the actual source first, followed by (FRED), to indicate that I obtained the data from that website.

2. Individually downloaded data from public sources. In cases where FRED did not have the data required, I obtained the data directly. In each of these cases, the raw data (in CSV format) is available on the book's website. In the chapter notes that follow, I cite the specific source for each of these one-off data sources.

1. Victims of Our Own Success

The idea that the growth slowdown predates the financial crisis can be found in Fernald (2014).

2. What Is the Growth Slowdown?

The data on real GDP per capita for the figures on the United States alone is from the BEA (FRED). The data on real GDP per capita for comparisons of the

United States and other countries is all from the Penn World Tables, Version 9, downloaded from https://www.rug.nl/ggdc/productivity/pwt/.

In terms of notation, let y_t be the level of real GDP per capita in year t. Define the absolute growth in real GDP per capita from period $t - 1$ to t to be

$$G_y = y_t - y_{t-1}. \tag{A.1}$$

The growth rate of real GDP per capita from period $t - 1$ to period t is defined as

$$g_y = \frac{y_t - y_{t-1}}{y_{t-1}}. \tag{A.2}$$

The other major calculation in the chapter is the 10-year average growth rate of real GDP per capita. This rate, which I denote $g_{y,10}$, is the annualized growth rate over the 10 years from time period $t - 10$ to time period t. Annualized means that it is the growth rate that would have to hold in each of those 10 years to match real GDP per capita level y_t given that we started at y_{t-10}. Hence it is something like the average growth rate of real GDP per capita across those 10 years.

In math, $g_{y,10}$ is defined as

$$\left(1 + g_{y,10}\right)^{10} = \frac{y_t}{y_{t-10}}. \tag{A.3}$$

In practical terms, I take natural logs of the prior equation and solve for

$$g_{y,10} \approx \frac{\ln y_t - \ln y_{t-10}}{10}, \tag{A.4}$$

where the approximation holds because $\ln(1 + g_{y,10}) \approx g_{y,10}$. This approximation is quite accurate when the growth rate is very close to 0, and as we are generally dealing with growth rates on the order of 1%–3%, that is the case here.

I used the term *average* growth rate, which isn't precisely right. But again, because all the yearly growth rates are small and close to 0, it is the case that $g_{y,10}$ is very close to the arithmetic average of the 10 yearly growth rates that hold from time $t - 10$ to time t. If you prefer to think about 10-year average growth rates as a simple average, you will not be making any major mistakes.

The financial crisis and recession play a role in the lower average growth rate during the twenty-first century. However, if you look just at the average of the growth rates in the twentieth century versus the twenty-first, but exclude 2008 and 2009, you still see the growth slowdown. That is, during the twentieth century, the average of yearly growth rates was about 2.4%. The average for 2000 to 2016, excluding 2008 and 2009, was 1.4%.

At the end of the chapter, I calculated the possible path of real GDP per capita. Start with y_{2000}, which is real GDP per capita in 2000 relative to real GDP per capita in 2009. Then, for each value of $t = 1$ through $t = 16$ (i.e., for 2001 through 2016), calculate

$$y_{2000+t} = y_{2000}(1 + 0.022)^t, \tag{A.5}$$

where 0.022 is the average growth rate that held from 1960 to 2000. This gives values for y_{2001} through y_{2016}, which are possible values for real GDP per capita in those years relative to actual GDP per capita in 2009.

The Meaning of Real GDP per Capita

I spent some time in the chapter making a few points about what counts as part of real GDP per capita and what does not. To get a better sense of what exactly is involved, I'd recommend Coyle (2015).

Understanding how real GDP is calculated is worth laying out, even if it does get to be a little tedious. The problem we have here is that not only are the real amounts of goods and services changing over time (which we want to measure), but their nominal prices are changing over time (which we do not). So we have to somehow remove the effect of general price inflation from our measures. Further, because there is no actual "unit" for real output, the best we can do is calculate real GDP in one year relative to another year.

Set things up this way. Let's assume there are two products, goods and services, a distinction that comes up a lot in the book. What we observe in a year t is nominal GDP, $P_G^t Y_G^t + P_S^t Y_S^t$, where P_G^t is the nominal price of "a good" in year t, and Y_G^t is the real quantity of goods we consume in year t. The terms with the S subscript are defined similarly for services. We also know nominal GDP in year b, the base year that the BEA chooses (currently 2009). Thus we know $P_G^b Y_G^b + P_S^b Y_S^b$.

The BEA also collects information on prices, so one way to compare real GDP in year t to the base year b is to calculate

$$\left(\frac{Y^t}{Y^b}\right)_A = \frac{P_G^t Y_G^t + P_S^t Y_S^t}{P_G^t Y_G^b + P_S^t Y_S^b}, \tag{A.6}$$

which compares the real amounts produced in year t to year b but uses the same prices. This ratio gives us a sense of the change in real GDP, because there is by definition no change in the prices involved. If $Y^t/Y^b > 1$, then we know real GDP went up, meaning that we had more real products in year t. This doesn't mean we had more of both goods and services, as perhaps we produced fewer goods and more services in year t, but the relative price of services is higher than that of goods; that is, they are considered more valuable than goods. Don't confuse this statement about relative prices with a statement about inflation. If $P_S^t > P_G^t$, this indicates only that we find services more valuable than goods. Regardless, if we find that $Y^t/Y^b > 1$, real GDP was higher in period t than in the base period.

But that's not the only way to compute this ratio. It would also make as much sense to do this:

$$\left(\frac{Y^t}{Y^b}\right)_B = \frac{P_G^b Y_G^t + P_S^b Y_S^t}{P_G^b Y_G^b + P_S^b Y_S^b}, \tag{A.7}$$

which does the same thing as above, but the prices used are from the *base* period, not period *t*. Again, if $Y^t/Y^b > 1$, this would indicate that real GDP went up. But because the relative value of goods and services could be different in *b* and *t*, it isn't the case that the first ratio we calculated is the same as the second. How different they are depends on how different the relative prices are in *b* and *t*.

This is a manifestation of the fact that there is no "right" way to measure real value. Either period *b* or period *t* could be used to compare goods to services, but neither is definitively correct. To account for this, the BEA tries to average the two ratios we calculated, *A* and *B*. But you cannot just average two ratios, so we need what is called the geometric average.

Here's the issue. If the *A* ratio were 2, indicating that real GDP doubled, but the *B* ratio were 0.5, indicating that real GDP halved, how should we compare those? We want to take both equally seriously. The "in-between" value of these ratios is really 1 (the doubling offsets the halving), whereas the naive average of the two ratios would be 1.25, suggesting that real GDP rose. The geometric average calculates the right in-between value as follows:

$$\left(\frac{Y^t}{Y^b}\right)_{Final} = \sqrt{\left(\frac{Y^t}{Y^b}\right)_A \left(\frac{Y^t}{Y^b}\right)_B}. \tag{A.8}$$

Yes, there is a square root involved here, but don't let that throw you off. All we're doing is trying to average two ratios. This *Final* ratio is the geometric average, and it gives us an indication of whether real GDP in year *t* is higher (the ratio is greater than 1) or lower (the ratio is less than 1) than in year *b*.

Just to be thorough, and because real GDP is often reported in this manner, let's set real GDP in the base year to arbitrarily equal 100. Then real GDP in year *t* is just

$$Y^t = 100 \times \left(\frac{Y^t}{Y^b}\right)_{Final}. \tag{A.9}$$

3. The Inputs to Economic Growth

The calculations of the human and physical capital stocks are an important component of the accounting done in chapter 4. As part of the human capital calculations, I refer to returns to education and experience. See below for details on how those returns are used.

The returns to education are from Card (1999), with corroboration from Lemieux (2006). The latter also provides evidence for the returns to experience. The numbers I select differ from, but are roughly consistent with, work done at the aggregate or cross-country level as in Klenow and Rodriguez-Clare (1997) and Hall and Jones (1999).

Human Capital

Data on total employees age 16 and older is from the BLS (FRED), and total population is from the US Census (FRED). Hours worked per week are from the BLS (FRED). For the purposes of the calculations that follow, let the number of employees be denoted by E, and the population be indicated by N. Let hours worked per week be *hours*. These three series are all used as is, without any modification.

The difficult part of calculating the stock of human capital is accounting for the role of education and education. To account for the human capital from education, I use data from the Current Population Survey (CPS; https://www.census.gov/data/tables/time-series/demo/educational-attainment/cps-historical-time-series.html) on the number of people age 25 and older with different levels of education. There are six levels: 0–4 years, 5–8 years, 9–11 years, 12 years (high school graduates), 13–15 years, and 16-plus years (college graduates and above). For each of these six groups, I assume that all people in the group have a single value for the years of schooling, s, as I do not know the distribution within these groups. The assumed values are 3 years (for those with 0–4 years), 7 years (for those with 5–8 years), 10 years (for those with 9–11 years), 12 years (for high school graduates), 14 years (for those with 13–15 years), and 16 years (for those with 16-plus years).

Each of the six groups j thus has years of schooling s_j, and the amount of human capital coming from education for each individual in group j is

$$\ln h_j^{Educ} = 0.10 \times s_j, \tag{A.10}$$

which says that each additional year of schooling adds 10% to the stock of human capital of an individual. In addition, I also know the number of people in each of those six education groups, N_j^{Educ}. Therefore the stock of human capital per capita coming from education can be written as

$$h^{Educ} = \frac{\sum_{j=1}^{6} N_j^{Educ} h_j^{Educ}}{\sum_{j=1}^{6} N_j^{Educ}}. \tag{A.11}$$

The numerator measures the total stock of human capital, by multiplying human capital per person in each group j by the number of people in that group, and then summing up over all six groups. That total is divided by the summation of people, giving me the human capital *from education* per capita.

There is a similar calculation for experience. From the Organisation for Economic Co-operation and Development (OECD) I have data on the number of people in nine different groups by age: 20–24 years old, 25–29, 30–34, 35–39, 40–44, 45–49, 50–54, 55–59, and 60–64. For each of these groups j, I use the midpoint age and call that x_j. For example, for 40- to 44-year-olds, I set $x_j = 42$. To calculate the human capital from experience in a given group, I use

$$\ln h_j^{Exp} = 0.05 \times x_j - 0.0007 \times x_j^2, \tag{A.12}$$

where the negative coefficient on the squared term means that the return on experience declines as people age. Given N_j^{Exp} total people in an age group, the total human capital from experience over the nine age groups can be calculated as

$$h^{Exp} = \frac{\sum_{j=1}^{9} N_j^{Exp} h_j^{Exp}}{\sum_{j=1}^{9} N_j^{Exp}}, \tag{A.13}$$

which has a similar structure to what I used for education.

Given the values of h^{Educ} and h^{Exp}, the overall stock of human capital per capita, h, is calculated by

$$h = \frac{h^{Educ} \times h^{Exp} \times hours \times E}{N}. \tag{A.14}$$

Here, the numerator measures the total human capital stock employed in the economy. This is the product of human capital per person from education, human capital per person from experience, hours worked per week, and total number of workers. That total stock is divided by the entire population.

There is a lot packed into this calculation. What the numerator assumes is that the education characteristics (h^{Educ}) of each worker (E) are the same as the education characteristics of all people age 25 and older. It also assumes that the experience characteristics of each worker are the same as the experience characteristics of all people age 20–64. These assumptions are not precisely right, of course. The actual people working, who make up the total E, are likely to have different characteristics from those populations. For example, people with more education are more likely to be employed, and some workers are younger than 25, or even younger than 20. And while my calculation of h is off in this sense, in practical terms the effect of this on the ultimate calculation of the importance of human capital in the growth slowdown will be small. What chapter 5 shows is that the dominant reason that h grew more slowly in the twenty-first century is that the ratio of E to N was falling. The change in growth rates of h^{Educ} and h^{Exp} are relatively unimportant.

Related to this point are the specific assumptions going into the calculation of h^{Educ} and h^{Exp}. My calculations make the implicit assumption that one can separate these two components of human capital from each other. That is, I did not allow the effect of education to depend on age or experience; nor did I allow the effect of experience to depend on education. It is likely true that in this latter case, the returns to experience are higher for those with more education (see Card 1999). Using the CPS data, which gives some crude information on age groups as well as educational attainment, I have done some calculations allowing the returns to experience to vary by education level and taking into account the differences in experience implied by the years spent in school (i.e., a 25-year-old who attended college has less possible work experience than someone who finished only high school). In no case did this alter the ultimate calculation of how important human capital was to the growth slowdown.

In a similar vein, the exact coefficients used to value human capital from education and experience are not crucial to the story in the book. I chose the value of 0.10 for the return to a year of experience because this appears to be something approaching the median estimate found in the literature (see Card 1999). I could adopt a higher (0.13) or lower return (0.08) and achieve similar results. I could also adopt a more refined relationship of years of schooling to human capital, assuming a higher return for earlier years of education, as is done in several cross-country studies (Klenow and Rodriguez-Clare 1997; Hall and Jones 1999), but this does not change the results.

The same obtains with respect to experience. The values I chose for the parameters, 0.05 and −0.0007, seemed to me a reasonable estimate given US evidence (see Lemieux 2006). In practice, my simple quadratic equation does not fit the data as well as a more complicated function (i.e., a quartic polynomial in x_j). My quadratic creates more variation in the human capital from experience over time than I would get using the quartic, and so probably overstates the role of experience. However, given that experience still plays a small role, this overstatement is not driving any of my conclusions.

Physical Capital

For the physical capital series, I draw from the BEA Fixed Asset tables, specifically table 2.1 (current cost of capital by type) and table 2.2 (quantity index of capital by type). The four types shown—residential structures, business structures, equipment, and intellectual property—make up the total private assets reported. This excludes public assets, which are mainly government structures. For each private asset type, I calculate its share of the total current cost of private assets in 2009. I then multiply the quantity index of the private asset type in each year by this share of current costs in 2009, giving me a way to plot the quantity of the private asset type relative to the total private asset stock in 2009.

I take the total capital stock from the BEA Fixed Asset tables, table 1.2, line 2 ("Fixed Assets"). This total capital stock is, as described in the text, a cumulated stock of the real spending on capital in the United States over time, with an allowance for depreciation. To be somewhat pedantic about things, I calculate physical capital per capita according to

$$k = \frac{K}{N} \tag{A.15}$$

in any given year, where K is the total capital stock, and N is the population taken from the US Census (FRED).

The total capital stock is not the only way to measure the capital used in production. In many cases, including the BLS's own calculations of multifactor productivity, the flow of capital services is imputed. This may arguably be a better measure of how capital is used, but I have avoided using it here. The first reason is that using the stock of capital is more straightforward, given that the imputation of capital services requires additional assumptions and data on things like rental rates, and one of my goals is to keep the analysis in this book accessible to a wider audience. The second reason is that if one did use the flow of capital services, the implied drop in growth rate of capital per capita would be less dramatic. This in turn would make the role of capital in the growth slowdown even less relevant than I find using the stock of capital. Using the capital services flow would thus not change anything material in the analysis here.

4. What Accounts for the Growth Slowdown?

The numbers that underlie the thesis of the book are calculated in this chapter. The details of this are described below. First, I offer several citations of work that either is referenced in the text or is used as the basis for my calculations.

The idea of calculating residual growth goes back to Tinbergen (1942), although it became widespread after the work in Solow (1957). A summary of the issues with calculating productivity growth can be found in Stiroh and Jorgenson (2000). A fuller discussion is in Jorgenson, Gollop, and Fraumeni (1987). The same kind of accounting has been used to account for growth across countries, as in Klenow and Rodriguez-Clare (1997).

Solow's residual calculations used labor costs as a share of total output, which was shown later to be a possible problem unless very strict conditions held. This was first made clear in Hall (1988, 1989).

The idea of adjusting the accounting to allow for the fact that capital is itself produced using GDP can be found in Klenow and Rodriguez-Clare (1997) and Hall and Jones (1999).

Finally, I mentioned that accounting for real GDP per capita is different from accounting for real GDP per worker. See Fernald and Jones (2014) or Fernald (2014) for an example. Perhaps the most thorough examination of this is in Fernald et al. (2017). Much of this relies on adjustments for utilization based on work by Kimball, Fernald, and Basu (2006).

Weights for Physical and Human Capital

I said in the main text that we could infer the elasticity of real GDP per capita with respect to physical capital per capita from the share of physical capital in total input costs. This follows from a simple problem of cost minimization by firms, combined with an assumption that production is constant returns to scale.

Consider a typical firm. Give it a production function of $Q = F(K, H)$, meaning that the output it produces, Q, is a function $F(\cdot, \cdot)$ of two types of inputs: physical capital, K, and human capital, H. Assume that each unit of capital costs the firm r to hire, and each unit of human capital costs the firm w.

Given some level of $\overline{Q}$ that the firm would like to produce, what are the cost-minimizing amounts of K and H to hire? To start, think of the marginal product of capital, $F_K(K, H)$, the derivative of the production function with respect to K. The ratio r/F_K is the dollar cost of raising output by one unit using physical capital. Similarly, the ratio w/F_H is the dollar cost of raising output by one unit using human capital. Intuitively, the firm should hire H and K until the two ratios are equal. If they were not equal, then the firm could lower costs by using less of the input with the higher dollar cost and more of the input with the lower dollar cost, all while keeping output the same. The marginal cost, MC, of production is equal to the ratios r/F_K and w/F_H when they are equalized, or

$$MC = \frac{r}{F_K} = \frac{w}{F_H}. \tag{A.16}$$

Working with the first equality in the above equation, we could rearrange it, multiply both sides by K, and divide both sides by $F(K, H)$:

$$\frac{F_K K}{F(K,H)} = \frac{rK}{MC \times F(K,H)}. \tag{A.17}$$

On the left is the elasticity of the production function with respect to K. On the right is the cost of capital, rK, divided by $MC \times F(K, H)$, marginal cost times total output. If we assume that the production function is constant returns to scale, then $MC \times F(K, H)$ is the total cost of inputs used. And that means the right-hand side of the equation is the ratio of capital costs to total costs.

Why is $MC \times F(K, H)$ equal to total costs when we have constant returns to scale? With constant returns to scale, it has to be that $1 = F_K K/F(K, H) + F_H H/F(K, H)$, or that the elasticities of real GDP with respect to physical and human capital have to add up to 1. If you raise both inputs by 10%, you'll get 10% more output, for example. Multiply both sides of this by $F(K, H)$, and use the $MC = r/F_K = w/F_H$ relationships from above, and you can write $F(K, H) = rK/MC + wH/MC$. This means that

$$MC \times F(K,H) = rK + wH, \tag{A.18}$$

which is just the total cost of production. Hence we have that the elasticity of real GDP with respect to K is equal to $rK/(rK + wH)$, and we'd get a similar statement for the elasticity of real GDP with respect to human capital and $wH/(rK + wH)$.

This cost-minimization problem gives us the ability to infer the size of the elasticity from cost data. I made no assumption about whether the firm here is maximizing its profits or has any kind of market power. The data used in the chapter shows that physical capital's share of costs is roughly 0.35 across time, and so I assume that the physical capital elasticity is also 0.35.

There are several ways my analysis could go wrong, in the sense that the capital elasticity may not be 0.35 even though the cost share of capital is 0.35. Most obvious is that the economy may not be operating to minimize costs. Perhaps firms have different goals (e.g., they may be public institutions), or feel some kind of social or political pressure to not minimize costs, or are just not very good at what they do. A related issue is that I showed the problem of cost minimization for one firm. If different firms have different cost shares and elasticities, then does it make sense to talk about a single aggregate cost share and elasticity?

It is impossible for me (or any economist) to provide evidence that 0.35 is *the* right answer for the elasticity of real GDP with respect to physical capital (or 0.65 for human capital). It is impossible for me (or any economist) to prove to you that it even makes sense to think about an aggregate elasticity in the first place. But doing analysis of an aggregate phenomenon like the growth slowdown requires making some assumptions about how the economy works. The fact that we can infer an aggregate elasticity from an aggregate cost share requires the least restrictive assumption—cost minimization—that we can introduce and still make headway at the aggregate level.

Running the Numbers

Let the growth rate of real GDP per capita be g_y. Given the elasticities for physical and human capital, the growth in real GDP per capita accounted for by just by growth in those two inputs, g_y^{Cap}, would be

$$g_y^{Cap} = \epsilon_K g_k + \epsilon_H g_h, \tag{A.19}$$

where ϵ_K and ϵ_H are the elasticities for physical and human capital, respectively, and g_k and g_h are the growth rates of physical capital per capita and human capital per capita, respectively.

Residual growth, g_y^{Res}, is the difference between actual growth, g_y, and growth accounted for by the two inputs, so

$$g_y^{Res} = g_y - g_y^{Cap} = g_y - \epsilon_K g_k - \epsilon_H g_h. \tag{A.20}$$

Given data on the actual growth rate, g_y, the growth rates of the two inputs, and the elasticities, calculating the growth rate of the residual is straightforward.

In table 4.1 in the main text, I use $\epsilon_K g_k$ to measure the contribution of physical capital. The growth rate g_K is the annualized growth rate of capital per capita for the given time period in the table. $\epsilon_H g_h$ measures the contribution of human capital per capita in a similar manner. The residual growth is calculated using the prior equation shown here.

Physical Capital Matters Less Than It Seems

I described in the text how we may be attributing too much to physical capital, as it depends itself on the growth rate of real GDP per capita. If real GDP per capita grows by 5%, for example, then we would expect that physical capital per capita would grow by 5% as well, holding our saving and investment behavior constant. So we don't want to attribute that 5% growth in real GDP per capita to the 5% growth in physical capital per capita. We should say that physical capital per capita contributes to growth only if it is growing faster than real GDP per capita, and detracts from growth only if it is growing slower than real GDP per capita.

To put this into mathematical terms, rearrange the equation for the residual to the following:

$$g_y = g_y^{Res} + \epsilon_K g_k + \epsilon_H g_h, \tag{A.21}$$

which just says that growth in real GDP per capita depends on residual, physical capital, and human capital growth. Now, we want to compare growth in physical capital to growth in real GDP per capita, so make the following subtraction on both sides:

$$g_y - \epsilon_K g_y = g_y^{Res} + \epsilon_K g_k - \epsilon_K g_y + \epsilon_H g_h, \tag{A.22}$$

which can now be manipulated to

$$g_y = \frac{g_y^{Res}}{1 - \epsilon_K} + \frac{\epsilon_K}{1 - \epsilon_K}(g_k - g_y) + g_h, \tag{A.23}$$

where the assumption of constant returns to scale means that $\epsilon_H = 1 - \epsilon_K$, and so the elasticity on g_h has disappeared.

What this tells us is that growth in real GDP per capita can be accounted for by, first, growth in human capital. This now has a larger elasticity equal to 1, allowing for both the direct effect of human capital and the additional effect of human capital on our ability to accumulate physical capital. The second component is the relative growth of physical capital to real GDP per capita, $g_k - g_y$, and this is scaled by $\epsilon_K/(1 - \epsilon_K)$. Finally, the term $g_y^{Res}/(1 - \epsilon_K)$. Note that this is our old value for residual growth but scaled up ($1 - \epsilon_K$ is a fraction) for the same reason that human capital was more important. Any residual growth has a direct effect on real GDP per capita and allows us to accumulate more physical capital.

In table 4.2, the physical capital column is therefore the term $\epsilon_K/(1 - \epsilon_K)(g_k - g_y)$. The human capital column is g_h. You can find the residual column as either $g_y^{Res}/(1 - \epsilon_K)$ using the residual numbers from table 4.1 or directly from $g_y - g_h - \epsilon_K/(1 - \epsilon_K)(g_k - g_y)$.

Beware of False Accuracy

I mentioned in the text that other economists account for the growth slowdown by looking at real GDP per worker as opposed to per capita.

To do things per worker, start by defining real GDP per worker as y^{Work}. Let physical capital per worker be

$$k^{Work} = \frac{K}{E},\qquad\qquad\qquad\qquad\qquad\text{(A.24)}$$

where E is the number of workers and K is as defined in chapter 3. The human capital stock per worker is now

$$h^{Work} = h^{Educ} \times h^{Exp} \times hours,\qquad\qquad\qquad\text{(A.25)}$$

where the three terms involved are all defined the same as in chapter 3. Residual growth in this case would be

$$g_y^{Res,Work} = g_y^{Work} - \epsilon_K g_k^{Work} - \epsilon_H g_h^{Work},\qquad\qquad\text{(A.26)}$$

and we could adjust this to account for the fact that physical capital depends on real GDP just as before.

Table A.1 shows the basic accounting per worker. The growth slowdown is evident, as the average growth rate from 1950 to 2000 was 1.80%, which fell to 1.35% in the twenty-first century. A small portion of this was due to a decline in the growth rate of physical capital per worker (from 0.49% to 0.39% per year) and a portion to a decline in the growth rate of human capital per worker (from 0.33% to 0.13% per year). Finally, residual growth fell from 0.98% per year to 0.82% per year. Compared to doing the accounting in per capita terms, the role of human capital is somewhat smaller.

Also as noted in the main text, these precise numbers would change under different assumptions about the exact nature of human capital. One particular set of different numbers is used in Fernald and Jones (2014). Their index of the amount of human capital per worker—meaning effects of experience, education, and sex—is drawn from Jorgenson, Ho, and Samuels (2013). To be clear, human capital per capita is calculated from

$$h = \frac{h^{FJ} \times hours \times E}{N},\qquad\qquad\qquad\text{(A.27)}$$

where h^{FJ} is the index from Fernald and Jones.

Table A.2 shows the results of doing the accounting using this alternative series for human capital. The index goes only through 2010, and to avoid muddying things with the financial crisis, I show the results for 2000–2007 only. What shows up is that the swing in the growth rate of human capital is not quite as large as in my original analysis, although that was based on 2000–2016, so if the Fernald and Jones numbers were extended it might look more similar. The relatively large effect of human capital, though, remains clear. The drop in the growth rate of productivity is similar to my original analysis.

5. The Effect of an Aging Population

The data on age structure and dependency ratios is from the OECD population database (https://stats.oecd.org/Index.aspx?DataSetCode=POP_PROJ).

Table A.1 Accounting for growth of real GDP per worker, by time period

Time period	Growth rate (%)			
	GDP per worker	Physical capital per worker	Human capital per worker	Residual
1950–2000	1.80	0.49	0.33	0.98
1950–1960	2.41	0.88	0.46	1.07
1960–1970	2.38	0.70	0.27	1.41
1970–1980	0.44	0.10	0.01	0.33
1980–1990	1.62	0.33	0.36	0.93
1990–2000	2.16	0.42	0.57	1.18
2000–2016	1.35	0.39	0.13	0.82
2006–2016	1.14	0.32	0.18	0.64

Note: The table shows the breakdown of actual growth in real GDP per worker (column 1) into the contribution from physical capital (column 2), human capital (column 3), and residual growth (column 4). The contributions of physical and human capital are calculated from their actual annualized growth rate over the given period of time, multiplied by their associated elasticity (0.35 for physical capital and 0.65 for human capital). The residual is simply the growth rate of real GDP per capita minus the listed contributions of physical and human capital. Because of rounding, columns 2–4 may not add up precisely to column 1. Each row of the table shows the same kind of accounting but limited to a given time period.

The data on fertility rates is from Our World in Data (downloaded from https://ourworldindata.org/fertility-rate). The figures in the chapter are all based on this raw data, without any additional calculations done by me.

Evidence on the relative importance of aging and the recent recession on participation in the labor force is from Eppsteiner, Furman, and Powell (2017). State-level evidence is from Maestas, Mullen, and Powell (2016).

Becker (1960) is the source for the logic behind living standards and family size. Evidence on the relationship of income and fertility over time in the US is from Jones and Tertilt (2008). They focus on completed fertility (children ever born), meaning the youngest cohort that they examine was born in 1958 (women

APPENDIX

Table A.2 Accounting for growth of real GDP per worker, alternative human capital

		Growth rate (%)		
Time period	GDP per worker	Physical capital per worker	Human capital per worker	Residual
1950–2000	2.25	–0.22	0.61	1.86
1950–1960	1.78	0.05	–0.09	1.82
1960–1970	2.92	–0.21	0.49	2.64
1970–1980	2.07	–0.08	1.19	0.96
1980–1990	2.32	–0.37	1.06	1.63
1990–2000	2.17	–0.52	0.43	2.26
2000–2007	1.54	–0.07	0.11	1.50

Note: The table shows the breakdown of actual growth in real GDP per worker (column 1) into the contribution from physical capital (column 2), human capital (column 3), and residual growth (column 4). The measure of human capital is built from estimates in Fernald and Jones (2014) rather than the original data I used for the book. The contributions of physical and human capital are calculated from their actual annualized growth rate over the given period of time, multiplied by their associated elasticity (0.35 for physical capital and 0.65 for human capital). The residual is simply the growth rate of real GDP per capita minus the listed contributions of physical and human capital. Because of rounding, columns 2–4 may not add up precisely to column 1. Each row of the table shows the same kind of accounting but limited to a given time period.

age 60 in 2018). By using children ever born, they ensure that they are not basing their analysis on changes in the timing of births during a woman's lifetime. Across countries, the data is from Chatterjee and Vogl (2018), who find that long-run increases in economic growth are associated with lower fertility, as well as delayed fertility, in all settings. For evidence and theory on the role of household technologies in marriage and labor force participation by women, see the review in Greenwood, Guner, and Vandenbroucke (2017). Two of the relevant papers in this area are Greenwood, Seshadri, and Yorukoglu (2005) and Greenwood, Seshadri, and Vandenbroucke (2005).

Evidence that the birth-control pill had a causal effect on first births before age 22, workforce participation, and increased work hours is from Bailey (2006). She uses variation in when states legalized the pill and tracks how these measures differed between states that had legalized and those that had not. One worry about this analysis was that it reflected not just access to the pill but other unobserved differences in states. To address that, in a second paper she used changes in laws associated with the legalization of the pill to show that it was in fact access to the pill that lowered marital fertility rates; see Bailey (2010). Goldin and Katz (2002) document that a similar change in contraceptive laws that gave unmarried young women access to the pill caused an increase in their entry to professions that required longer time periods in school, as well as raising their age at marriage.

Evidence cited on graduation rates is from Murnane (2013). Historical graduation rate information is from Goldin (2001) and Goldin and Katz (2007). This last paper contains source material from a book by the same authors, Goldin and Katz (2008).

Accounting for the Slowdown in Human Capital Growth

To do the accounting for human capital growth, I started with equation (A.14) from chapter 3, reproduced here:

$$h = \frac{h^{Educ} \times h^{Exp} \times hours \times E}{N}. \tag{A.28}$$

Taking growth rates of both sides, this implies that

$$g_h = g_{Educ} + g_{Exp} + g_{hours} + g_{E/N}. \tag{A.29}$$

The data in table 5.1 thus shows the elements of this equation, calculated over different time periods. For references on the sources of this data, see the notes on chapter 3 in this appendix.

The Preference for Smaller Families

There are two basic assumptions to Becker's theory of family size. First, parents get utility from both consuming (c) and having kids (n). Second, kids cost parents time. The most obvious way this might manifest is in one parent staying home and not working for wages while he or she cares for the kids. The problem Becker considered was thus asking parents to maximize a utility function $U = U(c, n)$ subject to a constraint that $w = c + w\tau n$, where w is the income they earn per unit of time, and τ is the time cost of each child. The value $w\tau$ is thus the cost of raising a child, in the sense that it reduces the amount of consumption that can be done. The cost of consumption is 1, in that \$1 of consumption requires \$1 of income. As in a standard problem of optimal choice, maximizing utility involves setting the ratio of marginal utilities equal to the ratio of marginal costs:

$$\frac{U_n}{U_c} = \frac{w\tau}{1}. \tag{A.30}$$

If w increases, then this implies that the marginal utility of kids must rise relative to the marginal utility of consumption. The marginal utility of children is higher the fewer there are (remember, this doesn't say anything about average utility, or whether parents care more or less about individual kids), so the family will shift toward fewer kids relative to consumption. There are a host of bells and whistles that one can add to this basic structure, but so long as children require some time commitment, the essential intuition will hold.

6. The Difference between Productivity and Technology

There are several recent books that discuss the possibility that slower technological change contributed to the growth slowdown. Gordon (2016) documents that productivity growth declined in the latter half of the twentieth century and into the twenty-first. His work is consistent with the calculations in this book on productivity growth, although I think he draws conclusions in that book about technological growth that are not necessarily backed up by the data. In a follow-up paper, Gordon (2018), there is a clearer discussion of the distinction between technology and productivity. There is a mix of technology and productivity at a few places in Cowen (2011). From the other side, a lot of time is spent arguing that technological advances will raise productivity growth despite their tenuous connection; see Brynjolfsson and McAfee (2011), as well as Brynjolfsson and McAfee (2014). I think their claim would be stronger if they argued that technologies would improve well-being even if they had no effect on measured productivity growth.

In terms of the measurement issues, the relevant articles are Feldstein (2017) and Syverson (2017). An additional paper that supports Syverson's position but is a bit more technical is Byrne, Fernald, and Reinsdorf (2016). Moulton (2018) details some of the history of the BEA's trying to deal with the quality adjustment issue.

The evidence on technologies becoming harder to find is from Bloom et al. (2017). The earlier papers with a similar set of aggregate evidence are C. I. Jones (1995a, 1995b).

The data on research workers over time is taken from https://stats.oecd.org /Index.aspx?DataSetCode=MSTI_PUB#. That data was downloaded directly by me and put into a spreadsheet available on the website for the book.

7. The Reallocation from Goods to Services

The industry-level KLEMS data used in all the analysis in this chapter is from http://www.euklems.net and uses the spreadsheets "US_output_17i.xlsx" and "US_capital_17i.xlsx." The BEA also hosts KLEMS data for the United States. The KLEMS data comes with breakdown into industries and subindustries. I use the main industries, denoted by the alphabetic codes (e.g., A, B). I exclude industry T (activities of households as employers) and U (activities of extraterritorial organizations and bodies). Code M-N is a combination for professional, scientific, technical, administrative, and support services, and R-S is a combination for arts, entertainment, recreation, and other services. O-U is the code for community and personal services, but I separate that into O (public administration), P (education), and Q (health and social work).

The Effect on Aggregate Productivity Growth

To calculate aggregate productivity growth from year $t-1$ to year t, the formula is

$$g_{Prod,t,t-1} = \sum_{i=1}^{17} \frac{VA_{i,t-1}}{GDP_{t-1}} g_{Prod,i,t}, \qquad (A.31)$$

where $g_{Prod,i,t}$ is the productivity growth rate for industry i from $t-1$ to t. $VA_{i,t-1}/GDP_{t-1}$ is the value-added share of industry i in GDP from time $t-1$. Productivity growth in a given year is thus a product of the weights (the value-added shares) and the individual growth rates of productivity.

The annualized growth rate of aggregate productivity from 2000 to 2015 is

$$g_{Prod,2015,2000} = \left(\prod_{t=2001}^{2015} \left(1 + g_{Prod,t,t-1} \right) \right)^{(1/15)} - 1, \qquad (A.32)$$

which simply rolls up the growth rates of productivity over the individual years from 2000 to 2015. This aggregate productivity growth term captures the effects of changes in the value-added shares of industries, because the individual year productivity growth rate terms are used.

As noted in the text, the productivity growth rate found using KLEMS for 2000 to 2015 does not match the productivity growth rate I calculated using aggregate data for 2000 to 2016. KLEMS differs from my calculations in using measures of labor and capital compensation to measure the flow of input services used, whereas I used stocks of human capital and physical capital. KLEMS also allows the elasticity of output with respect to physical capital and labor to vary by industry, whereas my aggregate calculation assumes a single elasticity. As noted in the text, this all results in my estimate of a larger growth rate of productivity in absolute terms.

One other note is that I am using the value-added TFP (total factor productivity) growth for each industry from KLEMS. This first calculates value-added (gross output minus intermediate input use) growth and then subtracts input growth to find productivity growth. For value-added TFP growth, the proper weights are value-added shares of GDP. An alternative would be to use gross-output TFP growth. This takes gross-output growth and subtracts input growth to find productivity growth. In this case the proper weights are "Domar weights," after Domar (1961), which are gross output relative to GDP. Note that Domar weights will add up to more than 1, as the productivity growth of an industry that provides intermediates to many others will create higher aggregate productivity growth. See Jorgenson and Stiroh (2000) for a short discussion of the difference.

The Effect of Reallocation on Productivity Growth

The counterfactual calculations alter the above math in one main way. The yearly productivity growth term is now

$$g^{CF}_{Prod,t,t-1} = \sum_{i=1}^{17} \frac{VA_{i,2000}}{GDP_{2000}} g_{Prod,i,t},$$ (A.33)

so that the weights are held constant at the year 2000 weights. For the calculations using 1990 or 1980 weights, simply substitute those weights in. Then the calculation of a counterfactual aggregate growth rate takes place exactly as described above, rolling up the individual year growth rates.

The Shift toward Services

The value-added share of an industry is a combination of its prices and its real value-added output relative to GDP. To be more concrete, the value-added shares are defined as

$$\frac{VA_i}{GDP} = \frac{P_i \, VA_i^Q}{\sum_{j=1}^{17} P_j \, VA_j^Q},$$ (A.34)

where P_i is the price index for production of industry i, and VA_i^Q is the real value-added of industry i. From this, you can see that the value-added share of industry i in GDP could go up or down depending on changes in price or in real value-added. But because GDP itself is just the sum of value-added across all seventeen industries, the value-added share of industry i depends on changes in price or real value-added relative to the changes in all industries. Hence both price and value-added can rise, as in manufacturing, but the share of GDP can fall because other prices and value-addeds are rising.

8. Baumol's Cost Disease

The articles I cited from Baumol are Baumol and Bowen (1965) and Baumol (1967). A recent book, Baumol (2012), offers a very nice introduction to his larger argument.

For an alternative story on the rise in health-care spending in particular, see Hall and Jones (2007). They propose that health-care spending rises as a proportion of income because as we get richer, extending our life span to enjoy a high consumption level is more valuable than increasing our consumption for a limited life span. Their theory doesn't necessarily explain the rise in the relative price of health care, however, as in Baumol's story.

The data on price levels for different types of products comes from BEA table 2.4.4, and I downloaded that directly. Data on the expenditures on services, durable goods, and nondurables comes from BEA table 2.3.5 (FRED).

The Cost Disease

If you care to see the formal logic behind Baumol's cost disease, consider the following setup. For goods, the production function is $Y_G = A_G L_G$, where A_G is the productivity of a worker, and L_G is the number of workers. For services, let $Y_S = A_S L_S$, with similar definitions.

In each industry, assume that firms are minimizing their costs and set the value of the marginal product of a worker equal to the wage rate, w. For goods, this means that $w_G = P_G A_G$, where P_G is the price for goods, and so $P_G A_G$ is the value (because we use the price) of the marginal product of a worker (A_G is the additional output from one additional worker). For services, the same idea holds, so $w_S = P_S A_S$.

If workers can move between the two industries freely, then the wage in the two industries will equalize, because if there were a difference, workers would flow from the low-wage to the high-wage industry. You can even allow that there is some fixed wedge between the two wages; it won't change Baumol's story. Setting the wages equal and rearranging we get

$$\frac{P_S}{P_G} = \frac{A_G}{A_S}. \tag{A.35}$$

On the left is the relative price of services to goods. On the right is the inverse of the relative productivity of services to goods, because when an industry gets more productive its relative price declines.

In growth rates

$$g_P^S - g_P^G = g_A^G - g_A^S, \tag{A.36}$$

where g_P^S is the growth rate of the price (P) of services (S), and the other terms all have similar definitions. Take Baumol's characterization of productivity growth differences seriously, meaning that $g_A^G > g_A^S$, or productivity in goods production is higher than in services. This then implies that $g_P^S > g_P^G$, or that service prices grow faster than goods prices.

To see what drives the shift into services despite their rapid price growth, we have to think about preferences of people. You could write down a utility function to arrive at the following, but I believe the following condition is fairly intuitive by itself:

$$\frac{C_G}{C_S} = \left(\frac{P_S}{P_G}\right)^{\sigma},$$

$$(A.37)$$

which says that the relative real consumption of goods to services (C_G/C_S) depends on the ratio of their prices. The value of σ, which is bigger than 0, is the elasticity of substitution between goods and services. It tells us how sensitive the ratio of real consumption is to the ratio of prices. The larger σ is, the more sensitive people are to the relative price, whereas the closer to 0 σ is, the less sensitive they are. But no matter how big σ may be, note that if the relative price of goods falls (P_S/P_G goes down), the ratio of goods consumption to service consumption rises.

Now, the amount consumed of both of these must come from somewhere, and it is produced by the industries, so $C_G = Y_G$ and $C_S = Y_S$. That, and multiplying both sides of the above equation by P_G/P_S gives us

$$\frac{P_G Y_G}{P_S Y_S} = \left(\frac{P_S}{P_G}\right)^{\sigma - 1}.$$

$$(A.38)$$

On the left is the relative amount of expenditure on goods compared to services, which is what we were looking at in the data. On the right is again the relative price of services to goods, but note that the exponent is now $\sigma - 1$, not σ.

From above, we established that the relative price of services went up over time because productivity grew faster in goods. With P_S/P_G rising, what happens to the expenditure on goods relative to services? If σ is less than 1, then the exponent is negative, and when P_S/P_G goes up, $P_G Y_G/P_S Y_S$ falls. If σ is less than 1 it means that the elasticity of substitution is less than 1, and that is the definition of complements.

When goods and services are complements, this means we are reluctant to change our real consumption behavior in response to prices. In turn, the expenditure share of goods falls even though goods get cheaper and cheaper. The increase in consumption of goods we do (C_G) is smaller in percentage terms than the percentage drop in the price of goods (P_G) that caused it. And so the total amount we spend on goods falls. By definition, that means that the amount we spend on services rises, even though services get more expensive.

The last thing to figure out is what happens to workers, and how many actual goods and services we get. Remember that $Y_G = A_G L_G$ and $Y_S = A_S L_S$. In addition, we saw that $P_G/P_S = A_S/A_G$. Put that in our last equation and after some cancelling we get

$$\frac{L_G}{L_S} = \left(\frac{P_S}{P_G}\right)^{\sigma - 1},$$

$$(A.39)$$

or that the ratio of workers in goods to services is also related to their relative price, the same way as expenditure is. When the service price goes up relative to goods, and $\sigma < 1$, then L_G falls relative to L_S. And given some fixed number of workers, that means that there are literally fewer goods workers, and more service workers.

More workers in services means that more services are produced. Even though productivity goes up slowly in services, we end up consuming more of them thanks to productivity growth in goods and our own unwillingness to substitute away from spending on services. In essence, we use the savings obtained from higher productivity in goods to buy more services.

For goods, total production goes up as well. Yes, L_G goes down, lowering output of goods, but A_G has gone up, raising output. Recall that when P_S/P_G rises, C_G/C_S rises as well. Although we use some of our savings from higher productivity growth in goods to buy more services, we also use those savings to buy more goods. We consume more of both products even when one has more rapid productivity growth than the other.

9. Market Power and Productivity

The basic calculation of economic profits—which I outline in detail here—is from Barkai (2017). The evidence on markups is taken from De Loecker and Eeckhout (2017). Additional evidence on markups and profits shares can be found in Gutiérrez and Philippon (2017), as well as Gutiérrez (2017). A possible methodological issue with measuring the average markup has to do with the weights on each firm, explained in Edmond, Midrigan, and Xu (2018). Despite this issue, those authors still find an increase in markups with effects on productivity similar to what is described in the text. Evidence that markups rose in other countries is in De Loecker and Eeckhout (2018) and Diez, Leigh, and Tambunlertchai (2018). For evidence that the rise in markups is not driven by a few megafirms, see Hall (2018).

The logic of the effect of market power on measured productivity comes first from Basu and Fernald (2002), and in particular from Baqaee and Farhi (2017). Both papers draw on some original insights from Hall (1988, 1989), which highlight the effect of markups on calculated productivity.

Measuring Market Power

To calculate economic profits, first note that gross value-added of a firm can be decomposed into four pieces:

$$VA = \text{Labor comp.} + \text{Production taxes} + \text{Capital payments} + \text{Economic profits}, \tag{A.40}$$

where *production taxes* are things like sales tax that are payable on the amount produced and that the firm has to remit back to the government. The problem mentioned in the chapter is that capital payments and economic profits are not reported separately but as *operating surplus*.

Following Barkai's work, if we make some assumptions about the required rental rate for capital, and we know the size of the capital stock firms use, then we can calculate an estimate of the capital payments and use them to back out the economic profits.

Barkai uses a technique dating back to a paper that makes some mild assumptions about how firms operate to back out what the authors called the "user cost of capital" (Hall and Jorgenson 1967). The upshot of their theory is that the real rate of return on capital, R, is

$$R = i - E[\pi] + \delta, \tag{A.41}$$

where i is the nominal interest rate that firms would face if they borrowed money, $E[\pi]$ is the expected inflation in the price of capital, and δ is the depreciation rate. The intuition of the three terms is straightforward. The higher i is, the more costly it is to borrow funds to buy capital (or the more costly it is to have funds locked up in physical capital), and hence the rate of return on capital must be higher. The higher the expected inflation in the price of capital is, the lower the rate of return necessary, as you can sell off the capital for more once you're done with it. The higher the depreciation rate is, the higher the required rate of return, as a greater proportion of your capital breaks down through use, leaving you with nothing.

To calculate R, I use data on the three pieces of information on the right-hand side. The nominal interest rate is the Moody's Aaa corporate bond rate (FRED). For expected inflation, I first calculate actual inflation in the price of capital goods. I use BEA data on historical cost (BEA table 2.3) and the quantity index (BEA table 2.2), divide, and get a price series. The growth rate of that price series is inflation in capital prices. As in Barkai, I then assume that expected inflation in a given year is equal to the actual inflation rate in capital prices. Unlike Barkai, I use the annualized growth rate of capital prices over the next 5 years, as opposed to 3 years. For example, the expected inflation rate of capital prices in 1980 is calculated as the annualized inflation rate of capital from 1980 to 1985. Finally, the depreciation rate I calculate using data on the reported consumption of fixed capital from BEA table 1.10 (FRED) divided by the historical cost of capital in the same year.

Given a calculated R, the total capital payments are $R \times K$, where K is the historical cost of capital from BEA table 2.3, "total labor compensation."

Finally, the share of economic profits is given by

$$s_{Profits} = 1 - \frac{RK + \text{Labor comp.}}{VA - \text{Prod. taxes}}. \tag{A.42}$$

Thus, economic profits are the fraction of gross value-added (minus the production taxes) that is not used to compensate capital or compensate labor. The fact that I do this as a fraction of gross value-added minus production taxes is not terribly relevant to the final number, as those taxes tend to be a small proportion of gross value-added.

The Paradox of Higher Markups and Productivity

To make sense of the idea that a shift into high-markup industries would be good for productivity growth, let's go back and think about how we value real GDP in the first place. In chapter 2, we were concerned with how to compare different years when the nominal prices differed. But here, we're interested in how to compare two different allocations across industries when the nominal prices are the same. So things are a bit more straightforward.

Similar to before, let's have two industries, goods and services. Let goods be produced using $Y_G = A_G L_G$ and services using $Y_S = A_S L_S$. The marginal cost of goods is thus $MC_G = 1/A_G$ and the marginal cost of services is $MC_S = 1/A_S$.

In addition, let us say that the markup of the goods price over marginal cost is $\mu_G = P_G/MC_G$ and the markup for services is $\mu_S = P_S/MC_S$. Finally, we're going to assume that services have a higher markup than goods, so that $\mu_S > \mu_G$.

The question is what happens to real output (and hence productivity) when we shift resources from producing goods (low markups) toward producing services (high markups). For our purposes, we don't care why this happens, we just want to see the implication for real output.

Let output, PY, be the sum of expenditure on goods, $P_G Y_G$, and services, $P_S Y_S$. Total expenditure is therefore $PY = P_G Y_G + P_S Y_S$. Now compare expenditure under a new allocation, PY^{New}, to expenditure under an old allocation, PY^{Old}. Note that the actual price level, P, is identical under the two allocations. This means we can write

$$\frac{Y^{New}}{Y^{Old}} = \frac{P_G Y_G^{New} + P_S Y_S^{New}}{P_G Y_G^{Old} + P_S Y_S^{Old}}, \tag{A.43}$$

where the fraction on the left is the ratio of real output under the new allocation to real output under the old allocation. On the right-hand side, you can see that this ratio might not be equal to 1 if the actual real amounts produced of the two goods are not the same.

As an aside, don't get confused by thinking that if we do shift labor or other inputs toward a high-markup industry, the price level P must be changing. P doesn't measure that. It measures only whether there is inflation in the prices of all goods and services. That is, P would change if both P_G and P_S rose, perhaps because the Fed printed more money and so the nominal amount that could be charged for both products increased. That's what we had to get rid of in chapter 2, so that we could compare real output over time. Here we don't have that issue.

If we fill in some things here, we can show that shifting the allocation toward a high-markup industry raises real output.

$$\frac{Y^{New}}{Y^{Old}} = \frac{\mu_G L_G^{New} + \mu_S L_S^{New}}{\mu_G L_G^{Old} + \mu_S L_S^{Old}}. \tag{A.44}$$

I got this by noting that $P_G = \mu_G MC_G$, which follows from the definition of the markup above. We then know that $MC_G = 1/A_G$, and that $Y_G^{New} = A_G L_G^{New}$. Thus $P_G Y_G^{New} = \mu_G/A_G \times A_G L_G^{New} = \mu_G L_G^{New}$. You can do the same process for each of the other terms.

From here, given that $\mu_S > \mu_G$, I think it is clear that if we reallocate labor toward services in the new allocation and away from goods, the ratio Y^{New}/Y^{Old} must be bigger than 1. That is, if $L_S^{New} > L_S^{Old}$, and $L_G^{New} < L_G^{Old}$, the numerator is larger than the denominator, because we are putting more weight on the high-value item—services—in the new allocation.

The key here is to remember that the markups measure the value of these products to us. Regardless of the reason for those markups—nefarious market power or the nature of our demand—pushing more inputs toward producing the high-markup items results in more real value. The economic pie gets bigger. Now, it may well be the case that the slice going toward the claimants on the economic profits of service firms grows by a lot, whereas the slice for workers or capital owners grows only a little, but it is true that the pie gets bigger.

10. Market Power and the Decline in Investment

The original work on investment rates that I draw on is from Gutiérrez and Philippon (2017). The data on investment rates and Q ratios is from the Federal Reserve (FRED). The net investment rates are simply reported absolute net investment divided by absolute operating surplus. The total net investment rate is found by taking the sum of absolute net investment for nonfinancial corporate and noncorporate businesses, and dividing that by the sum of absolute operating surplus of those same two groups.

For the Q ratio, the simple version is given by

$$Q^{Simple} = \frac{\text{Equities}}{\text{Nonfinancial assets}}, \tag{A.45}$$

while the complicated version is

$$Q^{Complex} = \frac{\text{Equities} + \text{Liabilities} - \text{Financial assets} - \text{Inventories}}{\text{Nonfinancial assets}}. \tag{A.46}$$

The figure on firm size is created using data from the US Census (https://www.census.gov/programs-surveys/susb/data/tables.html). I calculated the percentages using the reported numbers of firms in a given bin divided by the reported total number of firms.

11. The Necessity of Market Power

The two papers referenced as laying the groundwork for endogenous growth theory are Romer (1986, 1990). They built on the basic structure of the Solow (1956) model. Both of Romer's papers based growth on the idea of an expansion in the variety of goods produced. The origin of Schumpeterian endogenous growth theory, in which firms compete to replace one another in providing a given product, can be traced back to Aghion and Howitt (1992). For a paper that contains elements of both kinds of growth theory, see Grossman and Helpman (1991). A mathematical introduction to the whole span of growth theory can be found in Aghion and Howitt (2009).

The evidence on the U-shaped relationship of competition and innovation is from Aghion et al. (2005). For an expanded review of this evidence, see Aghion, Akcigit, and Howitt (2014) or Aghion and Griffith (2005).

Specific examples of laws and policies associated with competition and intellectual property are publicly available, but I was pointed to many by Lindsey and Teles (2017).

Data on the cases brought by the Department of Justice under the Sherman and Clayton Acts comes from https://www.justice.gov/atr/division-operations. I took their individual decadal reports and entered the data myself, and the data is available on the book's website.

The argument against intellectual property is drawn from two articles, Boldrin and Levine (2002, 2013). The same authors have also made this case in a book, Boldrin and Levine (2008).

12. Reallocations across Firms and Jobs

The evidence on the importance of reallocation for productivity growth comes from Foster, Haltiwanger, and Syverson (2008). For the retail sector, the evidence is from Foster, Haltiwanger, and Krizan (2006).

The data for both establishment and job turnover comes from the Business Dynamic Statistics (BDS) of the US Census (accessed at https://www2.census.gov /ces/bds/estab/bds_e_all_release.csv). The data is usable almost as is. The only calculation I did was to construct the net entry of establishments (jobs) by taking the number of entering establishments (creations) and subtracting the number of exits (destructions). The data underlying this comes from the Longitudinal Business Database, which you can find information about at https://www.census.gov /ces/dataproducts/datasets/lbd.html, but which requires authorized access through the US Census. The BDS data was developed as part of, and the patterns seen in the figures are consistent with, work in several papers by Ryan Decker, John Haltiwanger, Ron Jarmin, and Javier Miranda (Decker et al. 2014, 2016).

Estimates of the effect of the decline in reallocation are from Decker et al. (2017), figure 1. One note is that their calculation is for the change in growth of labor productivity, not residual productivity. The effect on residual productivity may well be smaller; it reflects reallocations of physical capital as well. The finding that the shocks hitting firms have been consistent but that reaction to shocks has declined is from Decker et al. (2018).

The paper linking demographic structure to firm and job dynamics is Hopenhayn, Neira, and Singhania (2018).

Is Slower Turnover a Problem?

In this section I sketched the argument that the response of firms to shocks will decline with their market power, something I drew from De Loecker and Eeckhout (2017). Here is a more formal demonstration of how this would work. Consider a firm that employs just one input, labor, so that $Y = AL$, where A is productivity and L is labor used. That labor costs w per unit. This isn't important for the math, and I could allow for several inputs if I wanted to.

Let the demand curve the firm faces be $P = Y^{-1/\epsilon}$, with $\epsilon > 0$. If we turn this around, this gives us $Y = P^{-\epsilon}$. From this, the elasticity of demand (Y) with respect to price (P) is $-\epsilon$. First, note that this means that as price goes up, demand falls, just as we want.

More important, as ϵ gets bigger, the elasticity gets bigger. If ϵ goes toward infinity, this would be like having a flat demand curve. If you raise the price, the amount people are willing to buy of your good drops a lot. A firm with a high elasticity of demand has little market power.

If ϵ goes toward 0, then the elasticity gets smaller. The demand curve gets steeper, if you are thinking of a simple supply and demand diagram. With low elasticity, a price change will not alter the amount purchased by much. A firm with low elasticity has a lot of market power.

Back to the firm. The firm's profits are

$$\pi = PY - wL. \tag{A.47}$$

Let the firm know or take into account the elasticity of price with respect to output when making their price-maximization decision. Thus, given their production function, I can write

$$\pi = (AL)^{1-1/\epsilon} - wL. \tag{A.48}$$

Maximizing profits, the firm will choose a value of L such that

$$w = (1 - 1/\epsilon)A^{1-1/\epsilon}L^{-1/\epsilon}, \tag{A.49}$$

which just says that the firm will set marginal cost (the wage) equal to the marginal revenue of an additional unit of labor. Solving this for L, you get

$$L^* = \left(\frac{\epsilon - 1}{\epsilon}\right)^{\epsilon} w^{-\epsilon} A^{\epsilon - 1}. \tag{A.50}$$

Now let's think about how responsive a firm is to shocks either to the cost of an input (the wage), or its own productivity. The elasticity of L^* with respect to wages is

$$\frac{\%\Delta L^*}{\%\Delta w} = -\epsilon. \tag{A.51}$$

A firm with little market power has a high value of ϵ, so the elasticity of labor with respect to the wage will be high as well. If the firm gets lower input costs, it can charge a lower price, and because its customers are very sensitive to prices, this allows it to sell a lot more. To sell a lot more, it has to hire a lot more workers. So firms with little market power are very sensitive to wages.

In contrast, a firm with a lot of market power has a low value of ϵ, so the elasticity is small as well. If the firm gets lower input costs, it can charge a lower price, but because its customers are insensitive to prices, this doesn't translate to many additional units sold. The firm does not need to hire many more workers. Firms with a lot of market power are insensitive to wages.

The elasticity of L^* with respect to productivity, A, is

$$\frac{\%\Delta L^*}{\%\Delta A} = \epsilon - 1. \tag{A.52}$$

Again, the same logic holds. A shock to productivity will have a big effect on the number of workers employed in a firm with little market power and a high value of ϵ, for the same reason as above. In a firm with a lot of market power and a low value of ϵ, the response to productivity shocks will be small, for the same reason as above.

In fact, what you can see here is that for a firm with a lot of market power, such that $\epsilon < 1$, the effect of a productivity increase can be lower employment. The firm's customers are so insensitive to price that they will continue to buy the same amount no matter what. So in response to higher productivity, the firm uses its advantage to shed workers.

Regardless of that interesting side note, the point is that firms with more market power (low elasticity) are optimally unresponsive to shocks, while firms without market power (high elasticity) are more sensitive to shocks.

13. The Drop in Geographic Mobility

The data on movers is from the US Census Bureau (https://www.census.gov /data/tables/time-series/demo/geographic-mobility/historic.html, table A.1). State-level GSP data is from the BEA (FRED).

For the MSAs, data on their output and output per capita is from https://www .bea.gov/regional/. Population is inferred from this data by dividing output by output per capita. Labor force data is from the BLS (https://www.bls.gov/lau/) in files by year that I merged manually. This labor force data is by county, not by

MSA. I use the FIPS codes (for counties), crosswalked to CBSA codes (for MSAs), to match labor force growth in counties to labor force growth in MSAs. There is thus some slight mismatch, as there are MSAs that cover part of a county, but not all of a county. I built the crosswalk table from data at the National Bureau of Economic Research (http://www.nber.org/data/cbsa-msa-fips-ssa-county-cross walk.html), and the actual file I use is available on the book's website. For temperature data, I use county-level data from the Centers for Disease Control and Prevention (https://wonder.cdc.gov/nasa-nldas.html) and merge that with the MSAs using the same crosswalk.

Evidence on the decline in mobility rates across different levels of administration is from Molloy, Smith, and Wozniak (2011).

For an excellent discussion of productivity differences across urban areas, see Moretti (2013).

The calculation of the lost GDP from housing regulations is from Hsieh and Moretti (forthcoming). Their work relies on elasticities from Saiz (2010).

The Profits of Housing

For the calculation of the economic profits of housing, I use the same methodology as in Barkai (2017). The rate of return on housing capital is calculated from

$$R = i - E[\pi] + \delta. \tag{A.53}$$

Here, the nominal interest rate is the 30-year average mortgage rate, where I use the first-available quote from FRED for a given year (quotes are quarterly). The price of housing is calculated by dividing the historical cost of residential capital (BEA table 2.3) by the quantity index (BEA table 2.2). I calculate inflation using this price series, with a lag of 3 years. Finally, the depreciation rate of residential capital comes from the historical cost of residential depreciation (BEA table 2.6) divided by the historical cost of residential capital.

Given the value of R, the economic profit share for housing is

$$s_{Profit} = 1 - \frac{R \times K_{House}}{Y_{House}}, \tag{A.54}$$

where K_{House} is the historical cost of the housing stock (BEA table 2.3), and Y_{House} is gross value-added of housing (FRED).

14. Did the Government Cause the Slowdown?

The finding on the effects of the 2003 dividend cut are from Yagan (2015) and Chetty and Saez (2005). The evidence on state taxation and innovation is from Akcigit et al. (2018). Evidence on the elasticity of taxable income with respect to individual tax rates is from Saez, Slemrod, and Giertz (2012).

One additional note here is that there is some evidence that the amount of taxable income reported for the highest-income individuals may be sensitive to the tax rate, at least for the 1986 and 1993 tax changes; see Saez (2004). However, the increase in tax rates in 2013 did not appear to have as large an effect (Saez 2016). Regardless, these studies all investigate reported taxable income, which is subject to retiming and can be sheltered from taxation for those with sufficient income (Chetty 2009). This has implications for fiscal policy but does not imply that there are material effects on human capital, physical capital, or productivity.

Regulation data was created by Al-Ubaydli and McLaughlin (2015). The estimation of the relationship of regulation and business dynamism is from Goldschlag and Tabarrok (2018).

The data on state-level GDP per worker and MSA level-GDP per worker is taken from the same sources as in chapter 13. The ALEC index of business conditions is from https://www.alec.org. This doesn't come in a spreadsheet, so I entered the values myself into a text file that is available on the website for this book.

The housing regulation data is originally from Gyourko, Saiz, and Summers (2008). I obtained their data from http://real.wharton.upenn.edu/~gyourko/land usesurvey.html, where I downloaded the Stata file from the link available. This file uses a slightly different set of codes for MSAs than the current set of codes, so I use a crosswalk that I built from the NBER (http://www.nber.org/data/cbsa-msa -fips-ssa-county-crosswalk.html) to match up MSAs. The exact codes and code to do the match are available on the website for this book.

The World Bank's *Doing Business* indicators are at http://www.doingbusiness .org.

Why Aren't There Big Effects on Growth?

To see the logic of why scale matters, consider a simple setup for a firm's profits. Let them be

$$\pi = (1 - \tau)(PY - wL), \tag{A.55}$$

where P is the price they can charge, Y is output, w is the wage, L is labor used. The value of τ is the implicit tax rate the firm pays when it operates, so it takes home only $(1 - \tau)$ of what is earned on selling its goods.

Let the demand for the firm's product be $Y = NP^{-\epsilon}$. The value of N scales this demand by the size of the market. This N could be the number of people (so the more people, the more demand there is for a good), or N could be something like total income (so the richer everyone is, the more demand there is). Either way, it tells us something about the scale of the market the firm operates in. Turning this around, you get $P = Y^{-1/\epsilon}N^{1/\epsilon}$.

Finally, let the firm produce output using $Y = AL$. Put this together with the profit function above, and you get

$$\pi = (1 - \tau)\left(N^{1/\epsilon}(AL)^{1-1/\epsilon} - wL\right). \tag{A.56}$$

Do the profit maximization problem here, and you get that

$$w = \frac{\epsilon - 1}{\epsilon} N^{1/\epsilon} A^{1-1/\epsilon} L^{-1/\epsilon}, \tag{A.57}$$

which is just that the marginal cost of labor should equal the marginal revenue product of labor. Note that the tax rate doesn't affect this. Solve this for labor and you get

$$L^* = N \left(\frac{\epsilon - 1}{\epsilon}\right)^\epsilon w^{-\epsilon} A^{\epsilon - 1}. \tag{A.58}$$

If you use this answer for L^*, the assumption that $Y = AL^*$, and the demand $Y = NP^{-\epsilon}$, you can solve for the price that the firm charges:

$$P^* = \frac{\epsilon}{\epsilon - 1} \frac{w}{A}, \tag{A.59}$$

which says that the price is a markup over the marginal cost, w/A. That markup, $\epsilon/(\epsilon - 1)$, depends on how elastic demand is to price. As ϵ goes up, customers are more sensitive, the demand curve is flatter, and the markup is lower. What determines this elasticity? It could be the desirability of the product or the regulations or restrictions involved in protecting the firm.

Using that price, you can solve for the profits of a firm as

$$\pi^* = (1 - \tau)\left(\frac{\epsilon}{\epsilon - 1} - 1\right) wL^*. \tag{A.60}$$

From this, you can see the three different forces at work on profits. First, the tax rate τ. The higher this is, the smaller are profits. Second, the markup, $\epsilon/(\epsilon - 1)$. The higher the markup, the higher the profits. Finally, the scale matters. Note that L^* depends directly on N. The more people, the higher the profits. Notice that this is directly proportional in this setting. If there are twice as many people, profits are twice as high. This is a feature of this little model where the markup and tax rate are constant. It need not be necessarily true that N works this way, but it illustrates the principle.

15. Did Inequality Cause the Slowdown?

I reference Piketty (2013). Data on the wage share of top incomes from that book was obtained from https://www.quandl.com/data/PIKETTY-Thomas-Pik etty, table S8.3. Data on the share of national income going to different income groups was produced by Piketty, Saez, and Zucman (2016). I obtained the data at http://gabriel-zucman.eu/usdina/.

The information about the occupation of the top .1% of the income distribution is from Bakija, Cole, and Heim (2008). The salary information on athletes and actors was obtained by me through copious Googling.

The National Center for Education Statistics information on college attendance rates by income comes from https://nces.ed.gov/programs/coe/indicator_cpa.asp.

There is no clear evidence that higher inequality is associated with slower or faster economic growth. One of the most thorough investigations is found in Banerjee and Duflo (2003). There is no monotonic relationship between inequality and growth in their specifications. Although it may be that high levels of severe poverty (e.g., less than $1 per day) are associated with slow growth, that does not apply in the case of the United States; see Ravallion (2012).

I mentioned in the text the role of education on inequality itself, which is primarily due to the change in the premium that college-educated workers earn over non-college-educated workers. The best discussion and history of this I know of is in Goldin and Katz (2008). A slightly different take on skills and inequality comes from thinking about job polarization, meaning that middle-skill positions are disappearing and only high- or low-skill positions remain. Some references here include Acemoglu and Autor (2011) and Autor and Dorn (2013). I found Autor (2013) a good summary of this line of research.

Expenditure shares by income were calculated in Boppart (2014). I took his reported expenditure share data directly from his paper.

The Effect of Higher Education Attainment

To do the calculation of the possible effects of raising educational attainment, I started with data on educational attainment by age group, from the US Census (https://www.census.gov/data/tables/time-series/demo/educational-attainment/cps-historical-time-series.html, table A.1).

In chapter 3, I calculated the human capital per capita using the equation

$$h^{Educ} = \frac{\sum_{j=1}^{6} N_j^{Educ} h_j^{Educ}}{\sum_{j=1}^{6} N_j^{Educ}}, \tag{A.61}$$

where h_j^{Educ} is the human capital from education for a given group, based on the assumption of a return of 10% per year. The numbers N_j^{Educ} were the number of people with each type of education. Each of those totals was made up of different numbers by age group, so

$$N_j^{Educ} = N_{j,25\text{-}34}^{Educ} + N_{j,35\text{-}54}^{Educ} + N_{j,55+}^{Educ}, \tag{A.62}$$

which is just the sum of individuals of the indicated age groups with education level j.

For my counterfactual calculation, what I did was change the numbers of the $N_{j,25\text{-}34}^{Educ}$ in each education group j. I set $N_{0\text{-}4,25\text{-}34}^{Educ} = 0$, meaning no one had 0–4 years of education, $N_{5\text{-}8,25\text{-}34}^{Educ} = 0$, and $N_{9\text{-}11,25\text{-}34}^{Educ} = 0$. I set $N_{12,25\text{-}34}^{Educ} = 0.2 \times N_{25\text{-}34}^{Educ}$, or 20% of the total number of people age 25–34 in the data. I set $N_{13\text{-}15,25\text{-}34}^{Educ} = 0.15 \times N_{25\text{-}34}^{Educ}$, and $N_{16+,25\text{-}34}^{Educ} = 0.65 \times N_{25\text{-}34}^{Educ}$. Then, with those numbers for workers age 25–34, I went back and calculated new counterfactual totals for N_j^{Educ} for each education level j. Using those new totals, I then recalculated human capital per capita. The code for this is available on the website for the book.

16. Did China Cause the Slowdown?

The data for the figures on GDP, imports, and the breakdown into consumption, investment, and government spending is all from BEA table 1.1.6 (FRED).

I draw on two papers that estimate the effect of trade on manufacturing employment or broader measures of employment: Autor, Dorn, and Hanson (2013, 2016). The numbers cited in the chapter are all drawn from their work. My own calculations of the implied effects are explained in the text itself.

17. The Future of Growth

Table 17.1 simply collects estimates of the effects of different economic forces that were calculated throughout the book.

The data on availability of various amenities (e.g., phones, cars, toilets) in China and the United States is all from the World Bank Development Indicators (https://data.worldbank.org/products/wdi).

Information on the number of legal immigrants to the US each year is from the Department of Homeland Security (https://www.dhs.gov/immigration-statistics /yearbook/2017/table1). The evidence on immigrant education levels is from the American Community Survey (https://www.census.gov/programs-surveys/acs/).

The research referenced on the effects of immigrants on native wages and employment comes from several papers: Peri (2012, 2016), Ottaviano and Peri (2012), Peri, Shih, and Sparber (2015), and Card and Peri (2016).

The idea that service productivity is mismeasured is from Young (2014). His idea is that workers have differences in their skill level depending on whether they are working in goods or in services. Assuming that people are able to move back and forth between activities, this means that people who have relatively high goods skills should work in goods, and those with service skills should work in services. As our spending shifts into services, though, this draws more and more workers into services, but over time we are drawing in people who have worse and worse service skills. All that is left in goods production are people who are very skilled with goods, but service work is done by people with relatively low skill levels in services. By assuming that all workers have similar skills regardless of industry, we are missing this difference, and this shows up as high residual productivity in goods and low residual productivity in services.

Keynes's prediction of fifteen-hour workweeks is from Keynes (1931). Jones's concept of high living standards reducing our willingness to risk innovation is from C. I. Jones (2016).

REFERENCES

Acemoglu, D., and D. Autor. 2011. "Skills, Tasks and Technologies: Implications for Employment and Earnings." In *Handbook of Labor Economics*, edited by O. Ashenfelter and D. Card, 4:1043–1171. Amsterdam: North Holland.

Aghion, P., U. Akcigit, and P. Howitt. 2014. "What Do We Learn from Schumpeterian Growth Theory?" In *Handbook of Economic Growth*, edited by P. Aghion and S. Durlauf, 2:515–63. Amsterdam: North Holland

Aghion, P., N. Bloom, R. Blundell, R. Griffith, and P. Howitt. 2005. "Competition and Innovation: An Inverted-U Relationship." *Quarterly Journal of Economics* 120 (2): 701–28.

Aghion, P., and R. Griffith. 2005. *Competition and Growth: Reconciling Theory and Evidence*. Cambridge, MA: MIT Press.

Aghion, P., and P. Howitt. 1992. "A Model of Growth through Creative Destruction." *Econometrica* 60 (2): 323–51.

Aghion, P., and P. Howitt. 2009. *The Economics of Growth*. Cambridge, MA: MIT Press.

Akcigit, U., J. Grigsby, T. Nicholas, and S. Stantcheva. 2018. "Taxation and Innovation in the 20th Century." Working Paper No. 24982, National Bureau of Economic Research, Cambridge, MA.

Al-Ubaydli, O., and P. A. McLaughlin. 2015. "RegData: A Numerical Database on Industry-Specific Regulations for All United States Industries and Federal Regulations, 1997–2012." *Regulation & Governance* 11 (1): 109–23. https://onlinelibrary.wiley.com/doi/pdf/10.1111/rego.12107.

Autor, D. H. 2013. "The Task Approach to Labor Markets: An Overview." *Journal for Labour Market Research* 46 (3): 185–99.

Autor, D. H., and D. Dorn. 2013. "The Growth of Low-Skill Service Jobs and the Polarization of the US Labor Market." *American Economic Review* 103 (5): 1553–97.

Autor, D. H., D. Dorn, and G. H. Hanson. 2013. "The China Syndrome: Local Labor Market Effects of Import Competition in the United States." *American Economic Review* 103 (6): 2121–68.

Autor, D. H., D. Dorn, and G. H. Hanson. 2016. "The China Shock: Learning from Labor-Market Adjustment to Large Changes in Trade." *Annual Review of Economics* 8 (1): 205–40.

Bailey, M. J. 2006. "More Power to the Pill: The Impact of Contraceptive Freedom on Women's Life Cycle Labor Supply." *Quarterly Journal of Economics* 121 (1): 289–320.

Bailey, M. J. 2010. "'Momma's Got the Pill': How Anthony Comstock and *Griswold v. Connecticut* Shaped US Childbearing." *American Economic Review* 100 (1): 98–129.

Bakija, J., A. Cole, and B. Heim. 2008. "Jobs and Income Growth of Top Earners and the Causes of Changing Income Inequality: Evidence from U.S. Tax Return Data." Department of Economics Working Paper 2010-22, Department of Economics, Williams College, Williamstown, MA.

Banerjee, A. V., and E. Duflo. 2003. "Inequality and Growth: What Can the Data Say?" *Journal of Economic Growth* 8 (3): 267–99.

Baqaee, D. R., and E. Farhi. 2017. "Productivity and Misallocation in General Equilibrium." Working Paper No. 24007, National Bureau of Economic Research, Cambridge, MA.

Barkai, S. 2017. "Declining Labor and Capital Shares." Working paper, London Business School.

Basu, S., and J. Fernald. 2002. "Aggregate Productivity and Aggregate Technology." *European Economic Review* 46: 963–91.

Baumol, W. J. 1967. "Macroeconomics of Unbalanced Growth: The Anatomy of Urban Crisis." *American Economic Review* 57 (3): 415–26.

Baumol, W. J. 2012. *The Cost Disease: Why Computers Get Cheaper but Healthcare Doesn't*. New Haven, CT: Yale University Press.

Baumol, W. J., and W. G. Bowen. 1965. "On the Performing Arts: The Anatomy of Their Economic Problems." *American Economic Review* 55 (1–2): 495–502.

Becker, G. S. 1960. "An Economic Analysis of Fertility." In *Demographic and Economic Change in Developed Countries*, edited by National Bureau of Economic Research, 209–40. New York: Columbia University Press.

Bloom, N., C. I. Jones, J. Van Reenen, and M. Webb. 2017. "Are Ideas Getting Harder to Find?" Working Paper No. 23782, National Bureau of Economic Research, Cambridge, MA.

Boldrin, M., and D. Levine. 2002. "The Case against Intellectual Property." *American Economic Review* 92 (2): 209–12.

Boldrin, M., and D. Levine. 2008. *Against Intellectual Monopoly*. Cambridge: Cambridge University Press.

Boldrin, M., and D. K. Levine. 2013. "The Case against Patents." *Journal of Economic Perspectives* 27 (1): 3–22.

Boppart, T. 2014. "Structural Change and the Kaldor Facts in a Growth Model with Relative Price Effects and Non-Gorman Preferences." *Econometrica* 82: 2167–96.

Brynjolfsson, E., and A. McAfee. 2011. *Race against the Machine*. N.p.: Digital Frontier Press.

Brynjolfsson, E., and A. McAfee. 2014. *The Second Machine Age: Work, Progress, and Prosperity in a Time of Brilliant Technologies*. New York: W. W. Norton and Co.

Byrne, D. M., J. G. Fernald, and M. B. Reinsdorf. 2016. "Does the United States Have a Productivity Slowdown or a Measurement Problem?" *Brookings Papers on Economic Activity* 47 (1): 109–82.

Card, D. 1999. "The Causal Effect of Education on Earnings." In *Handbook of Labor Economics*, edited by O. Ashenfelter and D. Card, 3:1801–63. Amsterdam: Elsevier.

Card, D., and G. Peri. 2016. "Immigration Economics by George J. Borjas: A Review Essay." *Journal of Economic Literature* 54 (4): 1333–49.

Chatterjee, S., and T. Vogl. 2018. "Escaping Malthus: Economic Growth and Fertility Change in the Developing World." *American Economic Review* 108 (6): 1440–67.

Chetty, R. 2009. "Is the Taxable Income Elasticity Sufficient to Calculate Deadweight Loss? The Implications of Evasion and Avoidance." *American Economic Journal: Economic Policy* 1 (2): 31–52.

Chetty, R., and E. Saez. 2005. "Dividend Taxes and Corporate Behavior: Evidence from the 2003 Dividend Tax Cut." *Quarterly Journal of Economics* 120 (3): 791–833.

Cowen, T. 2011. *The Great Stagnation: How America Ate All The Low-Hanging Fruit of Modern History, Got Sick, and Will (Eventually) Feel Better.* New York: Dutton.

Coyle, D. 2015. *GDP: A Brief but Affectionate History.* Princeton, NJ: Princeton University Press.

Decker, R., J. Haltiwanger, R. Jarmin, and J. Miranda. 2014. "The Role of Entrepreneurship in US Job Creation and Economic Dynamism." *Journal of Economic Perspectives* 28 (3): 3–24.

Decker, R. A., J. Haltiwanger, R. S. Jarmin, and J. Miranda. 2016. "Declining Business Dynamism: What We Know and the Way Forward." *American Economic Review* 106 (5): 203–7.

Decker, R. A., J. Haltiwanger, R. S. Jarmin, and J. Miranda. 2017. "Declining Dynamism, Allocative Efficiency, and the Productivity Slowdown." *American Economic Review* 107 (5): 322–26.

Decker, R. A., J. C. Haltiwanger, R. S. Jarmin, and J. Miranda. 2018. "Changing Business Dynamism and Productivity: Shocks vs. Responsiveness." Working Paper No. 24236, National Bureau of Economic Research, Cambridge, MA.

De Loecker, J., and J. Eeckhout. 2017. "The Rise of Market Power and the Macroeconomic Implications." Working Paper No. 23687, National Bureau of Economic Research, Cambridge, MA.

De Loecker, J., and J. Eeckhout. 2018. "Global Market Power." Working Paper No. 24768, National Bureau of Economic Research, Cambridge, MA.

Diez, F. J., D. Leigh, and S. Tambunlertchai. 2018. *Global Market Power and Its Macroeconomic Implications.* Technical report. Washington, DC: International Monetary Fund.

Edmond, C., V. Midrigan, and D. Y. Xu. 2018. "How Costly Are Markups?" Working Paper No. 24800, National Bureau of Economic Research, Cambridge, MA.

Eppsteiner, H., J. Furman, and W. Powell III. 2017. *An Aging Population Explains Most—But Not All—of the Decline in the US Labor Force Participation Rate since 2007*. Technical report. Washington, DC: Peterson Institute for International Economics.

Feldstein, M. 2017. "Underestimating the Real Growth of GDP, Personal Income, and Productivity." *Journal of Economic Perspectives* 31 (2): 145–64.

Fernald, J. G. 2014. "Productivity and Potential Output before, during, and after the Great Recession." Working Paper No. 20248, National Bureau of Economic Research, Cambridge, MA.

Fernald, J. G., R. E. Hall, J. H. Stock, and M. W. Watson. 2017. "The Disappointing Recovery of Output after 2009." Working Paper No. 23543, National Bureau of Economic Research, Cambridge, MA.

Fernald, J. G., and C. I. Jones. 2014. "The Future of US Economic Growth." *American Economic Review* 104 (5): 44–49.

Foster, L., J. Haltiwanger, and C. J. Krizan. 2006. "Market Selection, Reallocation, and Restructuring in the U.S. Retail Trade Sector in the 1990s." *Review of Economics and Statistics* 88 (4): 748–58.

Foster, L., J. Haltiwanger, and C. Syverson. 2008. "Reallocation, Firm Turnover, and Efficiency: Selection on Productivity or Profitability?" *American Economic Review* 98 (1): 394–425.

Goldin, C. 2001. "The Human-Capital Century and American Leadership: Virtues of the Past." *Journal of Economic History* 61 (02): 263–92.

Goldin, C., and L. F. Katz. 2002. "The Power of the Pill: Oral Contraceptives and Women's Career and Marriage Decisions." *Journal of Political Economy* 110 (4): 730–70. https://doi.org/10.1086/340778.

Goldin, C., and L. F. Katz. 2007. "The Race between Education and Technology: The Evolution of U.S. Educational Wage Differentials, 1890 to 2005." Working Paper No. 12984, National Bureau of Economic Research, Cambridge, MA.

Goldin, C., and L. F. Katz. 2008. *The Race between Education and Technology*. Cambridge, MA: Harvard University Press.

Goldschlag, N., and A. Tabarrok. 2018. "Is Regulation to Blame for the Decline in American Entrepreneurship?" *Economic Policy* 33 (93): 5–44. https://doi.org /10.1093/epolic/eix019.

Gordon, R. J. 2016. *The Rise and Fall of American Growth*. Princeton, NJ: Princeton University Press.

Gordon, R. J. 2018. "Declining American Economic Growth Despite Ongoing Innovation." *Explorations in Economic History* 69:1–12.

Greenwood, J., N. Guner, and G. Vandenbroucke. 2017. "Family Economics Writ Large." *Journal of Economic Literature* 55 (4): 1346–1434.

Greenwood, J., A. Seshadri, and G. Vandenbroucke. 2005. "The Baby Boom and Baby Bust." *American Economic Review* 95 (1): 183–207.

Greenwood, J., A. Seshadri, and M. Yorukoglu. 2005. "Engines of Liberation." *Review of Economic Studies* 72 (1): 109–33. https://doi.org/10.1111/0034-6527 .00326.

Grossman, G. M., and E. Helpman. 1991. "Quality Ladders in the Theory of Growth." *Review of Economic Studies* 58 (1): 43–61.

Gutiérrez, G. 2017. "Investigating Global Labor and Profit Shares." Working paper, NYU Stern School of Business.

Gutiérrez, G., and T. Philippon. 2017. "Investmentless Growth: An Empirical Investigation." *Brookings Papers on Economic Activity* 48 (2): 89–190.

Gyourko, J., A. Saiz, and A. Summers. 2008. "A New Measure of the Local Regulatory Environment for Housing Markets: The Wharton Residential Land Use Regulatory Index." *Urban Studies* 45 (3): 693–729.

Hall, R. E. 1988. "The Relation between Price and Marginal Cost in U.S. Industry." *Journal of Political Economy* 96 (5): 921–47.

Hall, R. E. 1989. "Invariance Properties of Solow's Productivity Residual." Working Paper No. 3034, National Bureau of Economic Research, Cambridge, MA.

Hall, R. E. 2018. "New Evidence on the Markup of Prices over Marginal Costs and the Role of Mega-Firms in the US Economy." Working Paper No. 24574, National Bureau of Economic Research, Cambridge, MA.

Hall, R. E., and C. I. Jones. 1999. "Why Do Some Countries Produce So Much More Output per Worker Than Others?" *Quarterly Journal of Economics* 114 (1): 83–116.

Hall, R. E., and C. I. Jones. 2007. "The Value of Life and the Rise in Health Spending." *Quarterly Journal of Economics* 122 (1): 39–72.

Hall, R. E., and D. W. Jorgenson. 1967. "Tax Policy and Investment Behavior." *American Economic Review* 57 (3): 391–414.

Hopenhayn, H., J. Neira, and R. Singhania. 2018. "From Population Growth to Firm Demographics: Implications for Concentration, Entrepreneurship and the Labor Share." Working Paper No. 25382, National Bureau of Economic Research, Cambridge, MA.

Hsieh, C.-T., and E. Moretti. Forthcoming. "Housing Constraints and Spatial Misallocation." *American Economic Journal: Macroeconomics.*

Jones, C. I. 1995a. "R&D-Based Models of Economics Growth." *Journal of Political Economy* 103: 759–84.

Jones, C. I. 1995b. "Time Series Test of Endogenous Growth Models." *Quarterly Journal of Economics* 110: 495–525.

Jones, C. I. 2016. "Life and Growth." *Journal of Political Economy* 124 (2): 539–78.

Jones, L. E., and M. Tertilt. 2008. "An Economic History of Fertility in the United

States: 1826–1960." In *Frontiers of Family Economics*, edited by P. Rupert, 1:165–230. Bingley, UK: Emerald Group.

Jorgenson, D. W., F. Gollop, and B. Fraumeni. 1987. *Productivity and U.S. Economic Growth*. Cambridge, MA: Harvard University Press.

Jorgenson, D. W., M. S. Ho, and J. D. Samuels. 2013. *Economic Growth in the Information Age*. Technical report. Boston: NBER Conference on Research in Income and Wealth, Summer Institute.

Keynes, J. M. 1931. "Economic Possibilities for Our Grandchildren." *Essays in Persuasion*. London: McMillan.

Kimball, M. S., J. G. Fernald, and S. Basu. 2006. "Are Technology Improvements Contractionary?" *American Economic Review* 96 (5): 1418–48.

Klenow, P. J., and A. Rodriguez-Clare. 1997. "The Neo-Classical Revival in Growth Economics: Has It Gone Too Far?" In *NBER Macroeconomics Annual*, vol. 12, edited by B. Bernanke and J. Rotemberg. Boston: MIT Press.

Lemieux, T. 2006. "The 'Mincer Equation' Thirty Years after Schooling, Experience, and Earnings." In *Jacob Mincer: A Pioneer of Modern Labor Economics*, edited by S. Grossbard, 127–45. Boston: Springer US.

Lindsey, B., and S. M. Teles. 2017. *The Captured Economy*. New York: Oxford University Press.

Maestas, N., K. J. Mullen, and D. Powell. 2016. "The Effect of Population Aging on Economic Growth, the Labor Force and Productivity." Working Paper No. 22452, National Bureau of Economic Research, Cambridge, MA.

Molloy, R., C. L. Smith, and A. Wozniak. 2011. "Internal Migration in the United States." *Journal of Economic Perspectives* 25 (3): 173–96.

Moretti, E. 2013. *The New Geography of Jobs*. Boston: Mariner Books.

Moulton, B. R. 2018. *The Measurement of Output, Prices, and Productivity: What's Changed since the Boskin Commission?* Technical report. Washington, DC: Hutchins Center of Fiscal and Monetary Policy.

Murnane, R. J. 2013. "U.S. High School Graduation Rates: Patterns and Explanations." *Journal of Economic Literature* 51 (2): 370–422.

Ottaviano, G. I. P., and G. Peri. 2012. "Rethinking the Effect of Immigration on Wages." *Journal of the European Economic Association* 10 (1): 152–97.

Peri, G. 2012. "The Effect of Immigration on Productivity: Evidence from U.S. States." *Review of Economics and Statistics* 94 (1): 348–58.

Peri, G. 2016. "Immigrants, Productivity, and Labor Markets." *Journal of Economic Perspectives* 30 (4): 3–30.

Peri, G., K. Shih, and C. Sparber. 2015. "STEM Workers, H-1B Visas, and Productivity in US Cities." *Journal of Labor Economics* 33 (S1): 225–55.

Piketty, T. 2013. *Capital in the Twenty-First Century*. Cambridge, MA: Harvard University Press.

Piketty, T., E. Saez, and G. Zucman. 2016. *Distributional National Accounts:*

Methods and Estimates for the United States. NBER Working Paper No. 22945, National Bureau of Economic Research, Cambridge, MA.

Romer, P. M. 1986. "Increasing Returns and Long-Run Growth." *Journal of Political Economy* 94 (5): 1002–37.

Romer, P. M. 1990. "Endogenous Technological Change." *Journal of Political Economy* 98 (5): S71–S102.

Saez, E. 2004. "Reported Incomes and Marginal Tax Rates, 1960–2000: Evidence and Policy Implications." In *Tax Policy and the Economy*, 18:117–74. Cambridge, MA: National Bureau of Economic Research.

Saez, E. 2016. "Taxing the Rich More: Preliminary Evidence from the 2013 Tax Increase." In *Tax Policy and the Economy*, 31:71–120. Cambridge, MA: National Bureau of Economic Research.

Saez, E., J. Slemrod, and S. H. Giertz. 2012. "The Elasticity of Taxable Income with Respect to Marginal Tax Rates: A Critical Review." *Journal of Economic Literature* 50 (1): 3–50.

Saiz, A. 2010. "The Geographic Determinants of Housing Supply." *Quarterly Journal of Economics* 125 (3): 1253–96.

Solow, R. M. 1956. "A Contribution to the Theory of Economic Growth." *Quarterly Journal of Economics* 70 (1): 65–94.

Solow, R. M. 1957. "Technical Change and the Aggregate Production Function." *Review of Economics and Statistics* 39 (3): 312–20.

Stiroh, K. J., and D. W. Jorgenson. 2000. "U.S. Economic Growth at the Industry Level." *American Economic Review* 90 (2): 161–67.

Syverson, C. 2017. "Challenges to Mismeasurement Explanations for the US Productivity Slowdown." *Journal of Economic Perspectives* 31 (2): 165–86.

Tinbergen, J. 1942. "Zur Theorie der Langfirstigen Wirtschaftsentwicklung." *Weltwirtschaftliches Archiv* 55:511–49.

Yagan, D. 2015. "Capital Tax Reform and the Real Economy: The Effects of the 2003 Dividend Tax Cut." *American Economic Review* 105 (12): 3531–63.

Young, A. 2014. "Structural Transformation, the Mismeasurement of Productivity Growth, and the Cost Disease of Services." *American Economic Review* 104 (11): 3635–67.

INDEX

accounting profits, 105
agricultural yields, 76
agriculture industry, 5, 85, 88
American Legislative Exchange Council, 175–77, 182, 183, 246
artificial intelligence, 8, 215

baby boom. *See* demographics
Baumol, William, 5, 94–98, 100, 101, 234, 235, 250
Boskin Commission, 74, 254

Canada, 111
China, 9, 19–23, 182. *See also* trade
Clayton Act, 136, 241
commuting zone, 201, 202
concentration: of firms, 105, 121–24, 137, 153, 154; of income, 185
constant returns to scale, 43, 224, 225, 227
construction industry, 74, 85, 165, 167, 181, 182, 209
contraception, 4, 68, 208, 231; birth control pill, 4, 35, 68, 124, 231
copyright, 130, 133
cost disease of services. *See* services
cost minimization, 44, 110, 224–26, 235
cost share of physical capital, 45, 226
creative destruction, 143

demographics, 5, 69, 138; age structure, 31, 32, 56, 68, 228; baby boom, 4, 33, 55, 56, 59, 64, 65, 154, 208; birth rate, 4, 55–57; dependency ratio, 59, 228; family size, 66, 68, 206–8, 231; fertility rate, 4, 56, 57, 60, 65, 67, 208, 229, 231; life expectancy, 60, 215; marriage, 4, 66–68, 208, 230, 231. *See also* contraception
durable goods, 34, 35, 102, 209, 235
dynamism. *See* reallocation

economic profits, 105–8, 111–14, 117, 122, 125, 138, 186, 210, 237, 238, 244. *See also* market power
education industry, 85, 88, 94, 97, 100, 101, 113
Environmental Protection Agency, 174
establishment, 6, 140, 142, 148, 150, 155, 241; entry, 143–46, 148, 151–53; exit, 143–46, 148, 151; number, 146; relationship to firms, 141
Europe, 111, 133, 250, 254
European Union, 133
excludable, 129, 133, 134

factor utilization, 54
finance industry, 85, 88, 190
financial crisis, 1, 3, 12, 13, 16, 32, 33, 39, 47, 65, 118, 120, 145, 148, 172, 217, 218, 228
food service industry, 85, 88, 96, 97
France, 18, 19, 201

Germany, 18, 19, 209
government, 8–10, 107, 170, 172, 175, 180, 184, 211, 217; antitrust enforcement, 135; economic activity, 44, 107, 196, 197, 199, 248; structures, 223. *See also* regulation; taxes
Great Depression, 1
Great Recession, 252
gross state product, 158
growth accounting. *See* real GDP per capita

health care industry, 78, 85, 88, 90, 94, 96, 101, 113, 162, 235; fraction of GDP, 83–84; labor requirement, 100; price level, 91, 97
housing, 45, 85, 155, 207, 209, 211, 212; economic profits, 164–68, 244; as physical capital, 34, 35, 37; price elasticity, 168, 169. *See also* regulation

human capital, 2–4, 10, 26, 28, 39, 40, 63, 72, 73, 79, 82, 87, 103, 104, 125, 128, 129, 154, 157, 169, 207; education, 4, 10, 28–31, 55, 61, 62, 64, 67–69, 158, 181, 185, 191–93, 208, 213, 220–23, 228, 246–48; effect on growth, 41–47, 49, 50, 52–54; experience, 29–31, 55, 61, 64, 68, 69, 220–23, 228; hours worked, 27, 28, 30–33, 64, 69, 203, 214, 221, 222; immigration, 212–14; inequality, 185, 191–95, 247, 248; labor force participation, 4, 27, 50, 59, 64, 65, 68, 153, 154, 162, 173, 174, 199, 201, 202, 208, 212, 229–31, 243, 244; measuring, 28–34, 220–31, 233; number of employees, 27, 28, 32, 35, 77, 106, 108, 121, 141, 172, 175, 203, 221; skill, 2, 28–30, 35, 43, 62, 129, 203, 213, 214, 247, 248; taxes, 170, 171, 173, 245; trade, 199, 202, 203

immigration, 212–14, 248
inequality, 9, 10, 170, 206; distribution of income, 185–88, 246; effect on growth, 191–94; top one percent, 188–90, 246
inflation, 17, 97, 107, 165, 219, 238, 239, 244
information and communication industry, 84–86, 88, 90, 113
innovation, 3, 5, 8, 100, 101, 160, 173, 180, 210, 215, 241; antitrust, 135–37, 210; competition, 79, 130–32, 180, 241; research effort, 51, 75–78, 116, 124–26, 130, 132, 134; scale, 180–83, 213, 215, 245, 246
institutional ownership, 123, 125
integrated circuits, 75, 76
Internal Revenue Service, 174
investment, 39, 126, 196, 197, 210; concentration of industries, 121–24, 132, 137; effect of inequality, 185; firm level, 112, 116–20, 191, 240, 248; institutional ownership of firms, 123–25; relationship with taxes and regulation, 170–72, 180–82. See also physical capital

Japan, 18–23, 209
job creation, 148–51, 174, 175, 241, 251
job destruction, 148, 149, 241, 249

labor force participation. See human capital
Lerner index, 131
linear regression, 123

manufacturing industry, 5, 9, 36, 78, 81, 83–85, 90–92, 100, 141, 142, 147, 170, 195, 202–5, 209, 234, 248
market power, 7, 10, 79, 80, 104, 105–11, 207, 210–12, 225; effect on aggregate productivity, 112–15, 237, 240; effect on investment, 122, 124, 125; housing, 162, 164–69; legal constraints, 135–38; reallocation, 152–54, 242, 243; relationship to inequality, 185, 194; relationship to innovation, 126, 127, 129–35, 241
markups, 79, 110, 111, 113, 125, 127, 130, 132, 133, 137, 180, 182, 185, 237, 239, 240. See also market power
merger, 136
metropolitan statistical area, 157, 159, 160–63, 167–69, 179, 180, 201, 243–45
mining industry, 85
mobility, 6, 155, 169, 206, 207, 212, 243, 244; measuring, 157; response to temperature, 162, 163; response to trade, 200
Moore's law, 75, 76
mortgage rates, 165, 166, 167, 244
multifactor productivity, 44. See also productivity

new molecular entity, 76
nondurable goods, 102, 103
nonrival, 127–30, 133, 134

Occupational Safety and Health Administration, 174
operating surplus, 116–18, 237, 240

pass-through business, 172
physical capital, 2, 3, 71, 72, 79, 111, 115, 118, 121, 124, 125, 128, 129, 138, 157, 242; depreciation, 35, 107, 116, 129, 165, 223, 238, 244; effect on growth, 42–45, 47–52, 54, 224–30, 233; equipment, 34, 107, 134, 223; in-

equality, 191; intellectual property, 2, 36, 210, 211, 223, 241; measuring, 26, 34, 35, 37–39, 220, 223; nonresidential, 35–37, 107; residential, 34–37, 39, 44, 107, 166, 223, 244; return on, 106–8, 238; taxes and regulation, 170, 245. *See also* investment

population aging. *See* demographics

productivity, 3, 9, 124–26, 128, 207, 209, 210, 214, 215, 248; definition, 70–73, 224; difference with technology, 8, 71, 75–78, 232; inequality, 191, 193, 245; market power, 7, 79, 105, 112–15, 130, 132, 137, 239; mobility, 155, 157, 160, 162–64, 167–69, 244; reallocation, 79, 80, 139–44, 147, 148, 150–52, 241–43; regulation, 170, 171, 175, 176, 178, 180; shift from goods to services, 5, 6, 81, 82, 84–89, 92–96, 98–100, 101, 103, 233–37; trade, 195, 199, 203–5. *See also* residual growth

professional services industry, 84, 85, 88, 90, 91, 94

Q ratio, 119–24, 240

real estate industry, 85

real GDP per capita: absolute growth, 14; accounting for growth rate, 46–54, 224–30, 239; across countries, 19–23; definition, 16–18, 184, 217, 218–20; errors in measuring, 73–75; growth rate, 12, 13, 77, 103, 208, 209, 215, 216; industrial composition, 83; level, 14, 15, 16; metropolitan statistical area level, 159; potential, 24; relationship to physical and human capital, 41–43, 45, 63, 65; state level, 157; trade, 197, 204

reallocation, 3, 79, 80, 152–54, 206, 207, 234, 241, 242; between establishments, 139–43; geographic, 155, 162, 164, 167, 178; from goods to services, 81, 82–89, 101; regulation, 171, 174, 175; trade, 201, 202

regulation, 3, 8–10, 170–72, 181–84, 206, 207, 210–12; business conditions, 181, 245; housing, 168, 178–80, 244–46; measurement, 174, 175; relationship with growth,

176, 177; relationship with investment, 124

residual growth, 3, 54, 157; calculation, 45–53, 224, 226–30, 242, 248; definition, 41, 42; equivalence with productivity, 70, 73; by industry, 75, 78, 82. *See also* productivity

rival. *See* nonrival

robot, 8, 35, 66

secular stagnation, 2

services, 2, 3, 4, 126, 137, 152, 162, 169, 215; from capital, 34, 36, 85, 165; cost disease, 95; effect on productivity growth, 85, 88, 89; income elasticity, 98–101, 103; inequality, 185, 193, 194; labor requirements, 94–96, 248; market power, 113, 114, 239, 240; price level, 90, 91, 96, 97; shift toward, 5, 6, 7, 10, 46, 78–83, 93, 102, 103, 138, 152, 155, 206–9, 233, 235, 236, 237; value of, 17, 26, 35, 72–75, 89, 91, 157, 183, 184, 197, 219, 220, 224

share buybacks, 111, 125, 210

Sherman Act, 135

Silicon Valley, 155, 160, 173, 179

Stigler Commission, 74

stock market, 17, 110

taxes, 3, 9, 10, 171, 173–78, 183, 184, 211, 244, 245; dividend tax, 9, 171, 172; income tax, 170, 173

technology, 46, 113, 128; difference from productivity, 71–73, 75

total factor productivity, 70, 86. *See also* productivity

tourism industry, 100

trade, 9, 10, 170, 195, 196, 199–206, 211, 212, 248; with China, 195, 197, 199–203, 205–7, 209, 210, 248, 249; exports, 195–97, 199; import penetration, 201; imports, 195–97, 199–201, 248; with Mexico, 195, 203

turnover. *See* reallocation

unemployment, 17, 202

United Kingdom, 19, 201

value-added: firm and establishment, 139, 141; housing, 164–67; industry shares, 83, 84, 86–89, 91, 92, 204, 233, 234

women, 4, 11; access to contraception, 68, 69, 103, 208, 231; fertility rate, 55–57, 209; labor force participation, 27, 67, 68, 173, 230; marriage age, 66

World Trade Organization, 195

zoning. *See* regulation